44959

CW00493744

# Reification,

*or*

# The Anxiety of Late Capitalism

DISCARDED

# Reification,

*or*

# The Anxiety of Late Capitalism

TIMOTHY BEWES

VERSO

London • New York

AIH-5384

303.4
BEW

First published by Verso 2002
© Timothy Bewes 2002
All rights reserved

The moral rights of the author have been asserted

1 3 5 7 9 10 8 6 4 2

**Verso**
UK: 6 Meard Street, London W1F 0EG
USA: 180 Varick Street, New York NY 10014–4606
www.versobooks.com

Verso is the imprint of New Left Books

ISBN 1–85984–685–8
ISBN 1–85984–456–1 (pbk)

**British Library Cataloguing in Publication Data**
A catalogue record for this book is available from the British Library

**Library of Congress Cataloging-in-Publication Data**
A catalog record for this book is available from the Library of Congress

Typeset in Bembo by M Rules
Printed in the UK by Biddles Ltd, Guildford and King's Lynn
www.biddles.co.uk

*For my parents and siblings:*
*Richard, Liz, Wendy, Stephen*

# Contents

## PART TWO
## Inversion



## PART THREE
## Redemption

# Acknowledgements

I wrote this book while I was a Post-doctoral Research Fellow at Liverpool John Moores University between 1999 and 2002, and I am very grateful to the Department of Literature and Cultural History, especially Pam Morris, for my appointment, without which the work would not have been possible. I would like to thank the following people for talking to me about the ideas and for reading drafts of the material: Matt Jordan, William Outhwaite, Charlotte Raven, Judith Williamson. I'd also like to thank Verso, and especially my editor Jane Hindle, for publishing the book. My family has been immensely supportive as always.

The illustrations on the following pages appear by courtesy of the copyright holders: p. 45: Stanley Spencer, *The Resurrection, Cookham* (1924–27). © Tate, London 2001. p. 237: Hieronymus Wierix, *Christ in the Wine Press* (c. 1600). © Copyright The British Museum. p. 256: The *Guardian* newspaper front cover (*G2* supplement), 9 July 2001. Artwork by Daniel Hansen. Thanks to The Organisation and the *Guardian*.

The photograph on p. 182 is by the author.

# Preface

This book is about the thingly quality of human experience: the ease with which the world as we encounter it, including our selves and the products of our labour, is transformed into a series of objects that are removed from us, and towards which we may feel a sense of reverence, or loss, or revulsion. It traces the fortunes of a once celebrated, lately disparaged metaphor used to describe that process – 'reification' – and considers its implications: that we are becoming ever more deeply inserted into epistemological categories which falsify our relation to the world; that a far-distant or long-lost world free from reification has existed; that it would be desirable – if it were possible – to reconnect with or rediscover that world; that present-day society is in a state of spiritual impoverishment which must somehow be reversed if calamity is to be avoided. The absence of these anxieties would imply either that the transformation is so complete that we are no longer aware of it, that reification has become the human condition as such, or, conversely, that the transformation has not even begun, that the civilization in question is still in that state of 'integration' which the young Georg Lukács ascribed to the world of the epic – an age of uninterrupted intimacy between world and self, where 'the fire that burns in the soul is of the same essential nature as the stars'.[1]

One of the propositions of this book, however, is that such

troubling feelings – in particular, the sense of anxiety towards reification – have become virtually universal in advanced capitalist societies. In a recent work of fiction by a prominent American novelist, subjectivity has become so invaded by the image that modern identity itself is a 'pretence' with no real – a mask which is no longer separable from what might once have been underneath. People, reflects the protagonist, have started pretending to be exactly who they are.[2] A young British artist claims, analogously, that artistic 'expression' has been eclipsed by the range of available 'techniques', exhausted in themselves. Art is reduced to self-parody; even Picasso ends his life making second-rate Picassos. Thus the output of contemporary artists is limited to witty but fatalistic commentaries upon the inevitability of repetition.[3] For a well-known writer on American film, the question of the reality of the 1950s, as opposed to its representation in the Hollywood cinema of the period, has become unbroachable. The 'innocence' which we ascribe to that decade, retrospectively, is nothing other than an image the fifties were trying to project *at the time*, a fantasy which they indulged about themselves, and to which there is no corresponding reality – true or otherwise.[4] 'Today there are only second acts in American lives', writes a literary critic in a similar spirit. 'To judge by the best of the new writing, the most urgent of the new films, the most watched television, American lives are now devoted to a wholesale inhabiting of the dead afternoon.'[5]

In such accounts the topographical model of signification has broken down completely; a crust has formed between reality and representation – indeed, the former has been displaced by the latter, to such a degree that a world uncorroded by the image is no longer accessible. A 'reified' society is one from which meaning has vanished, or in which meaningful statements have become impossible. Leszek Kolakowski describes its effects most succinctly:

> The transformation of all human products and individuals into goods comparable in quantitative terms; the disappearance of

> qualitative links between people; the gap between private and public life; the loss of personal responsibility and the reduction of human beings to executors of tasks imposed by a rationalized system; the resulting deformation of personality, the impoverishment of human contacts, the loss of solidarity, the absence of generally recognized criteria of artistic work, 'experimentation' as a universal creative principle; the loss of authentic culture owing to the segregation of the different spheres of life, in particular the domination of productive processes treated as an element independent of all others . . .[6]

The very idea of reification implies a society in a state of degeneration, and a prevailing sense of nostalgia for what has vanished: pathos, joy, immediacy, beauty – 'the meaning of the world made visible'.[7] In this respect, the concept has profoundly conservative implications. Did the world of the epic evoked longingly by Lukács several years before his turn to Bolshevism and his development of the theory of reification – a longing which tacitly informs that theory – ever exist? Is not the dream of a unification of subject and object and an end to reification an idealist, utopian one? How would one actually distinguish between a meaning-packed world, in which every sign breathes significance, and a world in which signs have become 'self-sufficient' – a society of 'hyperreality' in Jean Baudrillard's terms? Doesn't the yearning for the former carry us ever more recklessly into the latter? How would the dreamed-of unity between subject and object be distinguishable from their current 'collapse'?

Theodor Adorno draws a direct connection between the nostalgia latent in the concept of reification and social totalitarianism, in a provocative, somewhat overstated paragraph in *Minima Moralia*. In fact there is something almost totalitarian about the 'inexorability' of the logic that Adorno invokes here:

> Nothing is more touching than a loving woman's anxiety lest love and tenderness, her best possession just because they cannot be possessed, be stolen away by a newcomer, simply because of her newness. . . . But from this touching feeling, without which

> all warmth and protection would pass away, an irresistible path leads, by way of the little boy's aversion for his younger brother and the fraternity-student's contempt for his 'fag', to the immigration laws that exclude all non-Caucasians from Social-Democratic Australia, and right up to the Fascist eradication of the racial minority, in which, indeed, all warmth and shelter explode into nothingness.[8]

Quite what we are supposed to do with this observation is unclear; the apparent determinism of the passage illustrates the state of paralysis to which a philosophical temperament in which the concept of reification is central (as it is throughout Adorno's work) can lead. It is difficult, furthermore, to disentangle Adorno's own anxiety towards reification, as it appears here, from the 'loving woman's anxiety' over the prospect of losing a loved one – ostensibly the theme of the passage. The truth, as the present study seeks to show, is that a profound anxiety towards reification may be unearthed behind every piece of serious writing on the subject. Thus, the second major proposition of this book is that such feelings are *constitutive* of the experience of reification, that the latter is incomprehensible without taking into account the consciousness of the perceiving subject who creates it; that the anxiety towards reification suggests a static, frozen conception of the relation between reality and its representation; that the anxiety towards reification is *itself reifying*.

At certain moments in this book I have made use of my own coinage, 'thingitude', to express this state of entanglement, an obvious derivation of 'finitude'. It occurs to me, however, that this term might be open to a much more systematic elaboration than has been provided in these pages. One could draw an explicit analogy with Aimé Césaire's inversion of the pejorative term '*nègre*' to create 'negritude'. For Césaire 'negritude' is not, as has often been alleged, an 'essentialist' category, a politics of identity and thus of 'glorious resignation' towards the hegemonic powers which construct such identities,[9] but a mode of subjective insertion into what is unacceptable – a strategic, heavily inflected 'acceptance' of a situation which is thereby *materialized in its unacceptability*. Negritude is not a philosophy or a politics as such, but the defiant recognition and cold articulation of a situation in its brutal actuality: 'not a cephalic index any more or a plasma or a soma but measured with the compass of suffering', as Césaire wrote in his great poem *Cahier d'un retour au pays natal*,

> . . . and the nigger [nègre] every day more debased, more cowardly, more sterile, less deep, more spread out of himself, more estranged from himself, more cunning with himself, less immediate with himself,
>
> I accept, I accept all this . . .[10]

For Césaire at least, negritude is a way of turning a situation of suffering to account, a way of confronting a repressive society with the falsifying effects of its own racial-ideological apparatus.

Frantz Fanon, insisting upon this interpretation of negritude (as against Senghor's black-African essentialism, say) in the context of the emergence of 'the cult of the veil' in colonial Algeria, writes: 'It is the white man who creates the negro. But it is the negro who creates negritude.'[11] In a similar way, 'thingitude' might be introduced as a response to the reifying effects of capitalism, a 'poetics of objectification' arising out of a willingness *to name that process as such*, and a refusal to accede to its logic; a refusal, that is to say, to posit some essential identity outside reification to counterpose to it, for such a strategy would be complicit with the cycle of capitalist accumulation and appropriation. If it is capitalism that creates the thing, it is – in part at least – the thing that creates thingitude. Reification is inseparable from the consciousness of the person who experiences it, the person who takes upon him- or herself the thingly quality of the world, who celebrates it, denounces it, flees from it, or is driven insane by it – yet each of these responses is an affirmation of the world as it is; each takes seriously the process of reification and colludes in it by default. Like negritude, 'thingitude' may be invested with radically divergent political implications. It too is susceptible to a reified interpretation; but it too is open to inflection in a progressive, revolutionary direction.

Thus, a further implication of the passage from Adorno quoted above is also a third major argument of this book: reification is a reversible concept, as potentially liberating as it is potentially oppressive. This reversibility of the concept is there in Lukács's work too, but in the cruder, diachronically disjointed form of the historical repudiation of the theory in the wake of its initial formulation. The theory of reification put forward in the present work is an attempt to combine Lukács's theorization with his subsequent renunciation of it; to see both moments as identifiable with or presupposing each other, and as ultimately incoherent without each other. Reification and its obsolescence, or its repudiation, must be understood in a relation of intimacy and inseparability. Indeed, its reformulation along these lines represents nothing more than the correspondence of the concept with its own logic.

In a passage originally intended for *Minima Moralia*, Adorno writes: 'The only true ideas are those which transcend their own thesis.' There are no theories which escape reification. Every one, he continues, 'by virtue of its constitution as a fixed, coherent structure', eventually develops 'paranoid features'.[12] And there is no theory of which this is truer, presumably, than that of reification itself. The concept of reification is unable to survive its own theorization; this certainly seems to have been Lukács's experience. For Adorno truth is attainable only negatively, by means of concepts which are inadequate to it, which falsify it. 'To say in a precise sense that someone holds this or that theory,' he writes, 'is already to imply the stolid, blankly staring proclamation of grievances, immune to self-reflection.'[13] He mentions Rousseau's 'noble savage', Freud's Oedipus complex, and Nietzsche's *Übermensch* as examples; in each, the paranoid element is the source both of its truth and of its grotesque falsity. How could reification, of all theories, be exempt from this situation? How could Lukács, of all theoreticians, be oblivious to it? In its capacity to comprehend the ontological disjunction between truth and its representation, reification is a signifier of its own inadequacy. Reification is the purest of all theories – the most universal and the most concrete – and the concept which, *as anxiety and phenomenon*, speaks to our present condition more than any other. In order to do so adequately, however, it requires reformulation – precisely as the theory of its own inadequacy. This is the task that the present work sets itself.

PART ONE

# Fall

*I must say that I am perhaps not a very contemporary man. I can say that I have never felt frustration or any kind of complex in my life. I know what these mean, of course, from the literature of the twentieth century, and from having read Freud. But I have not experienced them myself.*

Georg Lukács[1]

# 1

# Obsolescence of a Concept

As a metaphor for the effects of capitalism on people, relationships, self-images, ideas, social life, art and culture, the concept of reification is brutal, unambiguous, and apparently straightforward enough to provide a 'total' if somewhat pessimistic narrative of modernity. Reification is unsurpassed in all these respects by any other category of Marxist theory. Inseparable from its utility, however, is the crudeness of the concept – a crudeness reflected in the term itself. The German word is *Verdinglichung* – 'thingification'; in Spanish the verb is *cosificar*, to 'thingify'. In Italian, French and English, the Latin root (from *res*, 'thing') obscures this crudeness – but this has not prevented the term from falling out of intellectual fashion, due largely to the perception that the perspective it springs from is implicitly paternalistic and therefore anachronistic. Reification is a pseudo-scientific abstraction which, moreover, is all too susceptible to the process it denotes. Reification seems far too simplistic a concept to apply to a modernizing, market-driven, multicultural society which, by definition, is in a state of continual reinvention and flux, rather than one of decline, stasis or stagnation.

Reification refers to the moment that a process or relation is generalized into an abstraction, and thereby turned into a 'thing'. In Marxist theories of labour, reification is what happens when workers are installed in a place within the capitalist mode of production, and thus reduced to the status of a machine part.[2] It is closely allied to the processes of alienation, objectification, and the fetishism of commodities, in which 'the definite social relation between men themselves [assumes] the fantastic form of a relation between things'.[3] Reification refers to the generation of a 'phantom objectivity', meaning that a human creation – an institution or an ideology, say – takes on the character of 'a force that controls human beings'.[4] In the broader socio-political sphere, reification is what happens in every instance of racism and sexism, where the objects of prejudice are perceived not as human beings but as things or 'types'. It is what happens in 'property booms', when houses are turned into investment opportunities rather than places of residence; or in situations of modern warfare, when a complex of competing state interests is represented as a force for 'good' (more often, 'justice' or 'stability') in confrontation with a force of 'evil' – and so on. In each case, reification is the process in which 'thing-hood' becomes the standard of objective reality; the 'given world', in other words, is taken to be the truth of the world.

Arguably, this double movement of abstraction and crystallization is one that is inherent in all representation – all art and all politics – and it suggests the loss of an original whole or integrity. The concept of reification has a poetic suggestiveness which translates easily into mythical, religious, literary, psychological or cultural-political terms. For the same reason it has a tendency to conceptual expansion: reification is what happens when Adam and Eve are expelled from the garden of Eden and forced to live out of the sight of God, since from that moment humanity is separated, categorically, from truth. It is what happens when the hubris of the Tower of Babel is punished by the fragmentation of human speech into the languages of the world, thereby cutting off the realm of words forever from that of things. Alternatively, reification is what happens when Socrates drinks the hemlock, martyring himself for the sake of a Platonic truth that supposedly *pre-exists* representation. In the modern age it is what happens when the domain of human knowledge, some time between the Renaissance and the Enlightenment, is rationalized into the spheres of cognition, ethics and beauty, and subsequently into the disciplines of science, politics and art. The Christian concept of the Incarnation may be taken as a metaphor or even a synonym for reification; when Christ becomes man – 'historically' or symbolically, in the sacraments of the Holy Communion – the divine is translated into worldly terms. Christian redemption is the promise of a non-worldly, thus a non-reified existence; it is structurally analogous to the Marxist promise of revolution, but projected in a metaphysical form that is categorically removed from the worldly activity of politics.

At its broadest, as here, the concept of reification is the concept at its least 'revolutionary'. Marx tends to avoid the term – on the grounds, suggests Gillian Rose, that it is insufficiently concrete, tending to obscure the link between objectification and 'a specific mode of production';[5] in the three volumes of *Capital* it occurs only once or twice. Hegel never uses the term, although the origin of the idea may be traced to the philosophy of history introduced in the *Phenomenology of Spirit*. This, at any rate, is the genealogy emphasized by Herbert Marcuse in *Reason and Revolution*, for whom the first three sections of the *Phenomenology* are nothing less than a critique of reification, a word used almost interchangeably by Marcuse with 'positivism', or 'the philosophy of common sense'.[6]

As such, the concept of reification presupposes a dialectic of modernity, a form in which, *pace* Marx, it is infused with complexity and ambiguity. Its lack of 'concretion', this is to say, is precisely the point. In the *Phenomenology of Spirit*, consciousness is determined by a historical cycle of reification and dereification; consciousness is the product of man objectifying his thought forms, and successively projecting himself in consciousness beyond those objectifications. Hegel's Absolute Knowledge is the speculative moment at which the philosopher transcends reification, the point at which 'spirit' (*Geist*) is fully transparent to itself. Reification is a process that, to an extent, we are all determined by and yet one which, through phenomenological reflection, we may come to recognize and to resist. The concept itself is a demand that we acknowledge the fact that, in Peter Berger and Stanley Pullberg's words, the reality of the world 'is given neither in itself nor once and for all' but must be continually realized as actualization and as recognition.[7] The 'given world' – *le monde comme donné*, in Lucien Goldmann's phrase[8] – insofar as it is understood as such, is a reification; it is easy to see how the concept might become severed from a political programme, and thereupon criticized as mystical or 'essentialist'.[9]

In the Hegelian Marxist tradition, 'dereification' is achieved through dialectical reflection, in which men come to know the world and themselves as mutually constitutive. For Georg Lukács – the thinker responsible for its most complete theorization – dereification is achieved in the moment of revolution, when subject and object are unified through the action of the proletariat, who represent Lukács's privileged subject of history precisely on account of their *subjection*. In throwing off the yoke of exploitation the proletariat remakes the objective world as one which the historical 'subject' has literally created.[10] The *realization* of the consciousness of the proletariat consists in the transformation from being to becoming, from facts to processes, from objects to relations. For Lucien Goldmann, the term reification circumscribes a collection of effects at the level of the superstructure – 'the *psychic and intellectual* consequences of the existence of production for the market in a purely capitalist society – liberal or monopolist – with little economic intervention by the state.'[11] Indeed, for Goldmann, it is precisely the generalizability of the theory of reification which has permitted what coherence there is between the various Marxist texts on the relation between base and superstructure to be established.[12] For Goldmann, as for Lukács, 'reified thought' seems to function as a simple oppositional term to 'dialectical thought'. Reification means 'identity thinking' – the thoughtless subsumption of words into things or, as Martin Jay puts it, 'the suppression of heterogeneity in the name of identity'.[13] It is the moment at which 'the totality of production disappears from consciousness' – an event which in various forms (the 'death' of God, the spread of individualism, the displacement of 'theory' by 'empiricism') seems as much a feature of modernity as of capitalist production *per se*.[14]

At a time when capitalism is widely proclaimed to have reached a stage of consolidation, the concept of reification ought to enjoy more currency than ever. Contemporary political reality, after all, is founded on the assumption that the globalized economy is 'the only possible world'. There seems no better example of a reified phenomenon than 'globalization', the intellectual product of a bourgeois ideology which always, for Lukács, polarizes reality into the details on one hand – over which people acquire increasing control – and the universal on the other, over which the possibility of intellectual control is progressively lost. The concept of globalization represents the 'totality' in a simplified, intellectually graspable but politically immutable form – like the concept of God in an earlier epoch. As such, globalization is the rarefied form of the logic of capitalism itself, a phenomenon forecast long ago by Marx and Engels in the *Communist Manifesto* as the 'cosmopolitan' effect of the expansion of the bourgeois mode of production. It is matched by the phenomenon of 'localization', its obverse and counterpart, which – understood in this way – is not a process which empowers people in the face of their political subjection, but a diversion from the truth of their subjection. Globalization, as Marx and Engels intuited, is a deeply contradictory structure, and it has led to correspondingly reified forms of consciousness at the micro-political level – from the turn to ethical values in political discourse to the growth in nationalistic or ethnocentric forms of consciousness. Globalization fulfills all the criteria of a reified phenomenon as described by Lukács in *History and Class Consciousness* – a 'man-made' reality which appears to man to be 'a natural phenomenon alien to himself', in which his activity is restricted to 'the exploitation of the inexorable fulfilment of certain individual laws for his own (egoistic) interests', and in which he remains 'the object and not the subject' of events, even of his own activity.[15] One might even speculate that the world is approaching that state of 'total reification' anticipated by Adorno at his most mordant, a point at which 'the will to live finds itself dependent on the denial of the will to live', as reality is increasingly bureaucratized, and all phenomena reduced to 'epiphenomena' – a level of objective reality that is merely secondary, derivative.[16] It seems surprising, therefore, that very little work in the humanities or the social sciences making explicit use of the concept of reification has been published in the last thirty years.[17] Yet this has as much to do, perhaps, with the changing perception of the possibility of dereification as with the status of the term as a credible description of contemporary reality.

Central to Lukács's theory is the status of reification as a phenomenon of class society. Both the proletariat and the bourgeoisie are 'repositories of reification in its acutest and direst form', writes Lukács – the only difference being, he says (quoting Marx), that the property-owning class 'feels at home in this self-alienation and feels itself confirmed by it; it recognizes alienation as its own instrument and in it it possesses the semblance of a human existence.' The proletariat, meanwhile, 'feels destroyed by this alienation and sees in it its own impotence and the reality of an inhuman existence.'[18] Reification is dependent upon being able to see it – on the existence of a proletarian or subaltern class which is not implicated in the hegemonic version of the world, and whose consciousness is by definition that of historical truth – meaning that its consciousness will be proven by future events to *have been* that of truth.[19]

The progress of capitalism, however, has been such that the consciousness of the proletariat – which for Lukács constitutes a perspective of truth by virtue of its subjection and marginalization alone – appears to have been utterly eroded. Power relations in capitalist societies are no longer characterized by violence or oppression, but by the progressive enfranchisement of citizens, by their material (and thus ideological) *recruitment*; the transformation is overwhelmingly from what Althusser termed 'repressive state apparatuses' to 'ideological state apparatuses'.[20] Capitalism has successfully *colonized* the position of marginality, bringing into being precisely Adorno's state of 'total reification', in which the subjectivity of men and women is completely dominated by consumer society, removing the possibility even of subjective, interior resistance. The effect of this is that reification itself fades from view – firstly as a perceivable phenomenon, and secondly as a category of critical-theoretical-sociological analysis. With the progressive evaporation of the possibility of recreating the world, the revolutionary mode of consciousness on which the concept depends falls into narcissism and obsolescence.

This is the concept of reification at its most straightforward (and abstract), a linear process inseparable from temporality and modernity; its implications, as can be seen, are politically paralysing rather than rousing or catalytic. Social theory becomes indeed that 'melancholy science' evoked by Adorno in the opening of *Minima Moralia* – a moribund discipline approaching a condition of 'intellectual neglect, sententious whimsy and finally oblivion'.[21] The most obvious criticism to level against this version of the concept is that reification has here been itself reified – turned into a mystical, autonomous and inevitable process, a purely 'objective' phenomenon impermeable to political intervention, a notion equivalent to and simultaneous with modernity and globalization. The situation it is meant to resolve – the alienation of subject and object – is on the contrary exacerbated, and imbued with a tragical character; in this defeatist vision the chasm between subject and object widens in direct proportion to the efforts exerted to bring them together. Tragic vision, however – the theme of which is that 'it is impossible to live a valid life in this world'[22] – is by no means the only or the most coherent of the various ideas of reification.

*

# 2

# Marxist Anxieties

In the twentieth century, theorists have invented different strategies for dealing with the 'threat' of reification. Within Marxist debates, some have tried to refine and rarefy the concept, endlessly differentiating its nuances from those of 'competing' concepts such as alienation, objectification, commodification, commodity fetishism, and so on. Taking this approach to an extreme, Gillian Rose insists that reification is not a concept at all, that to 'conceive' it as such is to 'reify' it.[1] Others, mostly from outside the Marxist paradigm, abandon any attempt at a 'concrete' elaboration of the concept – most notably Burke C. Thomason, whose 'constructionist' concept of reification avoids any parsimonious circumscription of the term, along with the project of finding causes for the phenomenon, the possibility or the desirability of devising strategies of liberation from it, and finally its negative connotations altogether.[2] Still others have discarded the concept, finding it unworkable, incoherent and potentially regressive – a symptom of the very anxieties it was intended to resolve. On the most basic critical account, reification is equated (as above) with a 'Fall of Man' scenario, and thence dismissed as essentialist and idealist. It's a simple enough point – indeed, as it turns out, far too simple: reification depends upon a totalizing narrative, a duality of distinct reified (existing) and non-reified (lost, or not yet realized) worlds, in which an immediate order of things, an integrated existence set in the remote past or future, is projected in contrast to a present-day, hopelessly mediated and insubstantial world.

Derrida's thought offers a theoretical rationale for a critique of the concept on this basis; indeed, in a body of work whose declared co-ordinates are precision, vigilance, specificity, Derrida has never even come close to using the term.[3] One implication of philosophical deconstruction and, in particular, postcolonial work in the humanities, is that such distinctions as that between a reified and a non-reified world reiterate a partial, implicitly patriarchal and thoroughly Western account of modernity which, by conceiving its relation to the 'other' in stark oppositional terms (the unknown, the primitive, the sublime, the unreified, the exploited, as opposed to the familiar, the civilized, the decadent, the malignant, the rapacious), preserves it in a state of absolute otherness. In this critique, 'non-reified' (primitive) societies and the 'dereified' society of the future are seen as idealistic projections, conceptually interdependent with and therefore inseparable from the 'reified' society in which they are conceived as such. For deconstruction and postcolonialism there is no escaping one's embeddedness in reification; yet, simultaneously, that recognition stands as an unstated and unstatable strategy of escape, a form of 'praxis' situated in what Homi Bhabha calls 'liminality' or 'hybridity', a political space in between necessity and accuracy.[4] Few postcolonial critics make reference to Lukács, or to any other figures within the 'Western Marxist' tradition. However Gayatri Spivak, a central figure in both deconstruction and postcolonialism, criticizes not Lukács's essay on reification itself but the 'philosophical presuppositions' of its 'Western Marxist readership' for privileging 'use-value as the concrete';[5] it is just such a binary conceptualization of Western modernity that the notion of reification is taken implicitly to depend upon and to reiterate.

That reification is caught up in an ostensibly linear narrative of history, however, is also the source of its utility and adaptability. Reification as an idea is equally applicable to belief in God in the modern age, and to the *dissolution* of belief in God (meaning the replacement of God by an equally reified notion of 'Man'). It may be applied at different socio-historical moments to marriage – a social form in which an essentially material, economic relation between two people appears in an abstract form as a thing – as well as to an aestheticized solitude which fetishizes its independence as a mode of immediacy or integrity that can only be *threatened* by social interaction or forms of institutional recognition (such as marriage). Reification is applicable to modernity itself, a social system which presupposes human omniscience; but also to pre-modernity as characterized by an ideological dependence on myth and mystification. The process of reification in capitalist society is one of embedding men and women in the particular, of hiding from them their implication in and constitution by a social and historical 'totality'; and of subsuming them beneath a false generality (such as their membership of families, states or nations) – an ideological process which must take different forms at different times. In each case, reification is opposed in principle to the failure to think the totality.

It is important to insist on this last point; for in one sense, as it is presented in the *Communist Manifesto*, capitalism might appear not as synchronous with the process of reification but as its complete opposite. After all, the process of globalization as represented in that text is one of constant revolutionizing of the means of production: 'All fixed, fast-frozen relations, with their train of ancient and venerable prejudices and opinions, are swept away, all new-formed ones become antiquated before they can ossify', etc.[6] The moment in which 'all that is solid melts into air, all that is holy is profaned', in Marx and Engels's famous phrase, is surely one primarily of dereification; as Ellen Meiksins Wood has pointed out, the real revolutionary hero of the *Communist Manifesto* is the bourgeoisie.[7] Its achievements are by no means purely malign; indeed they include the forcible eradication of racism – 'the barbarians' intensely obstinate hatred of foreigners' – and the dissolution of people's 'religious and political illusions'.[8] In such a situation the concept of reification appears more anachronistic than ever. Why, asks Spivak pertinently, 'are Marxist intellectuals interested in holding things together [with such totalizing concepts], when "history", "culture", "real-life" (big, difficult words) are forever on the move . . .?'[9]

Capitalism, says Meiksins Wood further, is for Marx and

Engels a *precondition* of socialism. It is this insight which might be seen to have imperilled the position of the concept of reification within radical theory, along with the wider project of a revolutionary Marxism predicated on the idea of overthrowing bourgeois society, including the 'reified consciousness' with which it co-exists. Neil Lazarus, developing this insight, writes that the 'socialist imaginary' of the Marxian tradition is 'made irrepressible' upon a conceptual basis established by capitalism. Not until the development of European capitalism, he observes (citing Samir Amin), had the idea of universalism been imagined on anything other than a purely speculative basis.[10] Gayatri Spivak is more formulistic when she writes, in *A Critique of Postcolonial Reason*, that 'Capitalism is . . . the *pharmakon* of Marxism. It produces the possibility of the operation of the dialectic that will produce socialism, but left to its own resources it is also that which blocks that operation.'[11] Such insights are exemplary of the logic according to which postcolonialism announces a shift from the oppositional (or dialectical) terminology of what has been termed 'Western Marxism' to the deconstructive language developed by post-structuralist thinkers such as Derrida and Michel Foucault.

Spivak's use of *pharmakon* alludes to Derrida's essay 'Plato's Pharmacy'; the word – taken from Plato's *Phaedrus*, and usually translated as 'remedy' – denotes, she says, 'poison that is medicinal when knowingly administered.' In other words, the *pharmakon* – like all of Derrida's central concepts – is a trope for non-reifiability, insofar as it signifies an entity *that has no truth in and of itself*.[12] A page later, introducing a discussion of what she calls 'the field of *différance* between capitalism and socialism', Spivak writes: 'There is no state on the globe today that is not part of the capitalist economic system or can want to eschew it fully.' As a result, she says, Marxism is now best conceived as a 'speculative morphology' which can operate in today's world 'only as a persistent critique of a system – micro-electronic post-industrial world capitalism – that a polity cannot not want to inhabit, for that is the "real" of the situation.' The implication is not only that capitalism and socialism are *historically* indissociable, but that, methodologically, the revolutionary anticipation of an Event inaugurating a break from a reified into a non-reified society is at best reductive, and at worst amounts to 'predictive social engineering' with all its 'violent and violating consequences'.[13] Lukács, in fact, claims something similar as a presupposition of his own theory of reification when he insists that the standpoint of the proletariat does not aim at an 'unrepeatable tearing of the veil' but at the dissolution of reality 'into processes and tendencies'.[14] For all that the concept of reification is criticized as embodying a dualistic topography of truth and appearance, use-value and exchange-value, transcendence and worldliness, pre-revolution and post-revolution, the consciousness of the bourgeoisie and the consciousness of the proletariat, etc., the concept elucidated by Lukács is at every moment set *against* such a dualistic topography. Reification, potentially, is as nuanced as any term within the post-structuralist arsenal of elaborate metaphors and 'non-originary' concepts. This, indeed, is one implication of Spivak's occasional insistence upon a certain 'minimal truth': that Marx and Derrida 'both belong to the dialectical tradition'[15] – a statement in which deconstruction, *read properly*, is declared to be nothing other than dialectical thinking, *read properly*; and vice versa.

# 3

# Reification and Colonialism

Nonetheless only Edward Said, in the huge body of work that has appeared under the sign of 'postcolonialism', has found a way to make systematic use of the concept of reification, albeit within rigorously controlled discursive boundaries, and while also acknowledging its 'complicity' with cultural imperialism. This complicity is worth exploring a little; for, notwithstanding the conceptual richness of Lukács's development of reification, the very idea of 'colonization' – an idea, as Marx puts it, of 'virgin soil colonized by free immigrants'[1] – is structurally analogous to a 'simple' concept of reification. It is one which has in principle been contested – not as historical fact, but as hermeneutical idea – by postcolonial theoreticians ever since the publication of Said's *Orientalism* in 1978. In recent years postcolonialist critics have explicitly refused the analogue of the Fall as a model for colonization, and it is easy to see that such a refusal might lead those same critics to be highly reticent towards the concept of reification.[2]

This structural analogy between reification and colonization may be mapped out at the most basic level as follows: the idea of a total theory which is similarly applicable to, for example, the killing of Stephen Lawrence, the Dreyfus case, the concept of Manifest Destiny in nineteenth-century America, and the concept of globalization at the turn of the twenty-first century, but also to the hate-fuelled demonization of the Lawrence suspects,[3] the colonial enterprise and the system of religious beliefs that legitimated it – such an idea is *de facto* an act of *theoretical* colonization, a reinscription of the relations of inequality which made possible those abuses in the first place, a way of stripping those events of their cultural and historical specificity, and a means of enforcing interpretative dominance over them.[4] Reification approximates everything to a single narrative, just as the colonial enterprise itself was founded on a single animating idea – that of the 'civilizing' or truth-bringing mission of the colonizing nations. Edward Said makes this point in the most economical of forms – the epigraph – on the first page of *Culture and Imperialism*, with a quotation from Joseph Conrad's *Heart of Darkness*:

> The conquest of the earth, which mostly means the taking it away from those who have a different complexion or slightly

> flatter noses than ourselves, is not a pretty thing when you look into it too much. What redeems it is the idea only. An idea at the back of it; not a sentimental pretence but an idea; and an unselfish belief in the idea – something you can set up, and bow down before, and offer a sacrifice to . . .[5]

The passage encapsulates the sheer inadequacy of the liberal queasiness towards the colonial project in a way that is instructive for the concept of reification. At the dawn of the modernist literary epoch, Joseph Conrad articulates a profound disquiet about modern civilization in terms which betray a continuing adherence to the Western narrative of history – a narrative which allocates every geographical place on earth a point on a linear chronology – and to the Western values underlying that project. As a critique of colonialism, *Heart of Darkness* falls desperately short; indeed the essential nobility of the colonial *idea* – above and beyond the contingent horrors of its historical implementation – is left more or less uninterrogated in Conrad's text.

The lessons for the concept of reification, however, are based on more than mere analogy. A characteristic of *Heart of Darkness*, indeed a theme of Conrad's writing in general, is a profound uneasiness over the ability of language itself to convey truth – an uneasiness alluded to in F. R. Leavis's famous deflating comment upon *Heart of Darkness*: 'Is anything added to the oppressive mysteriousness of the Congo by such sentences as: "It was the stillness of an implacable force brooding over an inscrutable intention –"?'[6] Said is more generous to Conrad when he writes of a tragic awareness apparent in his work that 'the chasm between words saying and words meaning [is] widened, not lessened, by a talent for words written.'[7] Conrad's writing has a certain endemic 'vagueness' about it, a refusal to commit itself to the exigencies of linguistic representation, or to concrete reality itself. His goal, as Said writes, is 'to make us see, or otherwise transcend the absence of everything but words, so that we may pass into a realm of vision beyond the words' – a realm which Said describes as

> a world of such uncomplicated coincidence between intention, word, and deed that the ghost of a fact, as Lord Jim has it, can be put to rest. There, the space separating ambition from activity is narrowed. Retrospective time and events are corrected for divergences. Or, still more radically, the writer's intention of wishing to say something very clearly is squared completely with the reader's seeing; by the labours of a solitary writer, words affixed to the page become the common unmediated property of the reader, who penetrates past the words to their author's visual intention, which is the same as his written presentation.[8]

This is a world, in other words, in which the disparity between word and thing, subject and object, has been abolished – a world without reification. *Heart of Darkness*, in particular, might be described as a straightforward 'reification narrative', the story of a man's quest for a locus of truth 'stripped of the cloak of time' – a quest which ends *successfully* at 'the heart of an impenetrable darkness'.[9] Marlow's tale, recounted on board the *Nellie*, is told to four representatives of a society in what Nietzsche would call an 'epigonal' state – including a director of companies, a lawyer, and an accountant – former seafarers reduced to 'performing on [their] respective tight-ropes for . . . half a crown a tumble', as Marlow remarks at one point in his narration.[10] Counterposed to these effete, mediocre figures is Marlow's discovery in the Congo of a race of 'black fellows', 'as natural and true as the surf along their coast'.[11] Yet this apparent admiration is inverted both by the 'horror' which he encounters further inland, and by his inability to give this horror linguistic form.

Conrad's writing is animated by anxiety, not only towards the brutality of the colonial enterprise, but towards the violence of language itself. Marlow laments to his listeners: 'No, it is impossible; it is impossible to convey the life-sensation of any given epoch of one's existence – that which makes its truth, its meaning – its subtle and penetrating essence. It is impossible. We live, as we dream – alone.'[12] Said characterizes Conrad's use of prose as 'negation', of itself and of what it dealt with – a product of 'his faith in the supremacy of the visible' combined with 'his radical doubt that written language could imitate what the eye saw'. Conrad's perception seeks, therefore, to transcend writing itself: 'For Conrad the meaning produced by writing was a kind of visual outline, which written language would approach only from the outside and from a distance that seemed to remain constant.'[13] Fredric Jameson locates Conrad's anxiety towards reification, similarly, in a stylistic 'impressionism' which sought a 'Utopian compensation for everything lost in the process of the development of capitalism – the place of quality in an increasingly quantified world, the place of the archaic and of feeling amid the desacralization of the market system, the place of sheer colour and intensity within the grayness of measurable extension and geometrical abstraction.'[14] Apparently free of the reservations which affect Said's reading of the work, Jameson's aesthetic validation of Conrad – his professed concern to 'respect the ambivalent value of Conrad's impressionism', his willingness to see his work as 'ideology and Utopia all at once'[15] – bespeaks not only the elevation of the sensual (the visual) over the textual, but the privileged status which the concept of reification enjoys in Jameson's own work.

With this 'privileged status', perhaps, the concept of reification becomes itself reified. Such is the implication of the critique which Sean Homer, for one, has levelled at Jameson's use of the term. Like Conrad's personal revulsion from the empirical reality of the colonial project, Jameson's aversion to reification risks embedding him in a culturally and historically specific 'aestheticism', in which the effects of reification are ameliorated, even negated, only by some form of existential activity (which, at certain ill-advised moments in his writing, Jameson makes specific). His interest in Conrad is precisely on the basis that Conrad's subjectivism emblematizes a strategy for dealing with reification which anticipates Jameson's own. The presupposition of this subjectivist approach is the 'total reification' of the world, an achieved dystopia which makes imperative some means, even if delusory, of access to the universal – a balm for the misery engendered by capitalist society or, as Perry Anderson puts it in relation to Jameson, 'a spray of wonder and pleasure – the chances of happiness in a stifling time', qualities which Anderson finds in the style of even Jameson's 'most ominous' reflections.[16]

Homer explains Jameson's theory of reification in just these totalizing terms: for Jameson, he says, 'the unremitting logic of reification and commodification has finally colonized the last areas of resistance: the unconscious, the aesthetic and the Third World.'[17] This presupposition is apparent in the concluding remarks to Jameson's book *The Geopolitical Aesthetic*, where he writes that reification and commodification 'have become so universalized as to seem well-nigh natural and organic entities and forms.'[18] Thus the formerly 'secondary' doctrines of reification and commodification in the domain of Marxist criticism are, in the present conjuncture of late capitalism, 'likely to come into their own and become the dominant instruments of analysis and struggle'. In such a context, a 'politics of daily life' emerges to displace what Jameson calls '"politics" itself' as 'the primary space of struggle'. Jameson's appeal, writes Perry Anderson, lies in his attempt 'to conjure into being what might be thought impossible – a lucid enchantment of the world.'[19] Just as Marx and Engels wrote of religion as the logic of an 'inverted' world in popular form and thus 'the opium of the people', so for Jameson the aesthetic – much less ambiguously than in Adorno's thought, for example – is a sphere for rekindling 'utopian longings' in a thoroughly reified society. And as long as that condition is as thoroughgoing as he implies, the cultural sphere will retain all the political significance that he attributes to it. Jameson's equanimity in the face of this situation, however, differentiates him markedly from the temperament embodied in Conrad's major protagonists.

An *obsession* with reification – meaning an overwhelming sense of the unreliability of language as a 'technology' of modernity, of the corrosiveness of representation itself, a quasi-religious idealization of 'timelessness' and the corresponding depreciation of 'history' – is entirely congruent with a revulsion from civilization itself and a pessimistic lapse into solitude and aestheticism. Conrad's attempt at a preservation of the self *against* the world masks, firstly, a nostalgic enchantment with the 'primitive', and secondly, an idealist, undialectical conception of truth as located outside history, and outside the bounds of human communication. His 'anti-imperialism' betrays a parochial vision, defensible only on the basis of his geographically and historically limited existence.

If Conrad's work is racist, as has been declared in the strongest terms by Chinua Achebe,[20] it is both in spite and because of this Eurocentric, self-reflexive anxiety – directed against every manifestation of civilization *per se*. The limitation of his vision finds an echo within Frankfurt School critical theory, in the elevation of reification itself into an inexorable and totalizing process, an analysis which contributes, as Ernest Mandel has pointed out (citing Adorno),[21] to the further mystification of 'late capitalism' itself.

# 4

# From Adorno to Jameson

Reification is described by Fredric Jameson as the most powerful of a series of tools variously employed by Marxist critique in a 'mediating' capacity: 'By being able to use the same language about . . . quite distinct objects or levels of an object,' he writes, 'we can restore, *at least methodologically*, the lost unity of social life, and demonstrate that widely distant elements of the social totality are ultimately part of the same global historical process.'[1] I shall leave aside, for the time being, the question of the substantiality of a merely 'methodological' restoration of unity. The charge haunting the concept of reification, which has led to its eclipse within philosophy, literary criticism and the social sciences, is that it originates in a Eurocentric perspective; that, in subordinating the concept of racism, say, to the logic of reification, the *experience* of racism is stripped of its specificity and prevented from being a thing in itself; that, in the final analysis, the concept of reification is imperialist and even implicitly racist. 'One must have tradition in oneself, to hate it properly', declared the great reification obsessive Theodor Adorno, apparently paving the way for the monopolization of *Ideologiekritik* by European bourgeois intellectuals:

> Late-comers and newcomers have an alarming affinity to positivism, from Carnap-worshippers in India to the stalwart defenders of the German masters Matthias Grünewald and Heinrich Schütz. It would be poor psychology to assume that exclusion arouses only hate and resentment; it arouses too a possessive, intolerant kind of love, and those whom repressive culture has held at a distance can easily enough become its most diehard defenders.[2]

The concept of reification presupposes the assimilation of all cultures to a single culture, whereupon they take a position somewhere on a line stretching between pure innocence, located near the dawn of the world, and decadence, situated in its twilight. This presupposition survives any attempt simply to invert the relation. In the same paragraph in *Minima Moralia*, Adorno opposes an 'uncompromising' (that is to say, critical) mind to 'primitivism, neophytism, or the "non-capitalist world"', and he lists among the attributes of the former 'historical memory', 'a fastidious intellect' and 'an ample measure of satiety' – all qualities which Conrad's 'savages', for example, are quite without, given that they lack any clear idea of time.[3]

The critical reflexivity of the intellectual hereby becomes a suspect value, insofar as it manifests a perspective which by *definition* – according to the conceptual structure described by Lukács in *History and Class Consciousness* – is unable to embody history in its person. The theoretician, as Adorno acknowledges in the notorious essay 'Resignation', is a 'relatively sensitive' figure who is himself 'deformed' by the division of labour, and thus most often characterized by 'subjective weakness'.[4] Appearing in a text which explicitly takes issue with the idea of the passivity and complicity of 'theory', this diagnosis seems resigned to the mere fact of the division of labour as a reifying force. 'Pseudo-activity', says Adorno in the same essay – disparaging a form of protest, direct action, that is often polemically counterposed to the activity of theoreticians – 'is generally the attempt to rescue enclaves of immediacy in the midst of a thoroughly mediated and rigidified society.'[5] If there is a difference between this attitude and that of Fredric Jameson, it is, firstly, the latter's unequivocal acceptance of the conclusivity of that 'rigidification', and secondly, his turn to the cultural as a means of liberation from it. In this move, says Perry Anderson, Jameson successfully leaves behind the current of 'historical pessimism' within the Western Marxist tradition.[6] For Jameson, apparently, the stance sometimes defended by Adornians as rhetorical exaggeration, intended to excite resistance against a progressively more exploitative society,[7] is a simple truth claim, or the prognostication of a future state of affairs which has now come into effect. While in Adorno the phenomenon of reification remains conceptually ambiguous – inescapable and yet, at every moment, potentially dissoluble – for Jameson the spheres of reification and aesthetic experience are more clearly differentiated, along the lines of another hermeneutic distinction which he makes between ideology and Utopia.[8] The cultural sphere is for Jameson the site of a liberating aesthetic engagement with the world; subject and object are maintained in their separation by default, such that he is able to write, quite earnestly, of the potential that inheres, in late capitalist society, in activities such as physical exercise and reading poetry to liberate people from reification.[9]

The same deterministic outlook was often attributed to Adorno, particularly in his later work. Mandel quotes the following passage – evidence, he says, of 'a tragic misreading of the facts', amounting to a defeatist and therefore complicitous relationship to the ideological objectives of the ruling class:

> The pseudo-revolutionary gesture is the complement of the technical impossibility of a spontaneous revolution, pointed out years ago by Jürgen von Kempski. Against those who control the bomb, barricades are ridiculous; one therefore plays at barricades, and the masters temporarily let the players have their way.[10]

'Pseudo-activity', according to Adorno, fails to comprehend the severity of the situation, consoling itself with futile posturing in the face of a vast, inexorable, all but omniscient state. Pseudo-activity has no genuine grasp of the totality, remaining in effect embedded in particularity. Like the pursuit of 'hobbies' which Adorno writes about elsewhere,[11] pseudo-activity is activity undertaken *on the basis of* a reified world – that is to say, in isolation from true knowledge of the totality; it functions entirely at the subjective level as a salve for the conscience, a mode of essentially aesthetic, or aestheticist *compensation*. Mandel identifies Adorno's attitude here simply as 'pessimism', a characteristic sensibility of modernist intellectuals, the effect of which is the further mystification of the reality of late capitalism.

In Jameson the same diagnosis is given a more optimistic gloss, a concomitant of his effective accommodation of the 'reality' of reification. It is worth elaborating Jameson's theory of reification in some detail, since he has been the most committed user, even popularizer, of the term since Adorno. The ambiguities of the concept are preserved in Jameson's work, but they are rendered quite differently from Adorno's usage. The most important factor to consider is Jameson's 'periodizing' approach, the basis of which is an alleged strain of 'Messianism' which takes its cue from Marx's early writings. It is on this foundation that Jameson's accommodation of the reality of reification is possible, along with his sustained commitment to the concept of culture 'for the time being'. Yet this same foundation has led to charges that the concept of reification – in particular Jameson's use of it – is idealist and even 'subjectivist'. Similar accusations were levelled at Lukács in the years following the publication of *History and Class Consciousness* in 1923. In a recently discovered manuscript, written in 1925 or 1926, Lukács strenuously, though privately, defended his work against such charges;[12] yet, before considering the substance of that defence, I shall examine the structural connection between 'Messianism' and the periodizing approach of Jameson's historical materialism.

# 5

# Messianism, Historical Materialism, Post-structuralism

As stated above, an apparently categorical antithesis operates in Jameson's thought, between reified consciousness and 'aesthetic' experience; the same antithesis is also present in his work in the form of a conceptual opposition between 'ideological' and 'Utopian' thought. While this opposition reiterates a conventional value structure – 'ideology' betokens a 'negative' Marxist hermeneutic of 'false consciousness' and domination, while 'Utopia' encompasses all forms of thought which promise liberation from the former, including that '*promesse de bonheur* most immediately inscribed in the aesthetic text'[1] – the opposition itself is also predicated upon a categorical distinction between a logic of the 'here and now' (a reality in which such oppositions are determining, constitutive and thus indispensable) and a projected 'logic of the collectivity', of *post-histoire*, in which such binarisms will dissolve.[2] Thus two levels are clearly differentiated: one of contingency, falsitude and necessity, and another of truth, liberation and other-worldliness. In the former, ideology and Utopia are polar opposites; that polarity is a product of 'reified' logic, but it also has truth value insofar as it has a constitutive bearing on present-day reality. The latter is a realm in which such oppositions are revealed in all their ideological clothing; yet to insist upon stripping them of it, without acknowledging that the 'good society' has little immediate prospect of being achieved, is to carry that insight to an extreme and perhaps politically despotic point. The only synthesis of these two dimensions of existence that is possible, in capitalist society, is 'methodological' or – in an alternative formulation – 'aesthetic'. Theoretical language, like poetry, is a means of disrupting the reification of everyday language. Theory, like poetry, 'reasserts its production of language and reinvents a center'; its difficulty is 'in direct proportion to the degree of reification of everyday speech'.[3] It is in Jameson's elaboration of the concept of culture, however, that these ambiguities attain their fullest explanation.

In *The Political Unconscious*, Jameson outlines his understanding of culture as having both an 'ideological' function of legitimizing the existing social order, as well as a 'Utopian' one in which substantial 'incentives' work to legitimize and subvert that ideology – to legitimize it, furthermore, *insofar* as they subvert it. The relation between ideology and Utopia is therefore dialectical and economic rather than positivistic and dualistic: the ideological cannot function adequately without offering Utopian incentives; simultaneously, Utopian incentives will in the present social system always be swiftly appropriated and dispersed. Even in its most 'ideological' manifestations, says Jameson, cultural production points towards a non-realized – perhaps non-realizable – sphere in which its own activity is annulled:

> Durkheim's view of religion (which we have expanded to include cultural activity generally) as a symbolic affirmation of human relationships, along with Heidegger's conception of the work of art as a symbolic enactment of the relationship of human beings to the nonhuman, to Nature and to Being, are in this society false and ideological; but they will know their truth and come into their own at the end of what Marx calls prehistory. At that moment, then, the problem of the opposition of the ideological to the Utopian, or the functional-instrumental to the collective, will have become a false one.[4]

The 'Utopian' function of such ideas, in other words, will in the final analysis (whatever that means) emerge from their purely 'reified' form like, we might suppose, a butterfly from a chrysalis. Meanwhile, in a reified society, religion, philosophy and poetry are indispensable to human happiness; they provide a form of access to the universal which is only false within the reified logic of capitalist society. Undoubtedly, dereified equivalents to God, truth, totality, or aesthetic experience are *addressed* by such concepts, yet the stage of human history at which such entities could be *named* as such is unforeseeable and unimaginable. Religion, art and philosophy offer us a momentary glimpse of a world without reification. The early Marxist aesthetician Max Raphael states this in the context of a favourable 'dialectical' appraisal of the paintings of Paul Cézanne, when he writes that art 'frees us from enslavement to words, concepts, and false moral values by showing us that life knows differentiations that cannot be reduced to concepts as well as situations which cannot be judged by accepted moral standards.'[5] It should at least be noted, however, that for Jameson the 'logic of a collectivity which has not yet come into being' is never elaborated in the form of anything more concrete than a 'logic' – and that for Jameson this limitation is inevitable in a reified society. In the passage quoted above, the term 'prehistory' is handled with a distancing mechanism ('what Marx calls'), as if to suggest that in the postmodern (or 'late capitalist') condition such an overtly Utopian phrase is antiquarian at best, teleological and idealistic at worst, and should certainly be bracketed off in any – albeit procedurally necessary – usage.

Thus Jameson's own critical methodology *presupposes* reification, insofar as it depends on 'an initial separation between means and ends – between Utopian gratification and ideological manipulation . . .'[6] This is the meaning of Sean Homer's objection that Jameson rewrites the concept of totality 'at a higher level of abstraction, as an absent cause, beyond representation'.[7] Jameson appears to want to have his cake and eat it; for, depending on whether he is floating in the alps of 'dialectical' thought, or slumming it in the 'lower and more practical level of cultural analysis',[8] he is both oppositional and immanentist, transcendentalist and materialistic. Jameson is committed variously to the moments of joy that can be rescued from the 'labour of the negative' and to the project of achieving that collective 'transparency' made possible by positioning the individual within the social totality.[9] A radically polarized distinction between theory and practice subsists in his thought as a corollary precisely of his commitment to 'reification' – even as he insists on their 'dialectical interpenetration'.

Jameson's claim to provide a genuinely historical and dialectical (rather than, say, idealist) account rests on the fact that he inflects ideology into Utopia and vice versa. A particular eschatology – a theory of final things – infuses his concept of reification. For all its claim to a revolutionary perspective, Jameson's thought might easily be accused, firstly, of *dissolving* all Utopian potential by means of this interpenetration with ideological forms. The domain of culture, in Jameson's thought, does not merely foreshadow the Messianic new world; it replaces it. Thus the projected moment of 'Utopia' is indeed purely methodological. Jameson's 'for the time being' comes to displace the teleological 'mirage' within Marxism – the moment at which 'the individual subject would be somehow fully conscious of his or her determination by class' and 'able to square the circle of ideological conditioning by sheer lucidity and the taking of thought.'[10] Marxism, in Jameson, is hereby reinvented as pure method. The 'higher level' at which his projected *Aufhebung* takes place is, for Homer at least, abstracted out of all consideration. The Messianic strain within historical materialism is inverted into its contrary – an abandonment of all Utopian strivings by default; a reformulation of the revolutionary *telos* as a critical practice, a process in which the end is displaced and recast as a guiding methodological principle, an objective which is endlessly deferred, even sublimated.

In an essay on the successive adaptation and appropriation of theoretical models in different geographical and historical contexts, Edward Said cites as an example Lucien Goldmann's reading of Lukács's *History and Class Consciousness* in *The Hidden God*. Goldmann, says Said, turns Lukács's theory of reification into an essentially scholastic rather than revolutionary mode of analysis, a modification which – having its own very sound social and historical reasons – is no less valid than its 'original', insists Said, but which makes the character of Goldmann's academic Marxism quite different from that of the revolutionary Lukács.[11] Jameson seems to owe more to Goldmann's reading of Lukács, in this regard, than he acknowledges. Just as Jameson writes of the end of Marxism as the 'decentring' of the individual consciousness in favour of a 'collective unity',[12] so Goldmann presents the Marxist version of faith, in contradistinction to that of Christianity, as invested in a collectivity – a 'future which men make for themselves in and through history' – rather than in an individualized, otherworldly beyond: 'The transcendental element present in this faith is not supernatural and does not take us outside or beyond history; it merely takes us beyond the individual.'[13]

It is a very fine line, of course, between abandoning the 'beyond' of history and abandoning history itself – that is to say, the aspiration to *change* history. Like Jameson, Goldmann sees the primary virtue of 'the dialectical method' as its avoidance of the 'ethical' terms inherent in the analytical methods of bourgeois ideology; this is the meaning of Goldmann's methodological insistence on a continual movement between 'the whole and the parts', which refuses to consider the artistic products of individuals in separation from the social totality – the 'world vision' – which brought them into being. In its reformulation as method, however, Marxism risks falling into academicism and political quietism. It is a fine line between abandoning the ethical structure of bourgeois ideology – in which the terms 'progressive' and 'reactionary', for example, are thoroughly implicated – and abandoning the revolutionary objectives of Marxism completely. Both Jameson's and Goldmann's writing are characterized by an apparently sublime equanimity with regard to the actually existing capitalist system. Jameson criticizes Lukács, for example, for presenting his theory of reification in 'ethical' – i.e. judgemental – terms, and for thereby 'ignoring the Utopian vocation' of certain processes of reification, such as the compensatory autonomy acquired by aesthetic experience in the face of capitalist 'dehumanization'.[14] It is a fine line, indeed, between history as 'the experience of Necessity' and history as the resignation to inevitability. Jameson's insistence on the 'omnipresence of culture'[15] lays him open to the charge of having restated – if only to renounce – a comprehension of the world which is essentially 'tragic' rather than 'dialectical', in which man 'refuses all compromise with the world and sets such limits on his actions that his chances of transcending his situation become almost non-existent'.[16] Jameson's culturalism represents an attempt to salvage what joy we can from a world which is progressively more administered by capital. His attempt at a purely 'methodological' restoration of unity presupposes a certain apostasy from the Marxist 'faith' in a future made by humanity, perhaps even a retreat into metaphysical 'agnosticism'.

Before writing Jameson off as an apostate, however, we need to distinguish carefully between the 'transcendental' and the 'supernatural' as they might relate to the project of a revolutionary Marxism. For Goldmann the 'transcendental element' in Marxism certainly exists, despite the obsolescence (without, of course, the disappearance) of superstition in modern society. The 'transcendent' is what distinguishes both tragic and dialectical thought from the relentless empiricism of the rationalist world view, represented by Descartes, Hume and Voltaire. Mary Evans, elucidating Goldmann's thought, observes that the difference between tragic and dialectical thought is merely that, 'whilst for the tragedy of refusal the wager, the gamble, is on eternity and a transcendent divinity, for dialectical thought the wager is on the future of man in the world.'[17] The dialectical 'wager' is no less a wager for the fact that, at a later historical moment, the speculation over the existence of God has been transformed into a speculation that, 'in the alternative facing humanity of a choice between socialism and barbarity, socialism will triumph.'[18] In each case the decisive factor is the wager 'on the existence of a force which transcends the individual'. The same is arguably true of Jameson, who inherits an idea of 'positive' (Utopian) hermeneutic from the essentially religious framework of Paul Ricoeur's thought – one of a series of vehicles for asserting 'a properly Marxian version of meaning beyond the purely ideological'.[19] The fact is that no mere fine line, but a world of difference separates culturalist defeatism (which, like 'rationalist and empiricist thought' for Goldmann, attributes 'no importance at all to the wager')[20] from the materialist dialectic as expounded by Goldmann or Jameson.

To describe these versions of Marxism as 'secular' or 'agnostic' would thus be quite inaccurate. Indeed, to posit the simple 'abolition' of religion, as opposed to its *Aufhebung* or radical transmutation, would be to 'dehistoricize' religious belief – and thus to go against what Jameson describes as the single absolute injunction of all dialectical thought ('Always historicize!').[21] In Jameson, rather, the possibility of 'rewriting' certain religious notions – such as Christian providence, the teleological historicism of Augustine's *City of God*, even primitive magic – is preserved in the dialectic, rendering pertinent the idea of a methodological continuity rather than a break between Marxism and religion. These religious concepts, says Jameson, represent 'anticipatory foreshadowings of historical materialism within precapitalist social formations in which scientific thinking is unavailable as such'.[22] For Goldmann, meanwhile, the transcendent betokens 'the existence of a reality which goes beyond [the objects of his study] as individuals and finds its expression in their work'.[23] In the thought of both of these thinkers, the Utopian spirit of historical materialism survives precisely in the moment of 'transcendentalism' – the wager on *a world other than what exists* – and for Jameson this 'wager' is to be found as much in the Utopian dreams of earlier religious thinkers, say, as in the dialectical analyses of contemporary Marxist theory.

A second implication of Jameson's periodizing methodology is its reiteration of an apparently straightforward linear narrative of history. Again, we might mention Goldmann as a comparison, for whom 'the tragic vision incorporates and goes beyond the findings of rationalism and empiricist individualism, and . . . is itself then incorporated and transcended by dialectical thought.'[24] Goldmann's narrative of the progress of European consciousness is complex yet undeniably evolutionary; the presupposition of his method, and of the very notion of 'world vision' which is central to it, is the essential *theoretical comprehensibility* of the human universe. 'World vision' denotes 'the whole complex of ideas, aspirations and feelings which links together the members of a social group (a group which, in most cases, assumes the existence of a social class) and which opposes them to members of other social groups.'[25] If, at the level of social processes, Goldmann's work is somewhat pessimistic – he talks elsewhere of the progressive and irretrievable disappearance of the 'collective consciousness' in market societies[26] – as a scholarly enterprise it is thoroughly optimistic, a methodological temperament he inherits from Hegel.[27]

Goldmann's project, it is generally acknowledged, was enormously ambitious; its most successful realization was *The Hidden God*, in which the written works of Pascal and Racine are extensively discussed by close reference to the influence of Jansenist religious doctrine on the *noblesse de robe* in seventeenth-century France. The treatment of the 'tragic vision' within Racine's plays – in which absolute values are seen as incompatible with a degraded social world – is regarded in the light of the progressive disfranchisement of the legal nobility under Louis XIV. Thus, in the course of a discussion of Racine's *Phèdre*, Goldmann writes of Phaedra herself as 'the incarnation of the character around whom the great battle between the Jansenists and the ecclesiastical authorities took place'.[28] For Goldmann, a huge amount of data is subordinated to a 'method' – dialectical or historical materialism – by which complex social processes and literary texts may be successfully and jointly comprehended within a 'totality'.

In *The Political Unconscious* Jameson cites Marx and Engels's explanation of 'all hitherto existing societies' as 'a history of class struggle' in the *Communist Manifesto*, and writes of the methodological necessity of presenting significant historical conflicts as episodes in a 'single vast unfinished plot'. For Jameson the 'function and necessity' of Marxist criticism is in 'detecting the traces of that uninterrupted narrative, in restoring to the surface of the text the repressed and buried reality of this fundamental history' – an approach in which, says Jameson, such events are restored to the unity of 'a single great collective story'.[29] These are bold, almost monumental statements to make in an era in which the dominant model of contemporary society is 'multiculturalism', in which no single 'culture' or 'ethnicity' is deemed to have the definitive version of history. In *A Critique of Postcolonial Reason*, Gayatri Spivak compares these sentiments of Jameson's to the 'Eurocentric arrogance' of Jean-Paul Sartre's declaration in *Existentialism and Humanism*: 'There is always some way of understanding an idiot, a child, a primitive man or a foreigner *if one has sufficient information*.'[30] Any such 'imperial conviction', she says, must be decisively laid to rest in today's world, along with the conception of the human adventure as 'a single great collective story'. Likewise, Goldmann's faith in the critical feasibility of 'a complete and coherent picture of the overall meaning of the work', and his unashamed talk of the 'real meaning of a passage',[31] sit oddly in an epoch of 'reader-oriented' criticism in which, as Barthes wrote in 'The Death of the Author', the claim to decipher a literary text 'becomes quite futile'; in which the idea of a single 'theological' meaning gives way to a conception of the text as a 'multi-dimensional space in which a variety of writings, none of them original, blend and clash'.[32]

If on one hand, then, Jameson's periodization of historical materialism is taken to imply a retreat from revolutionary activity into 'merely' cultural analysis (the standard Marxist critique of Jameson), on the other hand he seems equally open to the charge of methodological totalitarianism (the standard 'post-structuralist' critique). Such an assessment reads dialectical thought as a sociological surrogate of 'Christian historicism' – a theory which ascribes to history the same singleness of theological meaning as the doctrine of the Fall, and which has its classic representation in Augustine, who traces the development of the 'city of God' from 'this passing age, where she dwells by faith as a pilgrim among the ungodly' to 'the security of that eternal home which she now patiently awaits'.[33] Geoffrey Bennington, reviewing Jameson's *The Political Unconscious*, calls this dismissively 'the logic of the "not yet"', and writes that 'the unity of the transcendental narrative of history is essential to Jameson's project'.[34] The same inexorable teleology is postulated in Spivak's comparison of Jameson and Sartre.

Spivak, however, is certainly unfair to Sartre; perhaps she is unfair to Jameson too. A glance at the text of Sartre's from which she quotes reveals his expressed universalism to be as 'methodological' as Jameson's – a *principle* of critical activity, that is to say; a 'means' from which all explicit ends have been suspended, rather than an 'end' to which all means are diverted. Sartre's 'universality' is not something given, but a political formation in a state of constant production and renegotiation. 'I make this universality in choosing myself', he says in the same passage: 'I also make it by understanding the purpose of any other man, of whatever epoch. This absoluteness of the act of choice does not alter the relativity of each epoch.'[35] Universality is here an aspiration rather than a hegemony – an imposed or totalitarian cultural agenda. As implied above, the logic of the 'not yet' in Jameson, as in Hegel, may be understood as a dialectical critique, transcendence or *Aufhebung* of the opposition between the logic of the 'not yet' – Hegel's 'bad infinity' – and the logic of the 'here and now'. The theory of a 'reified' logic of the 'here and now' which is constitutive of present-day reality – a logic which lies, since the world it describes is a false one, but which also tells the truth, since its account is perfectly accurate, and derives authentically from that world – this theory, which is the theory of reification itself, manifests a sense of *achieved* liberation from the world as it is, even while it remains politically committed to changing that world. A 'materialist' dialectic, which re-reads Hegel in materialist (as opposed to idealist) terms, gestures methodologically towards a domain of freedom from the reified values of the here and now ('Absolute spirit'); yet it also establishes that freedom in every authentic product of human consciousness, which, insofar as spirit (*Geist*) inheres within it, is a vehicle of truth. This is the meaning of Hegel's insistence, quoted by Adorno from the *Encyclopaedia of the Philosophical Sciences*, that the content of philosophy – even at its most abstract and speculative – 'is no other than actuality'.[36] Hegelian dialectic is not a projection of the realization of *Geist* into the distant future; rather, the wager involved in the dialectic is one which, by the act of faith, wrests that moment of *Geist* into the here and now, simultaneously abolishing the metaphysical distinction between the imperfect present and the ideal future. It is only in the 'reified' logic of the 'here and now', in other words, that the realization of *Geist* is represented in apocalyptic terms.

Lukács writes that with Marx's overturning of Hegel 'it becomes clear how much . . . those categories that in Hegel himself, in the most abstract and idealist part of his *Logic* ('Logic of the Concept') form the peak of his system, become real, practical moments of the proletarian class struggle.'[37] This paradox also describes the status of the wager in Goldmann's thought. As Goldmann remarks, every objection to the materialist dialectic on the grounds that it embodies a contradiction between the 'historical inevitability' of socialism and the need to fight in order to bring it into being, fails to understand 'the dialectical nature of human reality'.[38] For Goldmann, Pascal's Christianity has the same paradoxical structure as dialectical thought; the wager that God exists is not opposed to the search for proofs; the search, rather, *constitutes* the wager, and represents simultaneously the truth of Christianity in Pascal's seventeenth century. Christianity is at this period 'in the unique position of being able to satisfy all man's needs'.[39] For dialectical thought, predicated on the inseparability of subject and object, this condition is both necessary and sufficient for it to be true.

Goldmann's insistence that his own project of 'scientific investigation' is 'a collective phenomenon which requires the co-operation of innumerable individual efforts', rather than a programme of any single scholar or regime, is a further implication of the concept of 'world vision' – his version of the Hegelian principle of embodied 'spirit'.[40] Goldmann's project is an ongoing one which presupposes the future collaboration of successive scholars. At the other end of the temporal equation, he assumes that his work is merely the latest contribution to an ongoing project which by no means began with Marx and Engels, or even with Hegel; the dialectical method, he insists, has always been spontaneously applied by philosophers 'when they wanted to understand the work of their predecessors.'[41] The process of understanding an earlier 'world vision' is one of tracing the *continuities* as much as the differences between that tradition and one's own. A clear distinction between 'post-structuralist' thought and the 'periodizing dialectic' represented by Goldmann and Jameson may be inferred from the fact that, in the latter, periodization is always 'suspended' by a commitment to the dialectical continuity of history. In post-structuralism, by contrast (and in apparent contradiction with this designation), there are no continuities as such; the idea that history's narratives inevitably converge upon a point of transparency – the 'objective knowledge' of human consciousness and society, the unity of subject and object – functions to legitimize and absorb resistance to what Nietzsche called 'real' or 'effective' history (*wirkliche Historie*) – the succession of violences, codified as a system of rules (in which the philosophy of history is also implicated), by which humanity 'proceeds from domination to domination'.[42]

The classic text of this post-structuralist critique is Michel Foucault's 1971 reading of Nietzsche against Hegel, 'Nietzsche, Genealogy, History'. On the basis, firstly, of Nietzsche's fervent denunciations of Hegelian philosophy of history, and secondly, of the structuralist dissolution of history into 'discourse', Foucault proposes to replace history with 'genealogy', a term he derives from Nietzsche, and which implies the dispersal of the object of historical research into a plurality of 'values, morality, asceticism and knowledge'.[43] It is worth unpacking these two propositions a little.

1. Foucault's 'genealogy' involves abandoning the thematics, along with the 'quest for origins', of the philosophy of history, for 'the accidents, the minute deviations – or conversely, the complete reversals – the errors, the false appraisals, and the faulty calculations that gave birth to those things that continue to exist and have value for us.' To pursue a genealogical approach, says Foucault further, is 'to discover that *truth* or *being* does not lie at the root of what we know and what we are, but *the exteriority of accidents*.'[44] The quest for objective meaning in history is displaced by a model of chance, subjective isolation and fragmentation – the alienation, rather than the mediation, of subject and object. Singular events (inversions of power relationships, *coups d'état*, the critical appropriation of a vocabulary, cultural lapses into decadence) are maintained in their specificity rather than dissolved 'into an ideal continuity'.[45] 'Effective' history thus amounts to a radical periodization of historical occurrences, masquerading as a critique of periodization. Significant 'moments' are isolated as such, cut loose from everything – in particular, from the idea of a 'primordial intention' and any drawing of conclusions – other than temporality. Their 'meanings' are derived from their 'haphazard' character – the degree to which they impact upon a world reconfigured as 'a profusion of random events'.

Thus Foucault outlines a practice of history and historiography delimited by the principle of material interests as the basis for human action, and of truth as found in immediacy and arrived at through precise attention to detail: 'the world of effective history knows only one kingdom, without providence or final cause, where there is only "the iron hand of necessity shaking the dice-box of chance".'[46] This statement represents a determined rejection of all ideas of teleology or eschatology; it asserts itself as 'the inverse of the Christian world', a negation of all Messianism and visions of history which assume a purpose beyond that most inexorable of principles, the will to power. In this extreme text, produced at what appears, retrospectively, as a critical moment in the history of ideas, it is as if the death of God is ratified by a secular methodology embedded in the here and now, confirming 'our existence among countless lost events, without a landmark or a point of reference.'[47] The contrast with Goldmann could not be greater. For Goldmann the idea of the detail as the ultimate unit of historiographical accuracy is predicated on the redundancy of the philosophy of history. The 'objective meaning' of a work is arrived at by attention to the 'world vision' of which it is the expression, rather than by considering the life and beliefs of the individual who created it. The important question is not whether Pascal was a Jansenist, but how his writing compares to a preestablished 'conceptual prototype' of Jansenism.[48] The methodological statements at the beginning of *The Hidden God* outline a position which favours schematicism and extrapolation 'for purposes of convenience'. While Hume, for example, was neither a complete sceptic nor consistently empirical, the truth of his philosophical position may be obtained only if he is discussed as such – as he was by Kant.[49] Descartes was no atheist, observes Goldmann, yet the substance of Cartesian rationalism is atheistic.[50] Spinoza, likewise, 'uses the word "God" in order to express a complete refusal of any really transcendental attitude'. The subjective (religious) attitudes of such thinkers function as 'old bottles which their new vision of the world has filled with completely new wine.'[51] The 'world vision' is a methodological tool by which 'the world as it is' may be overcome. Foucault's secularistic refusal of any world other than what exists, 'without providence or final cause', is hereby confronted with Goldmann's 'complete refusal to accept this world as the only one in which man could live, move and have his being' – a refusal which is no less substantial for the fact that it is 'merely' methodological.

2. The post-structuralist critique of history as a linear, progressive narrative, with an origin, a sense of direction and a *telos* – assumed, imputed or specific – is also predicated upon the structuralist motif of the linguistic origin of the world,

signification as the 'non-originary origin' of history itself.[52] For Derrida, elaborating this motif in his early essay 'Force and Signification', language precedes, indeed determines history, which is thereby revealed in *its* historicity. This linguistic determination extends to the philosophical moment ('structuralism') in which that insight appears. Thus 'the structuralist stance, as well as our own attitudes assumed before or within language, are not only moments of history. They are an astonishment, rather, by language as the origin of history. By historicity itself.' Structuralism, says Derrida, thereby 'escapes the classical history of ideas which already supposes structuralism's possibility'; for the history of ideas 'naively belongs to the province of language and propounds itself within it.' This situation comprehends an as yet undeclared moment of 'post-structuralism', a moment 'announced' and constituted in the body of Derrida's essay, which 'radicalizes' the structuralist moment by subjecting it relentlessly to its own logic. The post-structuralist ~~moment~~ is self-deconstructive, a theme inherited from structuralism and rendering all such moments of 'radicalization' problematic – conceivable (or inscribable) only 'under erasure' (*sous rature*). Thus Gayatri Spivak writes of the 'epistemic violation' perpetrated in any 'simulacrum' of historical continuity. 'The epistemic story of imperialism', she says, is 'the story of a series of interruptions, a repeated tearing of time that cannot be sutured.'[53] Likewise Derrida writes that 'to dream of reducing [the question of the sign (a signifier here for structuralism – T.B.)] to a sign of the times is to dream of violence'.[54] Structuralism is irreducible to a moment of intellectual fashion, and is 'unable to display itself in its entirety as a spectacle for the historian'; in fact structuralism confounds the historian by revealing the categories of historiography to be thoroughly anticipated by the system of signification, which 'always already' precedes it. As Derrida writes more plainly in *Of Grammatology*: 'The concepts of *present*, *past*, and *future*, everything in the concepts of time and history which implies evidence of them – the metaphysical concept of time in general – cannot adequately describe the structure of the trace.'[55] The operation of language, the *play* of signification denoted by the Derridean term 'trace', exceeds the rigid linearity of past-present-future. Geoffrey Bennington glosses this passage in relation to another central Derridean concept, *différance*, the implications of which, he says, include the fact that meaning is never fully present in the sign but is 'stretched or spread between a "past" and a "future" which themselves will never have been present (and which are thus not really a past and a future)' – in other words, that 'present' has no meaning without 'past' and 'future'. By extension, the meaning of any particular sign in the present, and indeed any condition of 'nowness', is never experienced fully, but is always 'anticipated' or 'reestablished after the event'.[56] In contrast to this procedure – described by Derrida as that of 'deconstructing the simplicity of presence' – a 'dialectical' elaboration of the concept of time is inadequate, since it preserves its 'fundamental successivity', thereby continuing to abide by a 'mundane' model of linearity. Deconstruction would imply rather an explosion of the terminology which reiterates such concepts as *time*, *now*, *anterior present*, *delay*, installing in its place, presumably, a discursive practice which would acknowledge in every iteration the inherent violence of all discourse.[57]

Yet the concepts of 'redemption' and 'totality', which operate in the dialectical tradition as a principle of the interpenetration of the present with the past and the future (and which are intrinsic to the concept of reification), already presuppose the irreducibility of meaning to the immediacy of 'presence'. The 'periodizing' methodology they suggest is no intellectual restriction within the 'mundane' limits of past-present-future, but rather – like the 'freedom from the law' represented and brought into effect by Christ's incarnation – a real liberation from worldliness, from the bridle of signification, and thus from any exhortation (such as Derrida's) to use language only with the full acknowledgement of its inadequacy, to maintain its capacity for meaning in a state of suspension. Where Paul writes, in the letter to the Romans, that 'the law has authority over a man only as long as he lives', he invokes a sphere beyond the earthly domain for those saved by Christ.[58] Likewise, the promise of 'absolute knowledge', or the anticipation of a moment at which society is recreated by – and in the image of – the proletariat, proposes a liberation from the anxiety of reification, and therefore, in effect, from reification itself.

If structuralism, as Goldmann observes, effects an artificial separation of function from structure,[59] deconstruction *presupposes* that same separation as a foundation for its own critical operations. Derrida's assertions are based on a structuralist, ahistorical and emphatically 'secular' conception of *langue* which a dialectical understanding of history has (always already) abolished from the outset. For all the local credibility of its readings, the insights of deconstruction are thus fundamentally banal – limited by, and lacking all resonance beyond, this ahistorical conception of *langue*. The truly 'mundane' strategy is that of *sous rature*, which betrays an interminable servitude to language, the order of signification. For Jameson, by contrast, the promise of redemption is *realizable* – methodologically and aesthetically – in the here and now. Hegel's concept of *Geist*, of embodied spirit, indissociable from 'absolute knowledge', is that of the immanence and the *materiality* of truth, not of its transcendentality. From a dialectical perspective, structuralism and post-structuralism belong to the history of ideas to at least the same degree that they 'escape' it. To conceive of these respective thematics as incompatible, an 'aporia', is to subordinate thought entirely to the 'reified' logic of the here and now.

★

# 6

# The Translation of God into Man

In *The World, the Text and the Critic* Edward Said distinguishes sharply between his own practice of 'secular criticism' and 'religious' discourse. The former is 'open', enabling 'a sense of history and of human production'; the latter 'serves as an agent of closure, shutting off human investigation, criticism and effort in deference to the authority of the more-than-human, the supernatural, the other-worldly'.[1] As such, religious discourse may be aligned with the imperialist and racist discourse which Said calls 'Orientalism'. Each represents a form of 'contemporary Manichaean theologizing of "the other"',[2] insofar as their intellectual investigations close prematurely with a final appeal 'to what cannot be thought through and explained, except by consensus and appeals to authority.'[3] Said's book, and his work as a whole, presents itself – in opposition to this 'Manichaean' tendency – on the side of 'secular' criticism, and against what he discerns as a new religious sensibility abroad in contemporary criticism – a symptom, he says, of intellectual and political 'exhaustion, consolation [and] disappointment'. Its prevailing conceptual forms – named here as unthinkability, undecidability and paradox – signal clearly the work of thinkers such as Derrida and Spivak. This same displacement of secular by religious criticism, he says, may be seen in the 'voguish' recreation of Walter Benjamin as a 'crypto-mystic', and the corresponding eclipse of Benjamin's Marxism. Feminism and psychoanalysis, meanwhile, are increasingly viewed in 'private and hermetic' – meaning quasi-religious – terms, rather than 'public and social' ones.

Said's use of the terms 'secular' and 'religious' in this context, however, threatens to reproduce the binary ('Manichaean') thought processes of 'reified' logic. To equate religion with 'closure' and secularism with 'openness' is to ignore a strain of religious writing, most notably within the Christian tradition, in which the complexity of faith is elaborated in ways that prefigure 'dialectical' thought. It is also to ignore a certain representation of the dialectic – derived in turn from Christianity – in which the relation between 'closure' and 'openness', along with that between 'hiddenness' and 'revelation', and between 'materiality' and 'spirituality', is complicated by a concept of 'mediation'. Christianity, after all, offers us a God who became man, a God who is simultaneously the mediator and the transcendent essence that is mediated; his manifestation in the figure of the Son is not simply the revelation of his being but, simultaneously, its *mediation* – a revelation, furthermore, *insofar* as it is a mediation. In the same way, the redemption of humanity proposed by Christianity is inseparable from the revelation of its corruption – an inseparability conveyed in the metaphor of the Fall, which posits sin and the awakening to sin as simultaneous, even synonymous. The mediating figure of Christ should be understood, dialectically, as bringing about not merely the interconnection of the transcendent and the human, but their *identification*.

Much of the work of the American Catholic writer Flannery O'Connor (which I shall consider in more detail in Part Three) is located thematically across the enigmatic distinction between 'earthly' redemption and the salvation attained after death. Her story 'The Artificial Nigger', about the once-in-a-lifetime journey of a God-fearing grandfather and grandson into the city – a journey that is compared explicitly in the text to the journeys of Virgil and Dante into Hell, and of Raphael and Tobias into Media – ends with a sense of the indissociability of the two concepts of redemption, as well as an insight into the simultaneity of sin and salvation. On their return home the grandfather, Mr Head, contemplates his denial of his grandson Nelson earlier in the day:

> He stood appalled, judging himself with the thoroughness of God, while the action of mercy covered his pride like a flame and

> consumed it. He had never thought himself a great sinner before but he saw now that his true depravity had been hidden from him lest it cause him despair. He realized that he was forgiven for sins from the beginning of time, *when he had conceived in his own heart the sin of Adam*, until the present, when he had denied poor Nelson. He saw that *no sin was too monstrous for him to claim as his own*, and since God loved in proportion as he forgave, *he felt ready at that instant to enter Paradise.*[4]

Christianity is affirmed here as a vehicle of certain 'dialectical' truths, such as the unity of what Marx calls 'species-being' and individual existence – Mr Head is as guilty of Adam's sin (the sin of the race) as he is of his own – and the unity of immediate, earthly redemption and the redemption vouchsafed in the next life (Paradise). Spiritual greatness, writes Goldmann, elucidating Pascal, is no mere hope or promise, but that which 'faith gives the unbeliever from this very moment'. Redemption, as Pascal explains it, is what the believer 'gains in this life'; but it is also something 'characterized – from the human point of view – by its inadequacy.'[5] These aspects of redemption are neither clearly delimited from each other nor are they left simply 'ambiguous' in dialectical thought. Rather, their *identity* is asserted, an implication of the periodizing methodology which proposes a future society that is unintelligible from the point of view of the present – a society, in other words, in which such distinctions as that between past, present and future, or between worldly and otherworldly redemption, will be comprehensible as the product of an inferior logic. Periodization hereby simultaneously annuls itself *qua* periodization; such paradoxes are inherent in the presupposition of a 'reified' logic of the present, and thus in any methodological strategy of periodization.

The same unity of 'outward' and 'inward' redemption, predicated upon the unknowability or unintelligibility of the life to come, is achieved in Stanley Spencer's painting *The Resurrection, Cookham* (1924–6), which transposes the return of Christ to Spencer's home town. The painting depicts people known to Spencer during his life – including the artist himself and several members of his family – physically arising from their graves in the parish cemetery. In the Christian narrative of apocalypse and final judgement, the narrative of the Second Coming, the disjunction between the beyond and the here and now – a disjunction punctuated by its inadequacy, by its actuality as the product of *worldly* logic – is given imaginative form. In Christian art, the same disjunction attains a sensuous form. Christianity and art have an almost symbiotic relationship, as thinkers including Hegel, Freud, Adorno and Georg Simmel have strongly intuited. Art, like Christianity, bridges the gap between human inadequacy – the logic of the here and now – and the unknowable beyond, in a dialectically satisfactory way. Artworks, writes Adorno, signalling this disjunction, 'point to a practice from which they abstain – the creation of a just life'[6] – meaning that they authentically bridge the chasm between reified and non-reified existence, transcending their own ineluctable embeddedness in worldly representation. Simmel describes this same paradox as a 'fundamental characteristic of Christianity', the intellectual form of which he locates in Tertullian's dictum *credo quia absurdum*:

> It is as if the stage of being 'possible' is simply omitted: confronted with the absolute demands of Christianity, the soul finds itself in a state of impossibility, and yet at the same time in a state of fulfillment and perfection. Christ as 'mediator' seems to make superfluous the stage of 'being able'; an ideal link comes into effect, which conveys that the soul is achieving something of which it is actually incapable.[7]

Paradox, in other words, is at the heart of Christianity: Christ, in the incarnation, took worldly form, became manifest, *reified*, in order to liberate humanity from sin, from worldly thingitude. The moment of reification is pregnant with the moment of liberation from reification. The ritual of the Holy Communion represents the same paradox, insofar as the bread and the wine become symbols of the body and blood of Christ – physical tokens, in other words, of the promised liberation from

Stanley Spencer, *The Resurrection, Cookham* (1924–27).

physicality. In Catholicism, the drama of the relation is further heightened by the belief in a material transsubstantiation of the bread and wine into the actual body and blood at the moment of ingestion, and by the insistence of the Church on the uniqueness and preeminence of the Eucharist (and thus the priesthood) in effecting that synthesis. This preeminence is illustrated in Raphael's famous fresco *The Disputation of the Sacrament* in the Vatican, in which the host occupies the sole point of mediation and inter-communication in a spectacular dualistic representation of the earthly and the heavenly domains. The 'symbolic' quality of the ritual, as it has been rationalized in the Protestant tradition, is thus preserved as a simultaneously physical transformation; the mysticism and obscurantism of 'ambiguity' is turned irretrievably into paradox, the very process which Lucien Goldmann identifies as that of Christianity in general.

Christ himself embodies contradictions which centre on his dual being as both God and man; these attributes are complementary rather than incompatible (the latter would imply an economic rather than dialectical relation between them). Christ is both fully human and fully divine, a signifier of the sheer inadequacy, or worldliness, of such categories.

> The Book of Revelation tells us he is [both] Alpha and Omega, the beginning and the end. But as Christianity evolved from a minority religion to a State religion, and as both the powerful and the oppressed rallied under his banner, Christ came to embody further dualities: Victor and Victim; Saviour and Sacrifice; King of kings and 'despised and rejected of men'.[8]

Thus paradox – contrary to Said's implication – is not a form of metaphysical closure at all but the opposite: an assertion of the limitedness of 'secular' reason, and an affirmation of openness to a non-theologized other. A commitment to 'secular' logic, including its realist implications – Said boasts of inhabiting 'a healthy scepticism about the various idols venerated by culture and by system' – signifies not ideological 'openness', freedom from false consciousness, but a complacent certitude as to the attainability of such freedom, in reality a form of conscription to the 'reified' anthropocentric logic of the here and now, and an extremely prosaic conception of the relation between art and truth.

The most moving and eloquent example of the Christian dialectical tradition in English literary writing is John Donne's fourteenth Holy Sonnet, addressed to a Providence whose magnitude both exceeds the logic of human (though God-given) rationality – 'Reason your viceroy in mee, mee should defend, / But is captiv'd, and proves weake or untrue', writes Donne – and makes necessary a form of poetic invention that has been equally celebrated and derided with the term 'metaphysical poetry'. The only possible comprehension of God is one which acknowledges the impossibility of full comprehension; thus the form of the logic sustained through Donne's poem is paradoxical. The sonnet concludes with a succession of highly compact dialectical images:

> Yet dearely I love you, and would be loved faine,
> But am betroth'd unto your enemie:
> Divorce mee, untie, or breake that knot againe,
> Take mee to you, imprison mee, for I
> Except you enthrall mee, never shall be free,
> Nor ever chast, except you ravish mee.

In the light of this profoundly religious and sensuous poem, the term 'secular' would seem more appropriate to a critical practice which, in the final analysis, *refuses* openness to the unknown, than to one which celebrates openness. *Pace* Said, the methodological refusal by certain 'post-structuralist' thinkers of the 'transcendentalism' of assuming an other to language, for example, is better conceived as a secular practice than a religious one. The presupposition of an other to language is a characteristic of dialectical, as of tragic and religious thought, and it signals a refusal to be determined by linguistic necessity, a refusal of the world in the 'reified' form in which it currently appears, which may be contrasted with the post-structuralist celebration of materiality – the 'always already' prioritization of the signifier over the signified. Said is right, therefore, to see the appearance within critical theory of terms such as 'unthinkability' and 'undecidability' as evidence of hermeneutical closure rather than openness.[9] 'Unthinkability' and 'undecidability' – particularly when elevated into central methodological concepts, as they are in Derrida's thought – are watchwords of agnosticism, which, rather than atheism, is the true antithesis of religious belief. What Goldmann says of Merleau-Ponty and Sartre is more true of Derrida: in the rationalization of contradiction into 'one of the principle themes of philosophical thought'[10] we see the *systematization* of ambiguity and thus, in essence, a critical acceptance of, rather than an ongoing struggle against, the fact of an unintelligible universe.

# 7

# Marxism and the Hidden God

The 'self-annulling periodization' of dialectical thought should be differentiated, therefore, from the trope of 'aporia' valorized in post-structuralist discourses – not least on the grounds that periodization makes possible a fundamentally redemptive rather than disabling approach to the 'naiveties' and 'inadequacies' of historical thought. It is by means of a narrative of redemption, for example, that Fredric Jameson refuses to write off Hegel on the basis of the apparent transcendentalism of the concept of Absolute Spirit. Hegel's concept is less the core of a fundamentally idealistic philosophy, says Jameson, than 'a symptom of a historical situation in which his thinking could go no further'.[1] It is his strategy of periodization – the insertion of Hegel into history – that makes this narrative possible: 'Rather than diagnosing some irremediable vice of "idealism" in Hegel's thought' he writes (indicating the procedure of deconstruction), 'we must more modestly accuse him of not having been able, in his historical moment, to become Marx.' It is precisely in its 'transcendental' or 'Messianic' aspects, the affirmation of an other to what exists – in the name of which what exists, or what has already existed, may be 'saved' – that Marxism retains its revolutionary and progressive potential. The 'mystical' version of Benjamin (*pace* Said, again) is not an optional extra, somehow decantable from his materialist 'essence', but is precisely constitutive of that essence. In other words – to restate Goldmann's distinction between the transcendental and the supernatural – there is nothing inconceivable *per se* about a materialist transcendentalism, or even a materialist theory of immortality.[2] Conceptual thought (there is no other kind) is by definition inadequate and vulgarizing; this condition extends to deconstruction, to historical materialism, to the concept of reification, to Jameson's periodizing methodology, and to all that is possible in the sphere of artistic and cultural expression – yet in that very acknowledgement lies the affirmation of something other. Jameson expresses this paradoxical relation in a formulation which avoids any need for a shift between registers: 'Works of culture come to us as signs in an all-but-forgotten code, as symptoms of diseases no longer even recognized as such, as fragments of a totality we have long since lost the organs to see.'[3] This formulation is not 'aporetic' or static, meaning impassable, but dialectical and kinetic. Its presupposition is a possible future world of wholeness and healthiness. For Jameson cultural works provide access, if only through a chink in the darkness, to a realm of completion and truth. The post-structuralist aporia, by contrast, is a metaphysical concept, a state of affairs in which decisions *as such* must be taken in the absence of any guide or 'principle' of action. A certain 'mysticism' is therefore dialectically interpenetrated with the materialism of the concept of reification. It is no separate discourse, however; indeed, the dialectical elaboration of the relation between 'mysticism' and 'materialism' is a facilitating rather than a proscriptive procedure, promising a level of understanding of historical-theoretical narratives which is precluded from any theoretical discourse which seeks to establish the rigorous differentiation of the two.

Thus – in *History and Class Consciousness* at least – Lukács makes almost no effort to distinguish the potentially 'mystical' implications of the concept of reification from its relevance in the context of a 'scientific' critique of capitalism. The same goes for the distinction between reification as a 'transhistorical' phenomenon – a fact of the human condition – and as a historical phenomenon specific to the capitalist mode of production; indeed, this distinction, where it is signposted at all in *History and Class Consciousness*, is explained on the plane of quantity rather than quality. Not only reification but commodity relations, notes Lukács, existed in primitive societies; only with the advent of modern capitalism does the commodity form begin 'to penetrate society in all its aspects and to remould it in its own image'.[4] This quantitative distinction has qualitative repercussions of course: 'Where the commodity is universal it manifests itself differently from the commodity as a particular, isolated, non-dominant phenomenon.' Nevertheless, this insistence on historical continuity is methodologically significant, since it implies that earlier 'world views' (most notably tragedy and Christianity) may be viewed – redemptively – as dialectical prefigurations of Marxist thought.

In opposition to crude accounts which speak of the 'lies' of Christianity, or the 'absolutism' of Hegel, or the 'bourgeois empiricism' of Kant, for Lucien Goldmann the articulation of such positions bespeaks a failure of historical comprehension, and the arrival of an ahistorical methodology. Goldmann goes further than Jameson when he states that in Pascal's seventeenth-century Christianity is effectively true; Christianity 'transforms ambiguity into paradox, and makes human life cease to be an absurd adventure and become instead a valid and necessary stage in the only path leading to goodness and truth'.[5] For Goldmann, historical materialism has a retroactive effect on our understanding of Christianity, the essence of which he declares in *The Hidden God* to be neither deistic nor atheistic – predicated, in other words, neither on a great and powerful God, nor an absent, illusory God, but rather on a 'paradoxical and contradictory God, and one whose nature corresponds exactly to everything which we know about man's nature and his hopes'. Indeed, neither of those alternative extremes available in the seventeenth century, deism and atheism, could hope to satisfy a race such as man, which is 'neither beast nor angel', and whose reality is also 'contradictory and paradoxical'.[6] The presentation of Christianity as a deistic religion is a critical retrojection emanating from a later historical moment, by which time Christianity had lost its quality of expressing the yearnings of human society – and the same goes for retrospective critiques of the 'metaphysical' foundation of Hegel's or Kant's thought, such as those offered by deconstruction.

Goldmann derives the concept of a 'hidden God' from Pascal, who in turn locates its origin in the Old Testament. *Deus absconditus* is a quotation from the book of Isaiah, in the Latin Vulgate: 'Verily thou art a God that hidest thyself', as the Authorised Version has it.[7] It is a concept which Goldmann associates with the situation of 'tragic' man, an archetype which appears in the modern world at a definite historical stage between Cartesian rationalism and the innovation of Hegelian dialectical thought. For Goldmann, *deus absconditus* denotes a God who 'no longer speaks directly to man' – as depicted in Racine's *Phèdre* (1677), for example, when Theseus laments the apparent refusal of Neptune to intervene on his behalf, leaving his (so he thinks) faithless son unpunished and his wife Phaedra unavenged; or when Phaedra soliloquizes to Venus as to 'an impassible and silent God' who seems to regard human affairs with the disinterest of a spectator viewing a play.[8] Jansenist doctrine, observes John Cairncross, demanded that divine interventions 'should appear natural to the sceptic, and their supernatural origin be clear only to the orthodox.'[9] Racine's later plays in particular, he says (apparently following Goldmann), represent a dramatization of this theology according to which God has withdrawn from view. Racine was educated at the famous Jansenist convent of

Port-Royal, and for Goldmann his plays must be understood, historically, in relation to 'the appearance and development of an ideology which asserted that it is impossible to live a valid life in this world'.[10] This ideology in turn may be understood, sociologically, as an expression of the political marginalization of a certain class faction under the absolutist regime of Louis XIV – yet what is most significant is the fact that Christianity is able to represent this state of affairs without apparently violating its own tenets or the truth of the world as it is. The hidden God is *simultaneously* an affirmation of the 'beyond' – meaning what is unknown, 'other' – and of the 'here and now', since it recognizes the inseparability of the concept of God from the historical circumstances of its production.

Pascal, who, like Racine, was closely associated with the community at Port-Royal, and who coined the term *le Dieu caché*, is the other representative of the idea of the hidden God for Goldmann. One of its implications is God's necessary transcendence of every material *and conceptual* representation of his presence – including therefore, in certain historical circumstances, the idea of God itself. It is this transcendence, a motif restated throughout Pascal's *Pensées* (1670), which suggests the affinity of Pascalian thought for Goldmann's Hegelian Marxism: 'Like any Christian,' writes Goldmann, 'Pascal himself gave the name of God to this reality which he spent his life trying to find. A rationalist would call it truth and fame, and a socialist the ideal community. They would each one of them be right, and there are many other ways of expressing this reality which men try to achieve.'[11] Goldmann himself opts for the concept of 'totality, or wholeness' – because, he says, of the relative freedom of these terms from 'ideological connotations'. That such terms have themselves become saturated with ideological connotations since Goldmann was writing suggests that the disappearance of God is a process that has vastly accelerated during that time; the difficulty of finding appropriate signifiers for the Absolute is a characteristic of modernity, and of the anxiety towards reification which saturates the present socio-cultural moment.

Nevertheless, the essence of the idea of the hidden God has no more adequate representation, according to Goldmann, than in the *structure* of dialectical thought – a structure which it shares with the tragic sensibility. The tragic universe, like the dialectical one, is defined by the existence of contradictory values that cannot be reconciled in this world. In Racine's *Phèdre*, these contradictions are located 'between passion and personal reputation, between absolute purity and forbidden love, between truth and life.'[12] In dialectical thought such values are translated into a methodological distinction between the here and now and the 'beyond'; thus, for both Goldmann and Fredric Jameson, we are enchained within an essentially tragic universe for as long as we are embedded in reification – yet that insight is the key to a liberation from reification, a promise which dialectical thought shares with Christianity. In Kierkegaard's *Fear and Trembling*, Abraham is represented as a tragic hero because his duty to God is radically at odds and incompatible with the ethical code of his worldly existence – with human law. The sacrifice of his only son which the Lord demands of him is necessarily a violation of the prohibition on infanticide, and of his responsibilities as a husband and parent. This contradiction is not *resolvable*; rather, it represents the fallen nature of worldly logic itself, which is incapable of grasping the beyond. It is precisely this incompatibility, this structural paradox, that for Kierkegaard, as for Pascal, as – centuries earlier – for Tertullian and Augustine, constitutes Christianity's truth and its strength.

The same might be said of Lukács's relation to Marxism, not only in the years immediately following his Marxist 'conversion' – before what is usually held to be his lapse into dogmatic Marxism in the 1930s and 1940s – but throughout his life, during which he maintained a certain notion of orthodox Marxism, 'equally impervious to any facts or events that might cast doubt on its truth.'[13] It is one's resolve in the face of all evidence to the contrary that evinces the true dialectical relation to the world, and the true sense of a paradoxical universe. Lukács's commitment to Marxism should be regarded, perhaps, in the light of the contradictions which animated Pascal's existence:

> [Pascal] denied the value of all worldly knowledge, yet went on with scientific research; he refused to compromise with authority, yet declared his obedience to the Church. He did not believe that truth and righteousness could triumph in this world, but he proclaimed that the whole of life should be devoted to fighting for them.[14]

If tragic feeling is the product of the insight that man is irreversibly and progressively sundered from truth, from the divine, and from self-fulfilment and self-realization, the rupture between this world and the next in Marxist revolutionary thought is of similarly epistemic proportions. Both tragic and dialectical thought refuse the world *while remaining in it* – this is the essence of any paradoxical world view.[15] While in tragedy the result of this irresolvable contradiction is pathos, in dialectical thinking the possibility of change is implicit in the realization – indissociable from the concept of reification – that in this world, subject and object are in a state of alienation. The overcoming of alienation would be at the same time the overcoming of a situation in which the transcendent and the material exist in isolation from each other – in which God presides over humanity's spiritual life, rather than being produced by it. The difference between tragic and dialectical thought is that the latter proceeds a crucial stage further towards the possibility of change, by its insight into the provisional nature of the epistemological categories in which we are embedded. The proposed break in or transformation of the order of things is by definition unforeseeable in advance, since it requires radically changing the categories which deny its possibility. The proposed transformation, writes Slavoj Žižek, 'cannot be accounted for in the terms of its pre-existing "objective conditions".'[16] Change must always seem premature in the context of the existing world; but, conversely and obviously, the 'prematurity' of the situation is a condition for change, for otherwise the event will already have taken place. This event, however, 'would radically change the "objective" relationship of forces itself, within which the initial situation appeared as "premature".'[17]

There is a structural analogy between Goldmann's concept of the 'hidden God' and Jameson's concept of history as 'absent cause' – a concept he takes from Althusser, who in turn derives it from Spinoza. As an absent cause, says Jameson, history 'is inaccessible to us except in textual form'; 'our approach to it and to the Real itself necessarily passes through its prior textualization, its narrativization in the political unconscious.'[18] Alternatively: 'history can be apprehended only through its effects, and never directly as some reified force.'[19] History – that is to say the *meaning* of history, the totality – is hidden, imputable, rather than empirically available to perceiving consciousness. In his expository book on Jameson, Sean Homer criticizes this idea for simply rewriting the concept of totality 'at a higher level of abstraction, . . . beyond representation'.[20] Such a process of 'rewriting', however, is nothing other than the dialectical movement of history itself – the perpetual withdrawal of God, one might say, behind ever more abstract forms of conceptualization; or, to invert this formulation, the incremental manifestation of God *as hidden*.[21] As the concept of 'totality' becomes itself laden with ideological baggage – a process described in the course of Homer's objection to Jameson's 'totalization' – this further abstraction, perhaps, takes the form of the appearance of the post-structuralist concepts of 'undecidability', 'aporia' and '*différance*' – surrogates for transcendentality, from which all notion of a teleology, a beyond, however obscured from view, have been expunged. Such terms, writes Jameson, merely 'reconfirm the status of the concept of totality by their very reaction against it' – a dialectic that is even more explicitly preserved, he indicates, in Adorno's development of a 'negative dialectic'.[22]

In taking this conciliatory, essentially *redemptive* attitude towards post-structuralism, Jameson is both magnanimous and consistent with his own methodological procedures. One might place this manoeuvre alongside his earlier, redemptive recuperation of Hegel: for Jameson, it seems, the apparent ahistoricism of post-structuralism may be comprehended sympathetically as the product of a historical moment in which it is *no longer* possible to be Marx. Jameson's methodological generosity owes more to Goldmann than he acknowledges; in *The Political Unconscious* he dismisses Goldmann's model of the 'homologies' – put forward in *The Hidden God* to explain the relation between class situations, world views and artistic forms – as 'simplistic and mechanical';[23] yet the 'redemptive' implications of Goldmann's theory are inherited more or less intact by Jameson's own periodization of history, in which the categories of past and present are regarded under a methodological principle of suspended abolition. Inspired in part by Walter Benjamin's fable of the 'angel of history' – a figure backed up against the present, contemplating the past, but blasted helplessly, backwards into the future – for Jameson a periodizing approach to history is always also an annihilation of all periodization. Intrinsic to Marxist periodization, that is to say, is another world in which past, present and future are transcended. 'As flowers turn toward the sun,' writes Benjamin, 'by dint of a secret heliotropism the past strives to turn toward that sun which is rising in the sky of history.'[24] This approach, Malcolm Bull has rightly observed, is not a matter of the present being redeemed by the future, nor even of the past being redeemed by the present, but 'of all times being redeemed from outside of time'[25] – from a place and a time, in other words, not bound by such worldly, reified conceptualizations as 'space' and 'time'. In the *Arcades Project* Benjamin writes of the dialectical image as a 'constellation' produced out of the impact of 'what has been' with the 'now'; this is a 'figural' rather than temporal relation, where 'each "now" is the now of a particular *recognizability*'.[26] The angel of history is just such a dialectical image; as is the mediating figure of Jesus Christ – who reveals to men both their corruption and their redemption, says Pascal;[27] as is the image of the world-changing, truth-revealing, history-creating revolutionary proletariat. The figural (or dialectical) elaboration of such images consists of wresting them out of the archaic domain of empirical history, charging them 'to the bursting point with time', and thereby annihilating what Benjamin calls the *intentio* – the immediate historical context which is more properly the concern of the human sciences. This explosive moment is simultaneously the 'birth of authentic historical time, the time of truth'. Thus, in Benjamin's idea of the dialectical image, at least, the affirmation of transcendence – of another world which is present at every moment in this one – is a central, ineluctable motif, inseparable from the task of intervening in this world. By contrast, the approach of post-structuralism appears fundamentally non-redemptive.

# 8

# Post-structuralism and the Absent God

In post-structuralism, it would seem, God finally disappears altogether, absents himself – this is the inevitable effect of the post-structuralist 'deconstruction' of the 'metaphysics of presence' – a procedure described by Derrida in *Positions* as 'a deconstitution of idealism or spiritualism in all their variants'.[1] The death of God, for the post-structuralist critique, is an accomplished event, a supposition underlying its elaboration of Saussurean, or Platonic, or Nietzschean thought. The very structure of belief in God is abolished in the post-structuralist critique, just as Gilles Deleuze and Félix Guattari seek to abolish the structure of belief in the Oedipal narrative – to achieve 'a *materialist reduction* of Oedipus as an ideological form', as they say in *Anti-Oedipus*.[2] Neither God nor the father ever existed, they insist – a fact that has no bearing whatever on the operation of belief, which continues, they say, irrespective of the death of God, or the death of the father. Belief itself is necessarily, *structurally* false: 'The question of the father is like that of God: born of an abstraction, it assumes the link to be already broken between man and nature, man and the world, so that man must be produced as man by something exterior to nature and to man.' 'Metaphysical' systems, in other words, like psychoanalysis and Christianity, are at once a product, symptom and cause of alienation, of the rupture between subject and object, man and world – indeed those categories are reproduced by psychoanalysis, which inherits them – along with its triangular structure – from religious thought. 'It is Oedipus who produces man', write Deleuze and Guattari,

> and who gives a structure to the false movement of infinite progression and regression: your father, and your father's father, a snowball gathering speed as it moves from Oedipus all the way to the father of the primal horde, to God and the Paleolithic age. It is Oedipus who makes us man, for better or for worse, say those who would make fools of us all.[3]

As that final clause merely confirms, *Anti-Oedipus* is a deeply anxious work, a text which betrays an enduring discomfort towards the tragic universe – a world of ever-widening alienation between subject and object. This is a world bequeathed to us, imply Deleuze and Guattari, by dialectical philosophies such as Kant's, which presents modernity as defined by the rationalization of intellectual life into the 'faculties'. The progressive alienation, and self-alienation, of men and women is identical to the process of reification, a product not only of modernity but of dialectical thought *per se*. *Anti-Oedipus* consequently refuses periodization, the differentiation of past-present-future; Deleuze and Guattari represent the antithesis of the 'redemptive' approach to history exemplified by the work of Jameson and Goldmann. Historical events and structures of thought are assimilated, in effect, to those of the present. God *was always* nothing other than a certain transhistorical structure of meaning. They write:

> To anyone who asks: "Do you believe in God?" we should reply in strictly Kantian or Schreberian terms: "Of course, but only as the master of the disjunctive syllogism, or as its a priori principle (God defined as the *Omnitudo realitatis*, from which all secondary realities are derived by a process of division).[4]

The tone and the emphasis of this insistence is quite contrary to the project of synthesis and *comprehension* fundamental to the work of historical materialists like Jameson and Goldmann. The non- or anti-dialectical 'atheism' of Deleuze and Guattari is equivalent to a deistic concept of God, a conceptualization which elevates him into a perfect, and thus unreachable, and thus effectively absent being.

This identity of atheism and deism is seen more clearly in the writings of the Jewish philosopher Emmanuel Levinas – an enormously influential figure for post-structuralist writing on faith and ethics. Levinas's conception of God is as an absent rather than a hidden being. In 'La trace de l'autre' he writes of God, from whom the other originates, as the 'absolutely absent', and in 'Dieu et la philosophie' of God as 'transcendent to the point of absence'.[5] This is a metaphysic which ends by *splitting* the concept of otherness itself along lines which follow the Kantian distinction between finitude and infinitude, thereby precluding the illumination of politics by true otherness, and vice versa. Such a split inflects otherness, as a political concept, towards the world *as it currently exists*; 'divine' otherness is correspondingly removed from the worldly domain entirely. In a conversation with Richard Kearney, Levinas assimilates the otherness of God explicitly to the otherness of the other person: '"Going towards God" is meaningless unless seen in terms of my primary going towards the other person. I can only go towards God by being ethically concerned by and for the other person. I am not saying that ethics presupposes belief. On the contrary, belief presupposes ethics as *that disruption of our being-in-the-world which opens us to the other.*'[6] Ethics itself, rather than arising out of what it means to be human, interrupts our primary ontological constitution as human beings. For Levinas we are subjects ontologically and constitutionally isolated from and independent of the world, rather than always already inserted into and inseparable from it. Levinasian ethics reiterates a dualism of self and other, the presupposition of which, it seems, is the initial absence of God, rather than the 'hiddenness' implied in the respective triangular metaphysical structures of Christianity, Marxism and psychoanalysis. In the same interview with Richard Kearney, Levinas states that

> our desire for God is without end or term: it is interminable and infinite because God reveals himself as absence rather than presence . . . What is a defect in the finite order becomes an excellence in the infinite order. In the infinite order, the absence of God is better than his presence; and the anguish of man's concern and searching for God is better than consummation or comfort.[7]

Indeed, it is with the absolute absence of God, his 'transcendence to the point of absence' [*jusqu' à l'absence*] – meaning 'to the point of a possible confusion with the stirring of the *there is* [*il y a*]'[8] – that the alterity of God is taken over by that of the neighbour; a confusion in which the relation with the neighbour 'gains in dis-interestedness, that is, in nobility', while 'the transcendence of the Infinite arises in glory' – i.e. becomes unfathomable, altogether abstracted from humanity.[9]

It is highly significant, therefore, that for Levinas the moment of truth in Genesis chapter 22 is absolutely *not* the moment in which Abraham responds, in the unfathomable solitude of faith, to God's command to slaughter his son, but the moment at which Abraham is pulled back from the brink of religious 'temptation', as the Biblical text has it, by the ethical. Indeed, Levinas objects to Kierkegaard's account of the episode in Moriah on these grounds.

> Abraham's attentiveness to the voice that led him back to the ethical order, in forbidding him to perform a human sacrifice, is the highest point in the drama. That he obeyed the first voice is astonishing: that he had sufficient distance with respect to that obedience to hear the second voice – that is the essential . . . It is here, in ethics, that there is an appeal to the uniqueness of the subject, and a bestowal of meaning to life, despite death.[10]

The structure of transcendence, as Levinas argues in 'God and Philosophy', is exemplified not by religious experience (the knife raised above the bound body of Isaac) – not by the singularity that is achieved in personal communion with God – but by the ethical, the *universality* represented by the relation with one's neighbour, which hauls Abraham back into the *prevailing* ethical universe. For Levinas, it seems, there are two alternatives, singularity and universality, which correspond approximately to what Kierkegaard calls the aesthetic and the ethical. Given Levinas's concept of an 'absent' God, Kierkegaard's third option – the religious – must appear for Levinas to be a deluded relapse into isolated singularity.

The difference between Levinasian and Kierkegaardian faith is the difference between a dualistic and a dialectical philosophy – between a conception of faith that is opposed to singularity, and one that is opposed to the *opposition* between universality and singularity. Kierkegaard's faith, contrary to received wisdom, is not immiserated in solitude, nor is it a form of unmediated singularity. The 'immediacy' of religious faith is achieved *on the basis* of that (ethical) mediation which is the universal, not as a negation of that mediation.[11] Faith constitutes the unity of the universal and the particular, not – as it seems to be for Levinas – merely the universal *as opposed to* the singular. The constitution of the third, religious stage in Kierkegaard's thought is the mediation of the false opposition between universality and singularity, between mediation and immediacy. By means of a non-administered, therefore transcendent, third term, Kierkegaard's philosophy, and dialectical thought in general, materially and substantially surpasses the world as it currently presents itself.

In this manner the concept of the hidden God simultaneously abolishes and preserves – preserves *in a state of abolition* – the received or the prevailing concept of God. The 'death of God', on the other hand, is inseparably attached to *the prevailing concept of God*; to pronounce the death of God is, paradoxically, to harness oneself to the received version of what God is, to preserve God in his existing conceptual form, and thus the world itself in the state it is in. 'Even the superlatives of wisdom, power and causality advanced by medieval ontology are inadequate to the absolute otherness of God', says Levinas, justifying the concept of a deistic, absent, irrelevant God.[12] Implicit in the idea of the 'hidden God', by contrast – the God who is *ontologically* hidden, whose identity is progressively revealed throughout history *as* hidden – is the simultaneity of God and man, the fundamental human-orientedness of God – an idea which takes nothing away from the otherness of God, nor from the divinity of the other, but rather brings that otherness *within the structure of reality itself.* Thus Christian marriage, a relation with the beloved mediated by the person of God, becomes explicable and – for Kierkegaard's Judge Wilhelm, say – defensible as 'the immediacy which has mediacy in itself, the infinity which has the finite in itself, an eternity which has the temporal in itself.'[13] Everyday reality is transcended, symbolically and materially altered, by the triangular structure of religious or dialectical thought which affirms something other than everyday reality as a constituent element of it.

## 9

# What is Imputed Class Consciousness?

The 'Messianic' affirmation or anticipation of something other, something unstatable which cannot be accounted for in systematic thought, is a common theme to both hostile and approbatory accounts of the Western Marxist tradition. Georg Lukács is described repeatedly in the critical and biographical literature as a figure who carries what was in essence a religious temperament into the political domain; this transfer takes place at precisely the moment at which he begins to develop his reification thesis. His Marxist 'turn' is described in the terms of a conversion narrative, as in the following, much quoted assessment by his friend Anna Lesznai: 'From one Sunday to the next he turned from Saul into Paul'.[1] Marshall Berman has described Lukács, approvingly, as 'communism's St Augustine', and compared his philosophical temperament during the 1910s and 1920s to those of Kierkegaard and Dostoevsky. George Steiner writes of Lukács's commitment to the cause of communism as his 'Devil's pact with historical necessity', and of his having, like Simone Weil, 'the soul of a Calvinist'.[2]

Fredric Jameson too has written of the attempt, intrinsic to Marxist criticism, 'to think another side, an outside, an external face of the concept which, like that of the moon, can never be directly visible or accessible to us.'[3] More recently still, Slavoj Žižek has written of the obligation of Marxism and Christianity jointly to save the element of Messianism in revolutionary thought, to 'fight on the same side of the barricade' in defence of 'the authentic Christian legacy', and in opposition to a fundamentalist tendency within both traditions, which fetishizes the person of Christ as against the 'institutionalization' of Christianity represented by St Paul, and the person of Marx as against the 'ossification' of his thought in the figure of Lenin.[4]

What these presentations of Marxism have in common is an affinity with the idea of a 'hidden God'. The implication is a political and intellectual continuity between Christianity and Marxism, where each is differently but *equally* unequal to the non-reified world of God's presence, of the unity of man and God, of subject and object, which each anticipates and imagines, differently and inadequately. It is this deep and originary affinity between Christianity and Marxism which Žižek wants to pursue – against the worldly limitations of each, and in the interests of what he calls the 'fragile absolute', or truth, itself.

Contrary to this is the idea of Marxism having simply replaced an 'obsolescent' God, an idea that leads inevitably to that of Marxism's own eventual obsolescence and failure. During the post-war years of disenchantment with Soviet communism on the left, Richard Crossman, in a book of essays by communist 'apostates', famously described communism as 'the God that failed', and wrote explicitly of the importance of the transferable Christian conscience to the one-time communist faith of his contributors:

> The emotional appeal of Communism lay precisely in the sacrifices – both material and spiritual – which it demanded of the convert . . . The Communist novice, subjecting his soul to the canon law of the Kremlin, felt something of the release which Catholicism also brings to the intellectual wearied and worried by the privilege of freedom.[5]

Žižek refers to this idea as a 'liberal slander' which seeks to discredit Marxism precisely by characterizing it as a 'secularized religious sect'.[6] Inherent in the idea of the 'God that failed' is a crude secularism, according to which Marxism, like Christianity, is fallacious *on account of* its covert religiosity, a transcendentalism which inevitably ossifies into dogmatism, and which is countered, supposedly, by ridding thought of all so-called 'isms'. 'Must we still cite Marx as an authority in order to say "I am not a Marxist"?' asks Jacques Derrida in *Specters of Marx*. 'What is the distinguishing trait of a Marxist statement? And who can still say "I am a Marxist"?'[7]

Deconstruction, one might say, is the latest, most sophisticated version of this liberal secularism, with its profound anxiety over 'metaphysics' and the crystallization of thought into 'dogma', an anxiety which results in the proliferation of textual strategies to avoid such crystallization – the inscription of words 'under erasure', the persistent coining of new words and figures of thought, and the interminable interrogation of texts for traces of a 'metaphysical' premise.[8] In *Specters of Marx*, Derrida writes of the necessary adaptation of Marxist critique to new conditions. He lists those aspects of Marxism that are obsolete: the 'socialist-Marxist International', the 'messiano-eschatological role of the universal union of the proletarians of all lands', and the 'dictatorship of the proletariat'.[9] Like the concept of God, however, the class consciousness of the proletariat and the 'socialist-Marxist International' can only be 'obsolete' if they are conceived in empirical terms – as objects in precise alignment with the most immediate and available conception of them. It is not the socialist-Marxist International that Derrida disbelieves in, or the proletarian revolution, but the very notion of 'Messianism', of a category of thought outside the circuit of immediate presentation, of an order of reference which, by definition and *par excellence*, exceeds its representation in the order of signification. In this spirit, Derrida declares himself in favour of 'a certain experience of the promise that one can try to liberate from any dogmatics and even from any metaphysico-religious determination, from any *messianism*', a promise which must not 'remain "spiritual" or "abstract", but [must] produce events, new effective forms of action, practice, organization, and so forth.'[10] This affirmation, signalled elsewhere in *Specters of Marx* as a distinction between Messianism and what Derrida calls 'messianicity', may be explicable as the introduction of otherness into the existing order of things, rather than the preservation of the other in a deistic (or atheistic) moment of mysticism. Like the 'materialist' refusal of God (atheism), however, Derrida's refusal of 'Messianism' could more convincingly be shown to be identical with its opposite – to be motivated precisely by a sense of the infinite preciosity of the messianic vocation and of the sanctity of the truly other.

The spirit of Marxist critique to be preserved against its messianic deterioration, says Derrida, is that which 'puts into question', interminably and vigilantly, the *concepts* of the ideal, of human rights (and its subsidiaries), of liberty, equality and fraternity, of capital, of the human (and, by extension, the divine and the animal), and finally of democracy, even the supposedly non-ontological concept of 'democracy to come'.[11] In this way, the very concept of the other (which is also the concept of the concept) is comprehensively and systematically demolished – stripped of its otherness. In *The Gift of Death*, in an attempt to avoid what he calls 'idolatrous stereotyping or representation', Derrida redefines God as 'the possibility I have of keeping a secret that is visible from the interior but not from the exterior.'[12] In *Specters of Marx* too, every possible receptacle of otherness is placed methodologically into question. The effect is a concept of the other which is split: on one hand, sublimated to the extent that it is effectively absent, beyond human reach – a God who is inaccessible, who turns away from the extended, unworthy hand of man; and on the other, predicated upon the violation of my own interiority, an entity which comes into being only 'at the instant of the infinite sharing of the secret'[13] – that is to say, in my ethical *going forth* towards every (or any) other person.

This methodological 'secularism', meaning the categorical removal of God – whether atheistically or deistically conceived – from human experience, contrasts with the authentic 'religiosity' of Marxist discourse. Historical materialism is an inheritor of the Christian dialectical tradition insofar as it affirms, methodologically and in principle, something other than what exists. Even such apparently 'concrete' terms as the proletariat and the party are, for Lukács and Goldmann, material *inasmuch* as they are ideal, projected into the future – towards a stage at which the consciousness of the individual may come to coincide with 'a particular typical position in the process of production' – and accessible as such precisely by consciousness in the present.[14] In *The Modern Prince*, Antonio Gramsci founds his idea of the revolutionary party on a similarly paradoxical conception of the agency of historical change. For Machiavelli, observes Gramsci, the archetypal prince had no real historical existence but was a 'pure theoretical abstraction – a symbol of the leader and ideal *condottiere*'.[15] In Machiavelli's final invocation of a prince (nominally Lorenzo de Medici) who 'really exists', therefore, occurs a synthesis of the ideal and the material, comparable to that which occurs in the Christian incarnation, or in the celebration of the Eucharist – or in the role of the party as Gramsci develops it by analogy:

> In the conclusion [to *The Prince*], Machiavelli merges with the people, becomes the people; not, however, some "generic" people, but the people whom he, Machiavelli, has convinced by the preceding argument – the people whose consciousness and whose expression he becomes and feels himself to be, with whom he feels identified. The entire "logical" argument now appears as nothing other than auto-reflection on the part of the people – an inner reasoning worked out in the popular consciousness, whose conclusion is a cry of passionate urgency.[16]

The wager that the prince (or God, or the proletariat) exists, and can change the world, is the very means by which that entity, and that change is brought about. The sense is similar to Lukács's presentation of class consciousness as 'imputed' or 'ascribed' (*zugerechnetes Bewusstsein*) rather than empirical or psychological, or to Lucien Goldmann's references to 'potential' or 'possible' class consciousness (*conscience possible*).[17] The 'revolutionary proletariat', like the image of salvation proposed by Christianity, is for Lukács a theoretical construction, not an empirical reality; it represents nothing other than the vehicle of that form of consciousness wherein 'the dialectical contradictions of the development as a whole become conscious'.[18] In the leap of faith that such a moment is possible, a leap of faith taken in defiance of all evidence to the contrary, this moment – a new state of consciousness – is actually brought into being; history itself is materially and substantially changed at the point at which the *particular* (or psychological) consciousness of the proletariat coincides with the universal consciousness: that coincidence is the moment of revolution, or at any rate is inseparable from it. Class struggle is thus revealed to be a struggle of the proletariat waged against *itself* – against 'the devastating and degrading effects of the capitalist system upon its class consciousness' – as much as against any external enemy. The objective theory of class consciousness, says Lukács, 'is the theory of its objective possibility', not of its empirical or psychological reality.[19]

Although Žižek explicitly disavows the term 'reification' (he writes of it as one of several motifs 'long ago appropriated . . . by the conservative critics of "consumer society"', by which he means the purely 'academic' tradition running from the early Frankfurt School to 'today's cultural studies'),[20] a strong concept of reification permeates his thesis in *The Fragile Absolute.* For Lukács, reification denotes not 'ossification' as such, but the 'opportunism' of capitalist ideology, which seeks to 'reduce the class consciousness of the proletariat to the level of the psychologically given'[21] – i.e., to effect an ideological corrosion of the possibility of anything other than what exists. The reified world, says Lukács, appears as 'the only possible world'.[22] Žižek, too, is explicit on this point: capitalism entails not only the suspension of the 'ghosts of tradition' but 'the radical secularization of social life', meaning that it 'mercilessly tears apart any aura of authentic nobility, sacredness, honour, and so on.'[23] This is the process of modernization recognized by Marx and Engels in the *Communist Manifesto* as inseparable from capitalism, which has 'drowned the most heavenly ecstasies of religious fervour, of chivalrous enthusiasm, of philistine sentimentalism, in the icy water of egotistical calculation'.[24] At the same time, says Žižek, a contrary process may be observed as inherent in this one of secularization – namely, the material process of production attains the status of a 'spiritual' truth given for all time, its 'spiritualization'. Radical secularization is a deistic, as much as an atheistic process. Capital creates 'its own monstrous ghosts', in the form of the mystical inevitability of its own expansion. The violence of capital, observes Žižek, 'is no longer attributable to concrete individuals and their "evil" intentions; it is purely "objective", systemic, anonymous.'[25] The idea that capitalism is a modernizing, demystifying force is the most powerful and seductive of the myths generated by the expansion of capital.[26] In fact, capitalism is less a demystifying than a radically secularizing force – the effect of which, paradoxically, is a deistic as much as an atheistic conception of a God who is absent from human experience. Thus is reiterated a conception of a world abandoned to a set of already existing ontological and epistemological categories. Reification is a process of radical secularization in this sense – one which can be found as much within the institutions of the Christian tradition as in the paradigms of humanist thought.

# 10

# Reification and Decolonization

As we have seen, postcolonial and post-structuralist theory provide a rationale for rejecting the concept of reification on the basis, primarily, of its inherent dualistic structure, a dualism which reiterates an imperialist and metaphysical distinction between self and other. This distinction is dramatized most effectively in colonial literature, and most famously in Joseph Conrad's *Heart of Darkness*. Reification, writes Spivak, implies a privileging of 'use value' as the concrete.[1] A myth of originary purity untouched by commodification underlies the concept, according to which 'primitive' societies enjoy access to a quality of existence that has been lost in 'developed' Western ones. The liberal horror at and revulsion from the colonial project is, on a fundamental level, a perpetuation of that project, insofar as it represents the other as an absence. In the projection of a pristine society, and of the malign effects of 'civilization' on that society, we may trace the continuation of a failure to acknowledge Africa, for example, as a continent with its own traditions, history, and culture. In the idea of the mystery and impenetrability of the 'heart of darkness', the other is *produced* as effectively transcendent: both a threat to –

since it is a radical negation of – the values of the self, and an outside against which that self is constituted as identity.

The substance of this postcolonial critique, then, is that the concept of reification, like the colonial project itself, is quasi- or potentially 'metaphysical'. Both colonialism and the critique of reification are legitimated by reference to some transcendent, ahistorical truth outside the text – the truth of Christianity for example, in the name of which the colonial project is undertaken, or the proposed moment of totality – the unification of particular and universal, of subject and object – which constitutes the revolutionary remaking of the world. The very identity of the European self, observe Michael Hardt and Antonio Negri, is produced in a movement of Manichaean exclusion, a process they call 'the dialectic of colonial sovereignty'; this is a variation on the mode of 'transcendence' which they see as central to the production of the modern concept of sovereignty, and which, in their book *Empire*, they counterpose to the revolutionary mode of 'immanence'.[2] Both the Marxist critique of reification and the colonial project hypostasize, implicitly or otherwise, a concept of God – a legitimizing authority external to the thing being legitimated.

Edward Said's discussion of the concept of reification, under the title 'Traveling Theory', is an analysis of its susceptibility, like all pioneering and potentially liberating ideas, to codification and institutionalization, to elevation into 'religious' dogma:

> To speak of the unceasing overthrow of objective forms, and to speak, as [Lukács] does in the essay on class consciousness, of how the logical end of overcoming reification is the self-annihilation of the revolutionary class itself, means that Lukács had pushed his theory farther forward and upward, unacceptably (in my opinion).[3]

Here the 'postcolonial' position, as implied in Said's critical position on Lukács, begins to look like a more subtle take on the liberal 'God that failed' thesis rather than a deconstruction of the metaphysical premises of the concept itself. Consequently, perhaps, of the major thinkers behind the influential body of work labelled postcolonialism, only Said has made any use at all of the model developed by Lukács in *History and Class Consciousness* to represent the colonial project. The link between Lukács's theory of class consciousness and postcolonialism is possible for Said on the basis of the speculative idea that Frantz Fanon, the great theorist of decolonization, adapted Lukács's model of the revolutionary proletariat to the colonial situation.

Fanon's categories of colonizer and native, like Lukács's categories of bourgeois and proletarian, have a paradigmatic, almost mythic quality. For Fanon, says Said, violence is 'the synthesis that overcomes the reification of white man as subject, black man as object.'[4] Decolonization is understood by Fanon as a 'historical' process;[5] thus the retention of reification as an explanatory tool is dependent on refashioning Lukács as the theoretician of a revolutionary archetype which is not limited to a narrow understanding of class struggle, but which may also become manifest in the struggle for independence in colonized countries – or, indeed, in any other struggle for liberation.

For Fanon, in fact, the theory of reification is *more* appropriate to colonial than to capitalist relations of exploitation. Fanon writes that colonial and capitalist societies work fundamentally differently; the former by violence, the latter by ideology.[6] The colonial context is therefore more 'transparent' that the capitalist one, because the apparatus of power is more immediately present; it speaks the language of pure force, rather than of moral exhortation or national pride. The task of the native, more easily than of Lukács's proletarian, is that of simply 'deciding to embody history in his own person'.[7] This idea might be read as a translation of the passage in *History and Class Consciousness* where Lukács writes that the ability of the worker to 'objectify himself against his existence' is the source of his resistance to reification, unlike the bureaucrat, whose very thoughts and feelings become reified.[8]

Said's thesis of the influence of Lukács on Fanon's *The Wretched of the Earth* is quite convincing, and not only because the dates fit (the French translation of *History and Class Consciousness* appeared in 1960, *Les Damnés de la terre* in 1961). Consider Fanon's description of colonial society: the colonial world, he says, is 'a world divided into compartments, a motionless, Manichaeistic world, a world of statues' – in other words, a thoroughly reified world. The process of decolonization – a *historical* process, stresses Fanon, meaning that it is inexorable and inevitable – is based upon a revelation of the reified status of that colonial world, and hence its unsustainability. 'All the Mediterranean [meaning Graeco-Roman, i.e. Western Enlightenment] values – the triumph of the human individual, of clarity and of beauty – become lifeless, colourless knick-knacks. All those speeches seem like collections of dead words; those values which seemed to uplift the soul are revealed as worthless . . .'[9] Fanon's approach is unashamedly 'binarist'; even the distinction between theory and practice is retained as one between the inadvertently complicit (such as the nationalist parties) and the truly subjugated. Thus 'some individuals', he writes, 'are convinced of the ineffectiveness of violent methods; for them, there is no doubt about it, every attempt to break colonial oppression by force is a hopeless effort, an attempt at suicide, because in the innermost recesses of their brains the settler's tanks and aeroplanes occupy a huge place.'[10] For the people, on the other hand, the violence of armed struggle is a unifying and 'cleansing' force; Fanon describes this in Lukácsian terms:

> It frees the native from his inferiority complex and from his despair and inaction; it makes him fearless and restores his self-respect. Even if the armed struggle has been symbolic and the nation is demobilized through a rapid movement of decolonization, the people have the time to see that the liberation has been the business of each and all and that the leader has no special merit . . . The action which has thrown them into a hand-to-hand struggle confers upon the masses a voracious taste for the concrete.[11]

In the light of Fanon's apparently Manichaeistic vision, the theoretical sophistication of an Adorno, say, resembles nothing other than the narcissism and decadence of an élite whose time is up; indeed, in places Adorno seems to acknowledge this himself, with his talk of a 'measure of both fortune and guilt' attaching to someone with his privileges, which he can do nothing about.[12] Jameson writes more explicitly about the decline of the Western intellectual, using a Hegelian framework derived from the Master–Slave dialectic described in the *Phenomenology of Spirit*. Jameson's passage is beautifully written – symptomatically so perhaps. Americans, he says, find themselves in the situation of the Master at the conclusion of Hegel's Master-Slave dialectic, 'condemned to idealism – to the luxury of a placeless freedom in which any consciousness of his own concrete situation flees like a dream, like a word unremembered on the tip of the tongue, a nagging doubt which the puzzled mind is unable to formulate.'[13] It is difficult to differentiate this 'dialectical' attitude very precisely from that of Joseph Conrad's narrator Marlow in *Heart of Darkness*, dismayed and yet reassured by the familiar mediocrity of Brussels, 'the sepulchral city', on returning from the Congo.[14] One might easily caricature Adorno, in particular, as a reification-obsessed, 'Eurocentrically limited' figure,[15] reduced to championing aesthetic works on the basis of their 'incomprehensibility', the sole remaining guarantee of resistance to the commodifying effects of the culture industry. It is similarly easy to counterpose the 'narcissism' of Adorno – especially in the light of his routine repudiations of revolutionary spontaneity[16] – to Fanon's firebrand militancy in *The Wretched of the Earth*. The concept of reification itself, a concept which is central to the works of Fanon and (more explicitly) Jameson and Adorno, seems tainted with just this form of essentialist thinking, which reproduces the Manichaeism found in Conrad's *Heart of Darkness*. In the relationship of Adorno and Fanon the extreme poles of the concept confront each other. Moribund, 'epistemologically crippled' Europe (Jameson's phrase)[17] contrasts with the disenfranchized superabundance of life in the 'Third World' in the same way as Hegel's Master to the Slave. At one point, Jameson even invests 'third-world culture' with a certain 'epistemological priority', further hinting that the premodernity of its 'allegorical vision' achieves a unification of subject and object that is forever obscured to 'the view from the top'.[18]

It is in explicit critique of such binary, therefore imperial models of thought that Gayatri Spivak mobilizes the *Communist Manifesto* itself, a text which – unlike the 'romantic anti-capitalist' readings to which certain pre-1848 writings are susceptible – emphasizes 'the dialectical embrace of the bourgeoisie and the proletariat on the one hand, and the impracticability of winning back the patriarchal or artisanal workshop on the other'.[19] For Spivak, oppositional thought is subject to a form of 'commodity pietism' which elevates the commodity, and the process of 'commodification', into something approximating an absolute evil, a signifier which takes on a quasi-theological significance.[20] The theory of the commodity developed in the volumes of *Capital*, rather, is a 'homoeopathic' form, meaning that it may be mobilized as a deconstructive rather than (or inasmuch as it is) a dialectical concept – like the presentation of capitalism itself in *The Communist Manifesto*. From Spivak's postcolonial-theoretical perspective (which, throughout *A Critique of Postcolonial Reason*, is treated with a circumspection intended to preserve its own 'homoeopathic' qualities), the circuit of commodity capital may be 'set to work' in the service of a critique of its own fetish-character – and she quotes (somewhat selectively) from the second volume of *Capital*: 'The commodity capital, as the direct product of the capitalist production process, recalls its origin and is therefore more rational in its form, less lacking in conceptual differentiation, than the money capital, in which every trace of this process has been effaced . . .'[21] Elsewhere, the commodity form is acclaimed by Spivak as a potential weapon of resistance to what is held to be one of the central political implications of postcolonialism itself: the recourse to a politics grounded in 'identity', a politics which cements people, by implication, into a different kind of thingitude. 'The rational calculus of commodification' she writes (opening a long, rather fascinating footnote), 'protects from the dangers of a merely fragmented identity politics'.[22] The meaning of this statement remains somewhat obscure in Spivak's own text, but becomes clearer if read in tandem with a passage in Adorno's *Minima Moralia*. 'The past life of émigrés is, as we know, annulled', writes Adorno – a consequence of intellectual experience being increasingly defined as 'non-transferable and unnaturalizable', a product specific to time and place. The passage is inspired by Adorno's own post-war displacement in the United States – but he could be talking about late twentieth-century multiculturalism, an ideology which holds differences between cultures to be not only sacrosanct, but (at its extreme) insurmountable. He continues:

> Anything that is not reified, cannot be counted and measured, ceases to exist. Not satisfied with this, however, reification spreads to its own opposite, the life that cannot be directly actualized; anything that lives on merely as thought and recollection. For this a special rubric has been invented. It is called 'background' and appears on the questionnaire as an appendix, after sex, age and profession.[23]

In a 'multiculturalist' society, reification flips over into its contrary, the respect for difference. A liberal policy of 'anti-racism' becomes, as Slavoj Žižek and Hardt and Negri have differently shown, the vehicle of a postmodern ideology of 'reflexive racism'. For Žižek, postmodern racism is articulated against, precisely, racism itself – as in the perception of the Balkans as 'the terrain of ethnic horrors and intolerance, of primitive irrational warring passions, to be opposed to the post-nation-state liberal-democratic process of solving conflicts through rational negotiation, compromise, and mutual respect.'[24] Racism – a process in which the *historical origin* of cultural differences is forgotten, in which those differences are 'naturalized' – is in turn reified as 'cultural intolerance'. In the emerging neo-liberal consensus, sexual intolerance, likewise, becomes increasingly unacceptable, such that 'standard normative heterosexuality' begins to be replaced with 'a proliferation of unstable shifting identities and/or orientations'.[25] For Hardt and Negri similarly, 'postmodern racism' is a form of segregation, not hierarchy, in which cultural difference comes to fill the role that biology and ethnicity once played. 'This pluralism accepts all the differences of who we are so long as we agree to act on the basis of these differences of identity, so long as we act our race.'[26] In this transformation, 'culture', 'difference', 'identity', 'tolerance', become the means by which *the struggle against reification is itself reified*. Slavoj Žižek counsels rejection of the 'fashionable motif' of reification on the grounds of its total appropriation by capital – a rejection that is complied with, though less fervently, by Spivak.[27] On the contrary, however, it is precisely this 'appropriation' of the motif of reification which makes a sustained theoretical engagement with the concept more timely and necessary than ever.

In this situation of progressive appropriation, implies Spivak, the commodity form itself may provide a means of genuine resistance. Commodification, after all, bestows a power of abstraction from one's immediate reality; commodity fetishism even offers a means of passage out of materialistic thingitude – physically, by way of the propensity of circulating goods to cross boundaries and frontiers, or imaginatively, by way of the transcendence which attaches to the object of fetishization – which constitutes that fetishization, and which elevates the thing itself above both instrumentality and exchange value. Consider the following fictional description of the Christmas transformation of a shop store by V.S. Naipaul:

> Then the Tulsi Store became a place of deep romance and endless delights, transformed from the austere emporium it was on other days, dark and silent . . . Now all day there was noise and bustle. Gramophones played in the Tulsi Store and all the other stores and even from the stalls in the market. Mechanical birds whistled; dolls squeaked; toy trumpets were tried out; tops hummed; cars shot across counters, were seized by hands, and held whining in mid-air. The enamel plates and the hairpins were pushed to the back, and their place was taken by black

> grapes in white boxes filled with aromatic sawdust; red Canadian apples whose scent overrode every other; by a multitude of toys and dolls and games in boxes, new and sparkling glassware, new china, all smelling of their newness . . .[28]

Here, perhaps, commodities function somewhat like artworks in a 'preartistic' age, a time before 'Art', when ephemerality, afunctionality and transcendence are in no sense incompatible with 'actuality', with thingness. For Adorno, a residue of such preartistic consciousness may be found in the modern appreciation of fireworks: 'Fireworks are apparitions *par excellence*: they appear empirically yet are liberated from the burden of the empirical, which is the obligation of duration; they are a sign from heaven yet artifactual, an ominous warning, a script that flashes up, vanishes, and indeed cannot be read for its meaning.'[29] What if an answer to the impoverishing effects of capitalism could be found, paradoxically, in the child's captivation by the auratic glow of goods for sale in the most commercial season of the year?

Spivak's intervention on behalf of the commodity is highly abstract, yet highly suggestive. We might think of Shakespeare's Cressida, described repeatedly in the text of *Troilus and Cressida*, not least by the character herself, in commodity terms. 'Men prize the thing ungained more than it is' she reflects, anticipating Marx's account of commodity fetishism two and a half centuries later. For her lover Troilus 'Her bed is India; there she lies, a pearl . . . Ourself the merchant' – indeed, she is later brutally exchanged by Troy for the release of a highly valued warrior, Antenor. On her arrival in the Greek camp, however, Cressida leaves behind her Trojan past, trading kisses with the Greek high command and, in a situation of apparent powerlessness, finally embracing her commodity status as a means – the only one available to her – of survival and advancement.[30] To identify the commodity form, as Spivak does,[31] with Derrida's concept of the *pharmakon* discussed earlier – a 'homoeopathic' concept, an entity that has no truth in and of itself – is to abjure any thought of a politics that seeks a return to a former undifferentiated unity of subject and object, or that sees reification as the evil to be combatted; for, increasingly, this would seem to be the tendency of the dominant ideology itself. Reification – in the form of religious belief, say, which contains the unknowability of life within an institutional, often exploitative ideological structure, or the sense of 'community', which functions to naturalize highly contingent, often exclusionary forms of social behaviour – may represent a barrier to, rather than a facilitator of the operations and the movements of capital. Correspondingly, the expansion of capitalism may function in part to liberate people from these structures, even as it embeds them in other, less visible ones perhaps.

All this is to say that capitalism is a situation which must generate its own solution; as 'the problem', capitalism itself is a reification. Spivak is right to locate her perspective in the wake of the 'mature' Marx, who, in the first volume of *Capital*, repeatedly criticizes those radicals who (like Conrad's Marlow) find everywhere 'the falsifying hand of civilization' – an attitude which, says Marx, 'knows how to judge and condemn the present, but not how to comprehend it'.[32] Adorno writes similarly in deprecation of Aldous Huxley's novel *Brave New World* – a curse upon the future, he says, which fails to realize that 'the past whose blessing [it] invokes is of the same nature'.[33] For Marx and Spivak, as indeed for Fanon and Adorno, 'there is no question of a return to Nature', and certainly not of a return to the unity of subject and object. For Adorno it is not civilization, or even the capitalist mode of production which should be obliterated, but 'the captivating spell of the old undifferentiatedness'.[34]

In her carefully phrased insistences, therefore, Spivak restages the complexity of Adorno's own relationship to reification, a relationship in which the concept itself is maintained (in apparent opposition to Lukács) as fully paradoxical. 'The meaningful times for whose return the early Lukács yearned' observes Adorno, 'were as much due to reification, to inhuman institutions, as he initially attested only to the bourgeois age [*wie er es erst den bürgerlichen attestierte*]. Contemporary representations of medieval towns', he points out further, 'usually look as if an execution were just taking place to cheer the populace.'[35] For Adorno the most recent example of a society in which subject and object were in near-total harmony, after all, was Hitler's Germany. Late capitalism may be described similarly as a stage in which the administration of reality reaches its logical conclusion – a society of perfectly disciplined, or self-disciplining, 'integrated' subjects, whose relationship to their labour seems less 'alienated' than 'organic'. In the recent appearance of 'organizational holism' as a discourse of business management, for example, workers are subject to what is in effect a new modality of the operation of power: spiritual integration – an ideology which coincides with the increasing disposability of the individual workers themselves:

> The consequence of [the] holistic vision seems to be a general implementation of corporate ideology so convincing that each employee will want to discipline her- or himself accordingly, without being directly controlled or managed by superiors. The happy result . . . is the disappearance of (Taylorist) 'mass logic and standard-controls' and a 'utilization of the collective intelligence and creativity of the united group of employees as a source for continual improvement'. Decisions are no longer transmitted hierarchically downwards, but rather 'grow out of the situation and [are] handled with reference to a common consciousness of the mission, vision and culture of the corporation . . .'[36]

In this situation, reification itself has become a barrier to the movement of capital. Like Shakespeare's Cressida, employees 'must become travelling, individualistic consumers of disposable authenticity, who will eagerly prepare themselves to adopt the "corporate religion" of their next new workplace.'[37] In a situation of enforced 'subjectification', a residual alienation between subject and object may provide a lever for the preservation, consolidation, and eventual 'objectification' or realization of freedom.

The question remains, however, as to whether a recognition of this structure affords anything like a progressive strategy for the long term. The commodity is potentially liberating, after all, only to the degree that it is potentially dominating. Commodification, or reification, is here revealed in its true reflexivity, a development I shall discuss in more detail in Parts Two and Three. The commodity represents process, dethingitude – the complexity of the relations of production, for example – as *thingitude*; it brings dethingitude, precisely, into the realm of visibility and representation, just as language brings the unknowable 'other' into cognition, necessarily violating it in the process. The commodity is a thing of abstraction, and thus of 'separation from individual intention'.[38] It may be conceived as a structural analogy to the reification inherent in every 'representative' politics – or the reification inherent in every religion which 'translates' the divine into earthly terms. Reification is not the antithesis of humanity but, as Adorno points out, an element of it; reification is not only 'the condition *from which* liberation is possible', but – in a reified society at least – the means by which 'subjective impulses are realized'.[39] The postcolonialist refusal of the concept on the basis, firstly, of its 'Eurocentric arrogance', and secondly, of its obsolescence, ignores the fact that the concept itself may, indeed must, be implicated in *its own* critique; the concept itself, in other words, is the product of reified consciousness. Reification is a condition which pertains as much to the idea of the primitive who preexists the subject's differentiation, as to that of the philosopher who regards himself with a sort of inverse narcissism, looking longingly, and self-disgustedly, to the other for salvation. The opposition between immediacy and fetishism – between primitive undifferentiatedness and capitalist reification – is a creation of reified consciousness, a category which is nevertheless simultaneously indispensable to any thoroughgoing critique of that opposition.

⋆

# 11

# Total Reification (I): Reading Fanon

Neither Adorno nor Fanon appear in Spivak's analysis, although both have suffered from 'Manichaean' misreadings at the hands of others. This is understandable, given the apparently incendiary rhetoric of the second, and the air of exhausted melancholy that attaches to the first. Neither writer has helped matters by his habits of self-presentation. Adorno subtitled *Minima Moralia*, perhaps his most widely read book, 'Reflections from Damaged Life', and described the perspective from which he was writing as a 'melancholy science'. Meanwhile it is claimed that the impassioned titles of Fanon's books – *The Wretched of the Earth*, *Black Skin White Masks*, *Toward the African Revolution* – exist in a state of dissociation from the temperament which animates the works. In an introduction to *Black Skin White Masks*, Homi Bhabha comments that Fanon's titles 'emptily echo a political spirit that is far from his own'. Fanon 'may yearn for the total transformation of Man and Society, but he speaks most effectively from the uncertain interstices of historical change.'[1] For Bhabha, the currency of Fanon's work among an audience looking for a symbol of revolutionary spontaneity – the kind of audience Fanon found among the English left during the 1970s, say – represents another means of containment of a thinker whose great significance lies not in the strength of his fervour, but in the substance of his contradictions. The 'ritual respect' accorded the name of Fanon is itself a Manichaeistic procedure, 'part of the ceremony of a polite, English refusal', which obscures the 'deep psychic uncertainty' characterizing the colonial relation itself.[2] As David Macey shows in his biography of Fanon, the 'refusal' of Fanon has its less polite forms also, such as Allan Bloom's talk of his 'murderous hatred of

Europeans and his espousal of terrorism', or Alain Finkielkraut's comparison of Fanon's revolutionary politics to *völkisch* nationalism – this despite Fanon's repeated insistence on the damage that occurs to national consciousness when race is privileged over nation, or tribe over state.[3]

For Fanon, crucially – and *pace* a certain interpretation of Lukács's account of the truth-bearing role of the proletariat – the real consciousness of the native in the colonial situation is no 'truer' than that of the settler. Fanon is intervening in a world in which all interventions are necessarily strategic; in which language, as a technology owned and controlled by the colonizing power, is falsifying and yet indispensable. In *Black Skin White Masks*, which is concerned in part with the way that language is implicated in colonial oppression, he quotes Valéry's description of language as 'the god gone astray in the flesh'.[4] Language is both alienating and – therefore – the necessary terrain of any possible disalienation. Thus the chapter 'Concerning Violence' in *The Wretched of the Earth* is nothing so simple as a call for the immediate, necessarily violent overthrow of the colonial regime (although it is that), but a 'homoeopathic' diagnosis, an appropriation of the tools of the existing order in the service of the eradication of that order. Nor is the chapter on spontaneity an apologia for the vibrancy and immediacy of the native way of life as opposed to the petrified mentality of the settlers; it is a critique of that very opposition as, paradoxically, *a creation of the latter.* When consciousness dawns, writes Fanon, it does so 'upon truths that are only partial, limited and unstable.'[5] The 'new history of Man' announced in *The Wretched of the Earth* is in no sense a reversion to or a preservation of something which preexisted colonialism, but is inaugurated in the postcolonial consciousness of the Third World. *The Wretched of the Earth*, with its overtones of violence, is like a story from the Old Testament: the description of a cleansing operation before the coming of the Messiah.

Madhu Dubey refers correctly to the 'dizzying complexity' which envelops Fanon's positioning on such issues.[6] In an anecdotal account of the antagonism characterizing the relation between doctor and patient in the colonial situation, which leads the colonized native to refuse or to mistrust the technically truthful diagnosis of the colonizer, Fanon inserts the following comment: 'The truth objectively expressed is constantly vitiated by the lie of the colonial situation.'[7] This is not a mystical statement in the slightest but one which presupposes the materialist inseparability of truth from the concrete circumstances of its enunciation. The colonizer's discourse is a lie, even when it tells the truth, because the relationship presupposed by and restated in every nuance 'makes of [the] life [of the native] something resembling an incomplete death.'[8] In the same book Fanon documents the historical significance of the revolutionary radio station *Voice of Algeria* to the Algerian struggle. In 1957 and 1958 the French army would regularly jam the station's broadcasts, meaning that the transmissions themselves were rarely, and then only imperfectly, heard. The mere existence of the station, however, was a powerful symbol, as testified by the practice of simply tuning into the noise of the static when this was the only sound attainable on the blocked wavelength. The people's claims to have listened to the station were thus a falsehood, but in some sense a true one, just like the 'true lie', as Fanon called it, of the Algerian nation. With the collapse of the occupying power vividly imagined behind each crackling modulation, writes Fanon, 'the enemy lost its density, and at the level of consciousness of the occupied, experienced a series of essential setbacks'.[9] It is easy to see that such a paradoxical relation between truth and falsehood affects every enunciation which takes place in a colonial context, and that this condition must therefore extend to Fanon's 'incendiary' writings themselves.

In fact, this dissociation at the heart of Fanon's works provides a clue to the concept of reification and, I want to claim, to the case for its reactivation. There is no version of Fanon's *Les Damnés de la terre* other than the one prefaced by Jean-Paul Sartre's insistence that this book 'is not addressed to us'.[10] There is no readership for the book, therefore, other than that which comes to it only to be told that it is not the intended readership. For whom, if not for its empirically existing readers, could the book be written? Yet Sartre's prefatory statement is more than a suggestive, paradoxical tease. It is a clue to the truth that *The Wretched of the Earth* is conceived as an intervention into a *totally reified* situation – one in which readership, author, and text are all implicated. Like the 'Manichaean' distinction between the body ('black skin') and the surface ('white masks') signalled in the title of the earlier book, the evocation of a distinction between native and colonizer in *The Wretched of the Earth*, and the accompanying opposition between theory and ideology, is grounded in an acknowledgement of the epistemological 'mutilation' inflicted by colonialism, and of the inevitable 'inferiority' of every mind touched by the colonial enterprise.[11] The archetypes who appear in Fanon's analysis are determined by the reified situation in which they appear. 'What is often called the black soul is a white man's artefact,' quotes Bhabha from *Black Skin White Masks*.[12] The other in whose name Fanon's analysis of the colonial situation is put forward is not the native, but the moment of truth which exists as an order of potentiality *outside* the entirely reified relationship between the native and the settler. Throughout the book Fanon offers further statements supporting this assertion of a totally reified society; and these achieve a degree of aphoristic economy in the final pages: 'The Negro is not. Any more than the white man.' 'There is no Negro mission; there is no white burden.'[13] If anything militates against Said's thesis that Fanon read *History and Class Consciousness* in 1960, it is that Fanon seems to have arrived at an independent understanding of the issues informing Lukács's theory of reification in *Black Skin White Masks*, published eight years earlier. Here Fanon anticipates the critique of 'Enlightenment' values in *The Wretched of the Earth*, and the concomitant insight into the reified nature of the colonial world – a condition in which both black and white identity are thoroughly implicated – in a measured rejection of the ideological apparatus of colonial liberalism: 'By calling on humanity, on the belief in dignity, on love, on charity, it would be easy to prove, or to win the admission, that the black is the equal of the white. But my purpose is quite different: What I want to do is help the black man to free himself of the arsenal of complexes that has been developed by the colonial environment.'[14]

In other words, there is no residue of truth to be salvaged from what Madhu Dubey calls the 'deformed reality of the colonial context'.[15] Dubey refers to the shiftiness of Fanon's writing as his 'double-voiced discourse', while Bhabha writes of the 'doubling of identity' in Fanon's work, a doubling which is broken down by Bhabha into the difference between *identity* and *identification*; one might further hypostasize this opposition (following Bhabha) as a categorical distinction between ontology and psychoanalysis, or between metaphysics and politics, or even between theory and practice.[16] 'Double-voiced' discourse, however, whether embodied in Adorno's relentlessly paradoxical 'negative dialectics' or in Fanon's strategic occupation of several apparently incommensurable subject positions, has only one conceivable rationale: the idea of a *thoroughly reified* world, in which language and discourse serve to sever us ever more firmly from truth, even as they promise and articulate that same truth – a world in which the theory of a 'totally reified' world is itself comprehensible as an effect and a symptom of reification.

# 12

# Total Reification (II): Reading Lukács

The Manichaean misreadings to which Fanon and Adorno have been subjected are as nothing beside the polarizations which have characterized accounts of Georg Lukács in Western Europe and America. In recent years, in particular, these have tended to delineate an acceptable (pre-Frankfurt School) and an unacceptable (Stalinist) Lukács. Marshall Berman, for example, identifies clearly a good and a bad Lukács, the break between the two occurring somewhere during the second half of *History and Class Consciousness*. In Berman's account the thought of the figure whose most celebrated success was the essay on reification was, by the last few chapters of that book, becoming itself 'reified'.[1] The strain of Bolshevism running through *History and Class Consciousness* is presented by Berman as a continuation and a refinement of Lukács's pre-Marxist writings (the aesthetic essays in *Soul and Form*, the classic study *The Theory of the Novel*), the predominant mood of which, says Berman approvingly, is one of 'religious anguish and longing'. According to Berman, the early Lukács represents a subversive strain of individualism and spirituality within Marxist thought, which in general gives him more in common with writers outside the Marxist tradition than with those within it.[2] Lukács's Marxism is richer for the fact that his 'kindred spirits' (Rousseau, Dostoevsky, Nietzsche) were all 'a lot weirder than Marx' – the implication being that the primary historical role of Marxism is that of an ideological repository for a number of eccentric and gifted individuals who might as easily have thrived in Berman's Paris of the 1850s or his New York of the 1960s.[3] In Berman's 'humanist Marxism' we see another permutation of the 'god that failed' thesis: it is when Lukács *betrays* his faith and enters the Soviet 'machine' that he becomes a symbol of decline.

Agnes Heller provides a corrective to this persistent Manichaeanism in her essay 'Lukács's Later Philosophy', where she argues that, far from a moment of apostasy, Lukács's 'Stalinist turn' represents a continuation along the road of faith – his progression to a 'stage' (to use Kierkegaard's term) beyond that at which one's actions need to be justified in the eyes of others: 'Lukács's repudiation of *History and Class Consciousness* was motivated both by the existential choice of an absolute and by the anxiety elicited by that very same absolute . . . Lukács believes in his God, yet at the same time he recognizes all the dirt and horror of "God's created world" and contrasts this extant world with an ideal world that would be commensurate with his God.'[4] The implications of this are severe for Berman's thesis of the two Lukácses, as Heller continues: 'All those who see in him the representative of Stalinism . . . are right, while those who see him as Stalin's greatest philosophical adversary are also right. For until his very last years, when his belief in the absolute became shaky, he was both.' There is no contradiction between the knight of faith of Budapest and the *apparatchik* of Moscow. We might express this in bolder, starker terms as follows: there is no contradiction between Lukács's theory of reification, as articulated in *History and Class Consciousness*, and his later repudiation of that theory – the latter being a necessary move and a corollary of the former. The paradox is that of Abraham, whose faith in God, at its purest and least worldly, is expressible only in the unfathomable and socially unacceptable form of the sacrifice of his son Isaac.

Reminiscing about Lukács, István Eörsi writes the following: 'Lukács chose Bolshevism, but without the innocence most of his contemporaries had. He was fully aware of committing a sin.'[5] To illustrate his point, Eörsi retells the story of when Lukács, attached to the Fifth Division of the Budapest Red Army as a political commissar during the Czech-Romanian offensive of 1919, ordered the execution of eight members of a battalion who had deserted their posts without firing a shot. 'By this means,' Lukács remarked later, 'I more or less managed to restore order.'[6] The 'contradiction' in Lukács between spiritual authenticity and submission to the party machine (like the opposition between the 'mystical' and the 'Marxist' Benjamin) is no more contradictory than Frantz Fanon's 'true lie' of national consciousness – a contradiction which vanishes in the light of the theory of reification, which absorbs and comprehends it. Indeed, it is precisely the development of this theory which makes possible Lukács's transition from a tragic intellectual stage, characterized by unresolvable contradiction and paralysis, to a stage at which that contradiction is fully resolved and transcended. In one of his last pre-Marxist essays, Lukács ends with an affirmation of democracy over Bolshevism, on the grounds that the Bolshevik assumption that good may be forged from evil – 'that it is possible, as Razumikhin says in *Crime and Punishment*, to lie our way through to the truth' – is a metaphysical abstraction. 'This writer cannot share this faith,' he concludes, 'and therefore sees at the root of Bolshevism an insuperable ethical dilemma'.[7] By the time he wrote 'Tactics and Ethics', just a few weeks later, this tragic knowledge had become for Lukács a basis for the authentically moral decision – that which takes thought to a plane beyond the reified, 'metaphysical' language of 'good' and 'bad'; a point at which the 'insuperable ethical dilemma' is radically contained and superseded:

> Only he who acknowledges unflinchingly and without any reservations that murder is under no circumstances to be sanctioned can commit the murderous deed that is truly – and tragically – moral. To express this sense of the most profound human tragedy in the incomparably beautiful words of Hebbel's Judith: 'Even if God had placed sin between me and the deed enjoined upon me – who am I to be able to escape it?'[8]

In a fallen, 'reified' world, lies are *all we have* to tell the truth, and sin the only means of attaining it. The distinction between the pre- and the post-'conversion' Lukács – the tragedian and the Bolshevik – signals not an epistemic break but a movement, in the Kierkegaardian sense, from one to another *stage* of spiritual life. Even in the early aesthetic work *The Theory of the Novel*, written in 1914–15, Lukács referred to his own age, using a phrase of Fichte's, as 'the epoch of absolute sinfulness' – a metaphor which directly anticipates the reification thesis of *History and Class Consciousness*.[9] And when István Eörsi asked Lukács what he meant by this use of the word 'sin' in his early writings, Lukács replied simply, 'Violence.'[10]

It is in this light that we should understand Frantz Fanon's ordinances on the use of violence in the colonial situation. In a world of complete sinfulness, of total reification, violence is an already determined quality of all action and all conceptualization. The task of revolutionary thought, for Fanon and Lukács, is to see the operation of this violence *as such* – to see the way of the world as sinfulness, as violence – and to implement the solution which cannot but pass by way of violence, since only violence can dislodge the petrified consciousness of an oppressed people. The idea that one may change a regime or a society peacefully is no less violent, in fact, than the use of revolutionary violence. Ideologically speaking it is more so, since it betokens a delusion as to the proximity and ready availability of a world without violence, without reification.

Even so, the reification thesis anticipates such a world, and is predicated upon its possibility – the realization of which would be the death of the theory of reification. The hypothesis of an 'age of absolute sinfulness', as Lukács remarked, defending *The Theory of the Novel* many years later, is the *transitional* diagnosis of a *transitional* epoch.[11] Immanent in the 'total reification' thesis is its own immediate repudiation – so hard on its heels as to be almost simultaneous with it. Reification is a self-reflexive, or dialectical concept; one invariably finds that the concept itself has played a part in any objection to it – yet, at the same time, the concept is always on the brink of succumbing to the very process it denotes. This reflexivity is the true explanation for the 'apostasy' of Lukács's Moscow period – a sharpening and elevation of his faith (rather than its collapse) which is entirely in accordance with the theory of reification itself. Lukács's repudiation of his theory was an enactment of its logic that was at worst 'premature', although this verdict too is incompatible with the logic of reification, according to which the notion of prematurity is a product of the very reified consciousness it is intended to replace.[12]

Consciousness of reification is constitutive of the concept itself; the idea of a reified object or a reified condition which nobody perceives as such is simply anomalous. The moment of reification is simultaneous with, or inseparable from, the moment of *awakening* to it. Thus it is to consciousness that we must look for any solution to the problem of reification – which is not to say that reification is an ideal structure, existing 'solely' at the level of consciousness; rather, the concept of reification alerts us to the dialectical interpenetration of consciousness (subject) and world (object), to the intimacy between thought and action, and to the necessary mediation of the opposition of materialism and idealism – an opposition that is left intact in any critique of the 'metaphysics of presence', for example. In the concept of reification all idealism or subjectivism cancels itself out, to paraphrase Adorno's defence of Hegelian dialectics – 'because no difference remains through which the subject would be identified as something distinct, as subject.'[13]

If it is true that we are approaching a condition of 'total reification', this is also, by implication, a state of imminent *liberation* from reification – firstly, since 'total reification' represents an identity of subject and object which would be, in turn, the end of reification; and secondly, since the theory of reification itself is unavoidably implicated in any such condition. In this formulation, the concept persists in a state of suspended annullment, inseparable from the consciousness that detects and, potentially, elevates itself beyond it. The vision of total reification as catastrophe is simply unsustainable in this theoretical context. It is in the light of this relation that the remobilization and rearticulation of the concept of reification is necessary. I shall attempt such a rearticulation in Part Two, where I will address the contemporary resonances of Lukács's theory of reification, and examine the representation of anxiety as it is played out across some of the major vehicles of the expression of consciousness in the modern age: art and aesthetics, literature and cultural theory, politics and social theory, religious belief and philosophy. In Part Three I shall present the other side of this relation in an exploration of Kierkegaard's theory of anxiety as in fact a theory of reification.

PART TWO

# Inversion

*Perhaps an object can provide a link, can enable one to go from one subject to another and so to live within society, to be together. But then, given the fact that social relationships are always ambiguous, given the fact that my thoughts create rifts as much as they unite, given the fact that my words establish contacts by being spoken and create isolation by remaining unspoken, given the fact that there is such a vast gap between the subjective certainty I have of myself and the objective reality that I represent to others, given the fact that I always find myself guilty although I feel I am innocent . . . I must go on listening. I must go on looking about me even more keenly than in the past.*

Jean-Luc Godard[1]

1

# The Reflexive Character of Reification

Writings that address the concept of reification are always troubled by a vein of anxiety concerning the susceptibility of the concept itself to the reifying process. In his essay on reification in *History and Class Consciousness*, Georg Lukács points out that the idea itself is vulnerable to a reified treatment by bourgeois consciousness, in the form of its conceptualization as 'the timeless model of human relations in general'. Such an analysis, he says, divorces the concept from its foundations in the economic base. For Lukács, the reified form of the concept of reification is an example of the process by which capitalism must 'embrace every manifestation of the life of society', turning even the hostile diagnosis of its own fundamental falsity into a 'phenomenon' – something both 'inevitable' and 'bewildering' in its complexity and apparent insuperability.[2] The category of reification is for Lukács inseparable from capitalism; thus any extension of the capitalist mode of production must result in the proliferation of reification. Conversely, overcoming reification, impossible in any case under Lukács's 'present conditions', is achievable only in the analysis offered by historical materialism, which disrupts 'by constant and constantly renewed efforts' the reified structure of existence.[3] To link reification directly with 'modernity' or 'progress', therefore, is to fail to interrogate those concepts sufficiently. To conceive of reification as a historically reversible (or irreversible) process of the incremental mediation of reality – a consequence of the division of labour, or the growing 'complexity' of life – is to maintain a reified notion of the concept itself, ruptured from its origin in capitalist exploitation.

The focus of this critique in Lukács's essay is the sociologist Georg Simmel, whose *The Philosophy of Money* puts forward a theory of 'subjective culture' in a state of being progressively encroached upon by the reifying processes of 'objective culture' – of which the growth of the money economy is a symptom and a vehicle. Simmel's analyses are part of a well-developed theory of modernity, written in a spirit of philosophical 'enquiry' and explicitly claiming the neutrality and objectivity which that implies: 'It is our task not to complain or to condone but only to understand', as he concludes his famous essay on metropolitan mental life.[4] This approach has led some commentators to think of Simmel as an alienated 'sociological flâneur', while others, such as Lukács, speak of him as a merely 'transitional' figure, a brilliant philosophical spirit with a 'missing centre', whose 'indecisiveness' is evidence of his own seduction by (and implication in) the phenomena he observes.[5]

In the work of later theorists meanwhile (including in his own subsequent writings), Lukács himself has fallen prey to the accusation of having reified or 'debased' the concept of reification. In *The Melancholy Science* Gillian Rose traces the various uses of the term by Marcuse, Benjamin, Adorno and Lukács to illustrate how reification (*Verdinglichung*) becomes synonymous with both alienation (*Entfremdung*) and objectification (*Versachlichung*). She cites Marcuse's misattribution of the term to Hegel, and Lukács's misattribution of it to Marx, in order to show how the concept is too easily freed from its grounding in 'a specific mode of production'. Reification is transformed into a generalization of Marx's theory of commodity fetishism, she says – and she too indicates Simmel as an example. Simmel's 'piecemeal social ontology' consists of 'things as well as objects considered as objectifications';[6] the apparent inevitability of this process for Simmel determines the essential ambivalence with which he theorizes it. Like Jean Baudrillard (whom he in some ways anticipates), Simmel hints at the potential measures by which 'the order of things' compensates for the triumph of objective culture: 'Every day and from all sides, the wealth of objective culture increases, but the individual mind can enrich the forms and contents of its own development only by distancing itself still further from that of culture and developing its own at a much slower pace.'[7] Simmel is an apologist for modernity by default; his prognosis of an ever increasing alienation between subjective and objective culture, and of the irrevocable and self-corrective nature of this process, is symptomatic of his reified treatment of the concept of reification itself. Simmel conceives of the subject–object relation as a binary, non-dialectical and therefore 'rigid' structure; in this way, writes Lukács, reification is made 'an eternal law of nature or a cultural value existing for all time.'[8]

Gillian Rose notes that in his later work Lukács also subscribes to a Simmelian concept of culture as a 'value in itself', one which may recover its authenticity and autonomy only once capitalism has ended. Yet such an opposition is also implicit in Lukács's privileging of the proletariat in *History and Class Consciousness*. While all men are reified and commodified under capitalism, the worker, he says, unlike the bureaucrat, preserves 'his humanity and his soul' – the very faculties that enable him to rebel against reification. Conversely, in the case of the bureaucrat, 'even his thoughts and feelings become reified.'[9] Thus a transhistorical, transsocial kernal of non-reifiable truth is maintained in Lukács's theory, accredited to the proletariat, and conceptualized as the motor of history. It seems inconceivable that any theory of reification which names itself as such, however, could avoid succumbing to its own critique. The ante is upped continually as a matter of course; what is presumed by the concept to be non-reified is inevitably reified in the moment of that very presumption.

The analysis of reification always eventually turns its anxiety against itself. One could go further: the analysis of reification is *structurally* disposed to find itself waiting at the end of every investigation into its most elusive manifestations. There is an essential incoherence to the concept: sometimes the concept of reification sides with the 'idealism' of politics against bureaucratic 'realism'; at other times it seems to side with material 'reality' against entrenched 'idealism'. In the name of the critique of reification, contradictory positions may find themselves championed with an effect of impassioned futility. An exemplary text juxtaposes the following declarations:

> Those who have set all idealists against each other, the enemies of vision in any form, surely they are the enemy. The grey nobodies and their organs, whose only aim is to regulate and organize all spontaneity, all intensity out of life, have won because they have divided the opposition.
>
> Why do all extremists fight when they have far more against the Centre than each other? Why do both cling to their useless ideologies when the total realization of either would result in a world of stultifying dullness?[10]

Reification is a self-reflective, neurotic category. It is also inherently paradoxical, since the hypothetical event of total reification would, logically at least, be the end of reification. Were concepts to become identical with their objects – were the triumph of 'objective culture', to use Simmel's terminology, to be assured, such that there was no longer any discrepancy between subject and object – the process would immediately lose its pernicious bearing, along with the reality principle itself. Reification both promises and denies the possibility of reconciliation between subject and object; likewise, the *critique* of reification, predicated upon the desirability of the 'restitution of immediacy', in the same moment presupposes its irrevocable loss.[11] The thesis of 'total reification' depends upon its impossibility; for, were it to be achieved, this dystopia would be at the same time a real utopia. Reification is indissociable from the anxiety which detects and laments it; indeed, reification as a concept would not exist without it.

Gillian Rose's discussion of the concept is appropriately entitled 'The Lament over Reification', a phrase taken from Adorno's *Negative Dialectics*.[12] She talks of Adorno's 'obsession' with the concept, as it recurs throughout his work, linking this with his 'eclectic' use of the term and his occasional generalization of it 'as a feature of all human activity'.[13] Yet Adorno is fully aware of the link between reification and anxiety, or alienation – 'the subjective state of consciousness that corresponds to it'.[14] He is also, as Rose points out, aware of the profound difficulty in making positive pronouncements about reification – of the risk thereby of reifying the concept itself. What he calls 'the lament about reification' is precisely such a reified version of the concept, one which is reduced to a subjective, socio-psychological category, 'the way conditions appear to people'.[15] The real problem, rather, is with 'the conditions that condemn mankind to impotence and apathy and would yet be changed by human action'. At every moment, the anxiety about reification threatens to flip over into a yearning for the reconciliation of subject and object, which would be simultaneously the *realization* of total reification and its *annihilation*.

> If a man looks upon thingness as radical evil, if he would like to dynamize all entity into pure actuality, he tends to be hostile to otherness, to the alien thing that has lent its name to alienation, and not in vain. He tends to that nonidentity which would be the deliverance, not of consciousness alone, but of reconciled mankind. Absolute dynamics, on the other hand, would be that absolute action whose violent satisfaction lies in itself, the action in which nonidentity is abused as a mere occasion.[16]

Any demand for a return to the former 'undifferentiatedness' of subject and object proposes a return to barbarism. Harmony between subject and object, Adorno makes clear, can only be attained by liquidation of the former – the solution of totalitarianism. The attachment to 'pure actuality' is a tyrannical, even hubristic urge. As Simon Jarvis has written, the hope of Adorno's thought is not, primarily, life without reification but life without domination.[17] Reification is a symbolic violence presupposed by one's insertion in the world, and by the distinction between ideality and actuality; it is for Adorno, therefore, an inevitable and necessary constituent of politics itself. To conceive of reification in the manner described above – to attach oneself 'positively' to nonidentity thinking – is to put oneself in the place of God, to deny one's *own* thingness, to approach sublimity as the polarized opposition to and negation of the world as it is.

Reification therefore, as a socio-political critique, co-exists with the anxiety towards reification; without its perpetual self-interrogation, the concept itself is reified. On the other hand, its possible conceptualization as a purely subjective category is brought into focus by any such discussion. The reduction of the concept to a species of eternal anxiety threatens to strip it of its critical-theoretical virility. If one version of the reification of reification is its conceptualization as the 'timeless model of human relations in general', the prevailing response might take the form of an existential withdrawal before the brutality and/or unpalatability of the world. The retreat into abstraction, say, or art, or 'decadence', or religion, or 'the provinces', on the basis of the modern world's conceptual violence and vulgarity, is accordingly a pathological one with no wider significance than to the mental well-being of the individual concerned. Such a solution is put forward to the chronically anxious protagonist of Nathanael West's novel *Miss Lonelyhearts*: 'She told him about her childhood on a farm and of her love for animals, about country sounds and country smells and of how fresh and clean everything in the country is. She said that he ought to live there and that if he did, he would find that all his troubles were city troubles.'[18] Any analysis of the concept must consider the nature of the anxiety which gives rise to it – more specifically, the question of the extent to which reification might be explicable as the 'objective' expression of a merely 'subjective' pathology.

★

# 2

# Total Illusion: The Triumph of Capital

At the conclusion of his essay, Lukács anticipates a time, associated with the decline of bourgeois society and the impending collapse of capitalism, in which the forms of reification 'gather themselves up' into their most extreme and brittle manifestations, simultaneously extending their grip and undermining their own credibility. At this point, two aspects of an immanent contradiction are in conflict: on one hand, the forms of reification are revealed as increasingly unable to 'do justice to' the phenomena: Lukács describes this as the 'cracking of the crust because of the inner emptiness'. On the other hand, we see a quantitative increase in the forms of reification, which are extended 'to cover the whole surface of manifest phenomena'. Two possibilities open up for the proletariat, says Lukács: (i) to 'substitute its own positive contents for the emptied and bursting husks' – in other words, to fulfil its revolutionary potential, enabling the eventual unification of subject and object; or (ii) to 'adapt itself ideologically to conform to these, the emptiest and most decadent forms of bourgeois culture' – that is to say, to collude, wittingly or otherwise, in the objectifying processes of capitalism, further eroding the subjective authenticity which Lukács attributes to the proletariat on account of its critical historical situatedness.[1]

Given that Lukács was writing as long ago as 1922; given that these two possibilities were based on observations made in two earlier texts – Bukharin's *Ökonomie der Transformationsperiode* of 1920[2] and a letter written by Ferdinand Lassalle to Marx dated

12 December 1851; given that Lassalle's letter is concerned with remarks already made by Hegel in his old age, and that these remarks are themselves anticipated in Hegel's first important work, the *Phenomenology of Spirit*, published in 1807 – we might conclude that the revolutionary 'substitution' sought by Lukács has been keenly awaited for a very long time indeed. The telos of Lukács's philosophy of history – the reconciliation of subject and object – is derived from the model of consciousness described in the *Phenomenology*. The 'goal' of philosophy, says Hegel, is the point at which 'knowledge no longer needs to go beyond itself, where knowledge finds itself, where Notion corresponds to object and object to Notion'.[3] The image of a society under a fragile blanket of reification, the dissolution of which is imminent, is similarly Hegelian. Hegel describes the replacement of superstition by enlightenment in the *Phenomenology* as a moment of social transformation long preceded by 'an invisible and imperceptible Spirit' which infiltrates existing society and lays hold of 'the marrow of spiritual life'. Spirit's previous shape, superstition, has by this time become merely an 'unconscious idol', a 'dead form' which is able to be cast aside as painlessly as 'a withered skin'.[4] If for Hegel the *philosophes* were the agents of this process, while for Lukács the proletariat, in theory, were to perform this role, the overriding impression in present times is that this position of revolutionary agent, the embodiment of 'true consciousness', has been finally abandoned. The ideological conformity of the proletariat with 'the emptiest and most decadent forms of bourgeois culture', imagined by Lukács as the momentary symptom of a prerevolutionary period, has proved to be not a temporary failure of revolutionary awareness, but the prevailing consciousness of late capitalism.

Acceptance of Lukács's theory requires that one accept, in perpetuity, the *imminence* of the proletarian awakening. After how much of the historical intransigence of the proletariat towards its symbolic role do we turn from Lukács to Simmel for the correct analysis? At what point does refusal of Lukács's 'idealism' demand an acceptance of Simmel's 'bourgeois' neutrality? At what point, if at all, does one accept one of three conclusions: (i) that the project outlined by Lukács – the liberation of society from, simultaneously, the phenomenon of reification and the dehumanizing capitalist economic system, by awakening the tendencies of history itself into consciousness through the agency of the proletariat – has failed conclusively; (ii) that there is something fundamentally flawed about Lukács's eschatological presentation of the theory of reification; or (iii) that to *await* the revolutionary moment is to vulgarize, to periodize Lukács's presentation – to turn what is, in essence, a theory of 'becoming' into one of 'being'?

There is a clear polarity here between Lukács's revolutionary faith in the purpose of history and Simmel's secular academicism. One could likewise draw an analogy between the three variations of revolutionary apostasy outlined above and those forms of religious apostasy enjoined by the 'death of God'. At one point in his reification essay Lukács opens the way for such an analogy by speaking of God and the soul as 'nothing but mythological expressions to denote the unified subject or, alternatively, the unified object of the totality of the objects of knowledge considered as perfect (and wholly known).'[5] Rejection of that unified subject/object, and reversion to Simmel's 'secularism', may take the three forms of defeatism, atheism and liberalism. The first, defeatism, concedes the triumph of the secular world and abandons its radicalism in a spirit of dejection. The second, atheism, concedes the falsity of its historical belief in the concept of reification, declaring the concept itself to be idealistic, oppressive, bourgeois and counter-revolutionary. The third, liberalism, concedes the impossibility of decreeing the nature or the timescale of the promised reunification of subject and object. It insists on reconceptualizing liberation from reification in a non-idealized sense, as a goal which is reinvented in successive periods and perpetually reenacted in political praxis: every age creates the form of liberation it requires.

Approaching Lukács's theory in the face of a 'refractory'

proletariat and the apparent triumph of capitalism seems to demand that one of these three positions is adopted. The alternative, of course, is to hold fast to the project, to keep reascending Mount Sinai in the ineradicable belief that the Second Coming is impending. Marxist revolutionaries, like pentecostal Christians and Jehovah's Witnesses, believe in the imminence of the meaningful Event, despite all indications to the contrary. There is a sense of 'keeping faith' in the ultimate objective – to be present at the approach of the Son in His splendour, or to raise to consciousness the underlying tendencies of history in the glory of revolution. Each – the revolutionary and the pilgrim – doggedly negates what exists, the world as it is; each, it might be said, refuses any negotiation with the present. Each also, in principle, writes off a society which has failed to perform in the way that, according to 'theory', it ought to have done.

Rather than the ideological 'conformity' or 'capitulation' of the proletariat, a more 'dialectical' explanation for the apparent non-realization of Lukács's vision might be that capitalism has proved to be extremely adept in appropriating the *forms* of revolutionary consciousness. This does not mean that resistance is futile, that the administration of reality is total, or that the link between reification and capitalism is false. Nor does it mean that revolutionary consciousness itself is successfully appropriated. On the contrary, what is implied is that the conception of revolutionary consciousness has been, or has need of being, utterly reconfigured in the wake of its apparent appropriation; furthermore, that such total appropriation is both always apparent and always illusory.

Such an explanation is opened up, to some extent, by Simmel's model of the conflict between 'subjective' and 'objective' culture, with its attempt to correlate the process of objectification with that of modernity, and his concomitant acceptance of the irreversibility of this process. In Simmel's theory, life – the non-administered 'humanity and soul' that Lukács ascribes to the proletariat – is engaged in a constant struggle against the forms that it generates for itself, and which acquire fixed identities in accordance with their own 'objectified' logic. These forms – works of art, religions, sciences and technologies, laws, etc. – thereby become alienated from 'the spiritual dynamic which created them and which makes them independent.'[6] Objective culture comes to predominate in the world over subjective culture, which seeks, perpetually and hopelessly, to transcend all forms and 'to appear in its naked immediacy'.[7] It is hereby that life 'provides the dynamics for this whole movement', while at the same time being constantly reduced and frustrated in its ambitions towards transcendence by the progressive rigidity of the forms. This dualistic model ends not in any dialectical resolution but in the further polarization of its primary terms. The relation between subjective and objective culture becomes one of radical alienation between the two. In *The Philosophy of Money* Simmel writes of modern man's simultaneous subservience to and domination over objective culture – a situation apparently indistinguishable from man's subjective retreat from the world, and which is strongly related to the development of a money economy:

> If modern man can, under favourable circumstances, secure an island of subjectivity, a secret, closed-off sphere of privacy – not in the social but in a deeper metaphysical sense – for his most personal existence, which to some extent compensates for the religious style of life of former times, then this is due to the fact that money relieves us to an ever-increasing extent of direct contact with things, while at the same time making it infinitely easier for us to dominate them and select from them what we require.[8]

Lukács describes exactly the same split in bourgeois consciousness, but with a vastly more critical emphasis: 'Our aim [is] to locate the point at which there appears in the thought of bourgeois society the double tendency characteristic of its evolution. On the one hand, it acquires increasing control over the details of its social existence, subjecting them to its needs. On the other hand it loses – likewise progressively – the possibility of gaining intellectual control of society as a whole and with that it loses its own qualifications for leadership.'[9] The end of bourgeois society is radical alienation, isolation and powerlessness for the vast majority of people, with the paltry compensation of complete domination over the 'details'. Capitalism offers unprecedented possibilities for the constitution of individual taste – in culture, cars or home furnishings – and the opportunity to develop a personal portfolio of emotional, political and philosophical sympathies – the means, in other words, of gratifying every subjective nuance of one's existential relation to the world.

The reconfiguration of revolutionary consciousness is not achieved in Simmel's alienated, isolated subjectivity; yet Simmel recognizes the irreducibility of the fact of the commodity form as a 'structuring principle' of modern society, a recognition that, for all his 'bourgeois' neutrality, ascribes him particular significance for any modern attempt to reexamine Lukács's theory of reification.[10] Simmel's model of modernity may, as Lukács suggests, be characterized by capitulation to the 'inevitability' of the subject–object divergence; history, however, has borne out Simmel's vision of a society in which 'objective culture' has effectively colonized every manifestation of subjective autonomy. Later thinkers such as Baudrillard have written of the mechanisms by which resistance, in a society whose administrative tendencies are no longer disciplinary but benevolent and inclusive, reconfigures itself not in terms of subjective articulation and liberation but as subjective 'disappearance'. The masses, says Baudrillard, have renounced the practices of the political subject – self-expression, voting, emancipation – for those of the object – 'infantilism, hyperconformity, total dependence, passivity, idiocy' – superior practices, speculates Baudrillard, in terms of their impact, but which bourgeois society now dismisses with the concepts of alienation and passivity.[11] In a culture characterized by an overwhelming ideological compulsion towards mass participation, the term 'cynicism', likewise, becomes a prevalent negative catchword. The response that it denotes and depreciates, suggests Baudrillard, is the most effective weapon of the masses, since by this means – silence, non-participation, apathy – power is confronted with an inertia which it has created, an absence which mirrors the logic of the system itself and which 'becomes the sign of its own death'.[12] The masses, says Baudrillard, no longer exist as such; any attempt to make them appear, to urge upon them their 'revolutionary vocation',[13] is completely beholden to the operations of power itself.

In 'Reflections on the Theory of Class', an essay written in 1942, Adorno provides a rationale for such a reconfiguration of revolutionary consciousness. In the administered world of late capitalism, he says, power 'disappears behind the concentration of capital':

> This makes it necessary to consider the concept of class closely enough so that it is both preserved and changed. Preserved: because the distinction between exploiters and exploited not only persists undiminished but grows in compulsion and fixity. Changed: because the oppressed, today in accordance with the forecast of theory the overwhelming majority of humanity, cannot experience themselves as a class.[14]

Adorno here comes close to Simmel's model of the polarization of subjective and objective culture (the 'exploited' and the 'exploiters'). What Simmel conceives as the progressive mediation of reality in modernity, as life increases in complexity, is accompanied, for Adorno, by the encoding of power within ever more impersonal institutional structures. Yet subjectivity is no privileged realm of truth, of freedom from reification, or locus of revolutionary consciousness. For Adorno, indeed, the process of self-isolation described by Simmel further contributes to, and is symptomatic of, the triumph of reification. At the same time as it loses its visible antagonist, revolutionary consciousness loses its self-identity. The subjective resistance to commodification, the illusion of intellectual autonomy, is as implicated in the processes of commodification as the blatant corrosiveness of the culture industry. The very notion of freedom of expression, for example, presupposes the 'marketability' of the mind: 'The network of the whole is drawn ever tighter, modelled after the act of exchange. It leaves the individual consciousness less and less room for evasion, preforms it more and more thoroughly, cuts it off *a priori* as it were from the possibility of differencing itself as all difference degenerates to a nuance in the monotony of supply.'[15]

Thus Adorno expressly rejects Lukács's 'idealist' conception of the proletariat as both subject and object of history, as well as Simmel's desire to preserve the ever smaller, yet ever more flexible, private space of the individual. That Adorno places under interrogation the basic critique of capitalism which equates power with reification and radicalism with dialectics is a direct corollary of this. For Adorno, the critique of reification is always itself at the point of becoming reified, and is thus always in need of self-interrogation. This problematic was outlined by Adorno as early as 1955; his reference here is to Marx's classic statement on the bankruptcy of philosophical idealism: 'Since the moment arrived when every advanced economic and political council agreed that what was important was to change the world and that to interpret it was *allotria*, it has become difficult simply to invoke the *Theses* against Feuerbach.'[16]

This statement informs the ambitions of the present work. With the global capitalist appropriation of the language of Marxian analysis ('all that is solid melts into air'), critique, to commandeer Peter Sloterdijk's memorable phrase, 'changes sides'.[17] In a situation of 'total administration' it is precisely power which seeks the reinvention and liquidation of every privileged, rigidified institution. The reification of the concept of reification takes the new form of a willingness to expel all traces of history from the present. The anxiety towards reification has become the prevailing cultural mindset. We are living in an unprecedentedly reflective world in which the desire for an unreified, untainted existence has become a mainstream cultural and political value.

⋆

# 3

# The 'Aesthetic Structure' of Reification

Linking reification directly to the anxiety towards it lends support to the view that reification is a merely psychological category, thus an insufficiently concrete one, and that this is the reason why Marx avoids the term. Simmel's *Philosophy of Money* is criticized on a similar basis – for approaching the phenomenon of exchange from the 'psychological' rather than the economic angle. A closely related implication – one which critics also drew from Lukács's use of the term – is that reification is a primarily aesthetic concept rather than one grounded in a 'scientific' analysis. Reification is a matter of sensibility, a temperament akin to a *taste* for the avant-garde, and having no positive bearing upon politics as such – in fact, the concept of reification aestheticizes politics. The 'constant and constantly renewed efforts' necessary to overcome the reified structure of existence are nothing other than the efforts of Ezra Pound to 'make it new', of Diogenes to 'remint the coinage', or the willingness of James Joyce to disregard 'with complete courage whatever seems to him adventitious', as Virginia Woolf wrote of him.[1] The concept itself arises from a misplaced aesthetic consciousness which develops in modernism and is transposed into a revolutionary political context, where it gives an individualistic emphasis to the objectives of revolution and, subsequently, creates an illusion of the unfeasibility of 'radical politics' in the consciousness of late capitalism. The theme of reification in political theory has been rendered anachronistic by structuralist and post-structuralist tendencies – which have substantially interrogated its ontological and eschatological presuppositions – and by historical developments, which have seen capitalism successfully mobilize the concept of reification against itself.

Inasmuch as Lukács's critique of reification takes issue with, and is critically intended to rectify, the progressive differentiation of subject and object, it certainly has structural similarities to the analytic of the beautiful as outlined in Kant's 'Critique of Aesthetic Judgement'. Lukács's concept of reification is necessarily oriented towards both subjective and objective culture, since the concept is directed against the bourgeois separation of the two. The proletariat, uniquely, is both subject and object of history; for Lukács only the proletarian class has the subjective potential to resist reification, an effect precisely of its objectification by the ruling class – Lukács's analysis here is directly informed by the master–slave dialectic in the *Phenomenology of Spirit* – and it is this position which enables the unification of subject and object potentially to inhere in the proletariat.

The analytic of the beautiful is similarly oriented towards both subject and object, and indeed forges a rapprochement of some kind between them – this is the meaning of Kant's seemingly paradoxical statement that the judgement of the beautiful has 'subjective universal validity'.[2] While the judgement of the *good* has objective universal validity – any fool can recognize a good tin-opener, since the use value to which it pertains is universally recognizable (the good is judged according to socially-entrenched concepts; a good tin-opener, for example, corresponds successfully to a non-contentious, specified idea of instrumentality) – and the judgement of the *agreeable* has only subjective validity – I cannot frame my subjective preference for comice over conference pears in universal terms, an evaluation prompted by the excitation of my *senses* (the agreeable causes a sensation which pleases us, and is therefore a judgement of sense rather than of taste) – the *beautiful* is a subjective judgement which demands objective recognition, but cannot compel it. I am unable to impose upon you my estimation of the 'beauty' of a landscape or a work of art, yet my estimation has the character of a demand that you assent to it. The category of beauty *demands* universal objective recognition, even though the objective world may decline to provide it. The judgement of taste only *imputes* agreement to everyone, says Kant; it does not *postulate* it; in other words the judgement of taste does not require as a necessary condition that everyone agree, it simply assumes that agreement in the abstract, and regards as at fault anybody who thinks otherwise.

Similarly, there seems little possibility of adjudicating over the concept of reification. Like beauty, reification is a subjective category which demands objective agreement without being able to compel such agreement. Thus, it is closely related to the aesthetic in being bound up with subjective perception; the arguments that it is a purely scientific (therefore objective), or a purely psychological (therefore subjective) category, are themselves forms in which the concept is reified. The militant critic of reified consciousness can only demand our recognition of and subscription to his belief that marriage, say, is the form in which love is rigidified and reified. In marriage, write the authors of *Life and its Replacement with a Dull Reflection of Itself*, the freshness and spontaneity of love is channelled into the institution, stripped of its authenticity and reality, turned from a 'protest against this consumption-besotted society' into a state-approved mechanism of social order, a 'lifeless drudge' and a state of security 'so firmly embraced that it always suffocates freedom'.[3] Can any arbitration take place between this position and that of Kierkegaard's Judge Wilhelm, for example, for whom marriage has a spiritual depth, and offers a route to eternity, that is simply inaccessible to the materialist philosopher who champions the immediacy of first love – an eternity which is inaccessible, therefore, to the critique of reification itself?[4]

Likewise, I can insist that a particular consumer's relation to a particular commodity is a 'fetishistic' one – that her taste for it is an 'aestheticization', effected through blindness to the processes by which its production and consumption constitute the means of her material and ideological exploitation – yet how can I enforce such a reading? If the consumer insists that she enjoys the contours of Ray and Charles Eames's lounge chair, say, or the ironic textures of Yasmina Reza's play *Art*; if this partiality, furthermore, appears as a generalized, even a 'cultural' one, why should the conviction that such taste is delusory be any more deserving of recognition than the simple enjoyment of it? Insight into the processes by which capitalism produces a reified and administered subject is removed from certainty to the same degree as aesthetic judgement itself; if it were not, indeed, the category of reification would be a category of the administered world, to be applied with a precision which only a thoroughly reified consciousness would have access to. The relationship of the critique of reification with aesthetic judgement – analyses which seem antithetical – is in fact quite intimate, as Adorno recognized; indeed his whole aesthetic theory is founded upon this recognition.

If it is still to be useful, the concept of reification must be reconfigured so as to incorporate the anxiety towards it – which means making the case that the revanchist, perpetual rarefaction of the concept, *pace* Gillian Rose, is a violation of it; that reification as a concept is inseparable from its application in various contexts; that to conceive of an 'authorized' or originary conception of it is the grossest reification. As Adorno's writings on art demonstrate, reification is by no means simply soluble; nor is there any verifiable example in history of a non-reified society, or one in which subjectivity is unmediated by the object. If reification is the most extreme because the most abstract model of capitalism's destructive consequences, this abstraction is also the very reason why it can and should be remobilized as a tool for understanding capitalism's contemporary phase.

★

# 4

# Post-structuralism: Anxiety Reified as *Différance*

In an age in which capitalism is apparently consolidating its global dominance, the concept of reification has largely been replaced in social theory by concepts such as 'globalization' and 'reflexive modernization' – ideas which carry all the trappings that Lukács associates with bourgeois thought: inevitability and inexorability. One might see this replacement as facilitated, or in any case mediated, by the theoretical phase of post-structuralism, in which the concept of reification comes under an implicit critique.

In post-structuralist theory, terms like '*différance*' and 'logocentrism' appear as strategies of resistance to reification – both as a real process threatening the integrity of its own thought, and as a concept which itself falls into incoherence when pushed to its logical extreme. Gillian Rose's claim, in *The Melancholy Science*, that reification is not a 'concept' at all mirrors Jacques Derrida's insistence that his coinage *différance* is 'neither a word nor a concept'.[1] This insistence on Derrida's part is necessary precisely in order to avoid the reification of his own term, although whether it is sufficient to do so is highly questionable. The meaning of *différance*, insofar as it can be articulated, is *non-reifiability*; *différance*, punning on Saussure's system of signifying difference and the French word *différer*, meaning both 'differ' and 'defer', implies that meaning is never fully present in the word. Meaning is structured by the difference between terms and between concepts within any signifying system, and it is characterized by deferral; meaning is a promise that is never honoured – or, more accurately, a promise which may always never have been honoured. Thus the term *différance* proposes a means of perpetually out-manoeuvring the processes of reification always threatening the versatility and plasticity of language.

*Différance*, however, also implies that the concept of reification is problematic *per se*. Reification posits a distinction between true and false consciousness, between meaning which is fully present in the concept and meaning which has in some sense departed from it, leaving the signifier as an 'empty husk'. Like Lukács's imagined reconciliation of subject and object – a reconciliation which, as Adorno points out, is both the origin and the goal of Lukács's philosophy of history – the idea that the proletariat might have or ever had an intimate relationship with truth is quite contrary to deconstruction's radical critique of ontological/teleological metaphysics.

The place where Derrida comes closest to addressing the concept of reification is his reading, in *Specters of Marx*, of Marx's account of commodity fetishism.[2] The reading focuses around the opposition between use value and exchange value, and the metaphors of 'spectrality' (haunting, mysticism, obscurantism, phantasmagoria, supernaturalism, supersensuality) with which Marx characterizes the fetishistic relation to the commodity. Derrida's interrogation of the opposition seeks to demonstrate how use value and exchange value are mutually interdependent – in particular, how the currency of exchange value is necessary in order to evaluate a supposedly preceding use value.

Marx's account of commodity production, for all its mythic quality, has a strict temporal logic: the archetypal wooden table described in the first chapter of *Capital* continues to be 'that common, everyday thing, wood', up until the moment when it 'steps forth as a commodity' – at which point 'it is changed into something transcendent'.[3] Similarly, he describes the decisive if hypothetical moment at which the 'mysticism' of the commodity will one day disappear, along with the market economy: 'The whole mystery of commodities, all the magic and necromancy that surrounds the products of labour on the basis of commodity production, vanishes therefore as soon as we come to [*flüchten*] other forms of production.'[4] Like Lukács, Marx sees the alienation of worker from the object of his labour as a moment embedded within linear history; the theory posits a purity, pertaining to use value, which has been lost in the present, but which might be regained in the future, and this purity constitutes both the goal and the origin of history. Yet for Derrida exchange value, as the very presupposition of substitution, exchangeability, iterability, etc., is necessary even for one to form the concept of use value, 'or of value in general, or inform any matter whatsoever, or determine any table . . .'[5] Exchange value here performs the same role in Derrida's critique of Marx as does the concept of writing in his deconstruction of the opposition between speech and writing in Saussure, Rousseau and Plato. The metaphors with which Plato demonizes writing in the *Phaedrus*, for example, are comparable to those with which Marx conceptualizes exchange value: with the development of writing, thought is encapsulated in a form which is unalterable. Thereupon it takes on *a life of its own*, circulating 'equally among those who understand the subject and those who have no business with it'.[6] Derrida expands on this, drawing out its *phantasmagorical* aspect: 'Writing is not an independent order of signification; it is weakened speech, something not completely dead: a living-dead, a revived corpse, a deferred life, a semblance of breath.'[7] Likewise, the temporal quality attributed to the distinction between use value and exchange value in the first chapter of *Capital*, says Derrida, implies that use value is intact, 'identical to itself',[8] until the appearance of the commodity-form 'on the stage'; the latter is thereby reduced to a derivative of the former, its mere 'spectre' (this is the basis of Derrida's elaborate analogy between exchange value and the ghost of Hamlet's father, both of which appear 'belatedly').

The historical and philosophical privileging of speech at the expense of writing is, for Derrida, an archetype of the binary logic of 'Western metaphysics'. The logic of 'commodification', and thus the concept of reification too, is another expression of this logic. Reification privileges, or seems to privilege, use value over exchange value, nature over culture, speech (or thought) over writing, immediacy over mediation, instinct over rationality, emotion over intellect, spontaneity over routine, the invisible over the visible, morning over evening, youth and innocence over age and knowledge, and love at first sight over marriage. Despite this, even thinkers who have sought to debunk the terms of Western philosophy have not been able to resist putting the concept tacitly into play. 'Alas, and yet what are you, my written and painted thoughts!' lyricizes Nietzsche in the closing pages of *Beyond Good and Evil*:

> You have already taken off your novelty and some of you, I fear, are on the point of becoming truths: they already look so immortal, so pathetically righteous, so boring! . . . It is only your *afternoon*, my written and painted thoughts, for which alone I have the colours, many colours perhaps, many many-coloured tendernesses and fifty yellows and browns and greens and reds: – but no one will divine from these how you looked in your morning, you sudden sparks and wonders of my solitude, you my old beloved – *wicked* thoughts![9]

As an expression of the simultaneous joy and anguish of artistic creativity, born precisely of the anxiety towards reification, this passage from Nietzsche is exemplary. A deconstructive critique of the logic of reification, however, exposes even Nietzsche the great anti-Socratic thinker as an inverse Platonist and a metaphysician.

The most sympathetic accounts of deconstruction maintain that Derrida's writing comes as close as possible to a critical practice free from reification; that by 'deconstructing' the logic presupposed by reification his work makes the case for 'thinking differently' the concept; that metaphysics itself is reconfigured, in deconstruction, by means of a 'non-originary origin'; that the only non-reified philosophy, paradoxically, is one which affirms the ubiquity of reification. Whether or not such claims are justified, what is certain is that deconstruction is not by any means free from the *anxiety* towards reification that, I have been arguing, is central to the emergence of the concept itself. Derrida's writing is characterized by the proliferation of mechanisms intended to insulate his work from violent misreading and from 'metaphysical' interpretations. The textual richness of Derrida's writing, the words preserved 'under erasure', the endlessly paradoxical statements which simultaneously affirm and deny the possibility of eluding 'metaphysical discourse', reinscribe the concept as central to his work, at the very point of its exclusion and denial.

Inevitably, in the wider intellectual sphere, liberated from the control exerted within Derrida's own writing, deconstruction has also, in a very straightforward sense, proved to be susceptible to the reifying process which it has sought to confound. The idea of 'reflexive modernization', for example, takes the critical procedures of postmodernism and deconstruction (the diagnosis of an incredulity towards grand narratives, the interrogation of the linear progression of history, the Althusserian link between subjectivity and ideology, the deconstruction of oppositions such as nature/culture, speech/writing, interior/exterior) as ontological truths, evidence of the *non-reifiable* nature of the world, of the end of the domination of the world by reason – little acknowledging the fact that the idea of such a truth about the world is itself a proposition of the triumph of reason and the intellectual mastery of reality.

The concept of modernization put forward in Beck's *Risk Society* is that of the progressive colonization or mediation of the natural (non-Western) world, a process which is actually, or virtually, at the point of completion. The critical *interrogation* of the nature/culture opposition in deconstruction is hereby transformed into its ontological *dissolution*: in its moment of 'victory', industrial modernization turns against itself, beginning a process of 'creative (self)-destruction' and the replacement of one kind of modernization (expansive, assertive, indubitable) by another (reflexive, self-confrontational, doubtful).[10]

In reflexive modernization the idea of society as

simultaneously reified and non-reifiable is established in a politically respectable form. Reflexive modernization, writes Beck, 'abolishes boundaries – of classes, business sectors, nations, continents, families, gender roles and so on.'[11] But here the concept of reflexive modernization is indistinguishable from the process of capitalist expansion as described, for example, in the *Communist Manifesto*. For Beck this erosion of 'boundaries' is the response to and of a world which has been effectively mastered – not the process by which the world is mastered. Slavoj Žižek describes the implications of this theory as follows: 'All our impulses, from sexual orientation to ethnic belonging, are more and more often experienced as matters of choice. Things which once seemed self-evident – how to feed and educate a child, how to proceed in sexual seduction, how and what to eat, how to relax and amuse oneself – have now been "colonized" by reflexivity, and are experienced as something to be learned and decided on.'[12]

This is a situation which recalls the Frankfurt School hypothesis of 'total administration'. Where there is no longer any non-administered realm of human existence, for Beck everything becomes knowable and therefore negotiable, a matter of choice. Beck's thesis of the impossibility of intellectual mastery of the world is, in essence, little different from its apparent converse, Simmel's thesis of the inevitability of reification; and like Simmel, Beck cannot afford to see this in wholly negative terms. The difference between Beck and the analysis put forward in *Dialectic of Enlightenment* is that for Adorno and Horkheimer 'total administration' is only a hypothesis, and must remain so. By proposing that such a condition of 'total administration' has been attained, and by the methodological 'immunity' with which it asserts that diagnosis, reflexive modernization implies the permanent suspension of the concept of reification from social theory. Beck's thought, it turns out, is not reflexive *enough*. Reflexive modernization requires a theory of genuine *reversibility* to complete it – to produce a version of the inseparability of the progressive administration of society from its liberation, which would imply not the facile affirmation of the existing world but its revolutionary annihilation. Such a theory must involve a radicalized concept of reification.

Reflexive modernization is a *positivistic* theory; like globalization, it is almost disconcertingly explicable by reference to Lukács's theory of reification. Reflexive modernization is a contemporary *mythology*, something which functions to reproduce, in imagination, the problem in its *insolubility*.[13] Man in capitalist society, writes Lukács,

> confronts a reality 'made' by himself (as a class) which appears to him to be a natural phenomenon alien to himself; he is wholly at the mercy of its 'laws', his activity is confined to the exploitation of the inexorable fulfilment of certain individual laws for his own (egoistic) interests. But even while 'acting' he remains, in the nature of the case, the object and not the subject of events. The field of his activity thus becomes wholly internalized: it consists on the one hand of the awareness of the laws which he uses and, on the other, of his awareness of his inner reactions to the course taken by events.[14]

In such passages Lukács seems thoroughly contemporary; his analysis has not been rendered obsolete, merely outpaced, by historical events. Reflexive modernization represents the *bringing to self-consciousness* of the fact of reality's constructedness by man, whilst preserving the condition of man's objectification. Reflexive modernization thus, in a certain sense, presents the reconciliation of subject and object sought by Lukács, but in reverse; rather than the proletariat awakening to its objective historical role, uniting political subjectivity and objective history in the moment of revolution, reflexive modernization accredits the objective world with autonomy and agency – 'subjectivity'. The revolution it announces is an anonymous one of social transformation, taking place 'unintended and unpolitically, bypassing all the forums for political decisions'.[15] Modernity itself becomes an autonomous event boasting all the qualities of a natural process, within whose laws only are human beings able to act. Its 'inevitability' is in Lukács's terms a pure reification, signalled by the lack of discordance with its 'constructedness'. Thus the corollaries of reflexive modernization are such oxymoronic concepts as 'constructed certitude', the 'risk society', and 'naturalization' (the simulation of the natural) in place of nature. Like Fukuyama's 'end of history' thesis – an idea which in *Risk Society* Beck dismisses as a 'mad joke'[16] – reflexive modernization posits the triumph of Western capitalism, meaning its decisive mastery over *everything that it is not*, and the ontological 'withering away' of everything that has rigidified. Reflexive modernization represents the fantasy of total reification as, precisely, the end of reification, thereby enacting the obsolescence of the theory of reification. By this means, however, reflexive modernization reveals itself not only as a reified form of postmodern theory and of the 'contemporary historical moment', but implicitly the moment in which the concept of reification is itself reified.

# 5

# Reflexive Modernization: Anxiety Reified as Risk

Like that other contemporary mythology, 'globalization' – the irrefutability of which, as a 'fact' of modern life, it presupposes – reflexive modernization proclaims itself as the return to immediate reality after the ideological mediatedness of earlier, 'linear' theories of modernization. Such competing theories, says Beck, mentioning functionalism and Marxism, posit themselves as absolutes; they exempt themselves from their own critical premises, articulating their denunciations of society from a position outside it. This is the reason they are able to make use of categorical narratives like commodification, alienation, objectification and reification. In our contemporary, 'post-traditional' social order, writes Beck, where modernity itself has need of being modernized in accordance with the processes of globalization, where no institution – either intellectual, methodological or revolutionary – should expect to escape the modernizing process, such theories have become 'antiquated and ossified, the ideological relic of their own pretensions.'[1] The intellectual context for the theory of reification, in other words, is an anachronism, a 'site of privilege' which is itself in need of modernization – meaning that it resides in a condition of complacency, passively contemplating its own lack of implication in the reified world, a condition that is itself, implies Beck, a completely reified one.

Here is confirmed the most basic inference of Lukács's theory of reification – namely, that narratives of immediacy and mediation, of truth and false consciousness, are constitutive even – and especially – of those theories which attempt to situate themselves beyond them. To claim to have transcended the dialectic of modernization and counter-modernization in a new order of 'reflexive modernization', to claim the virtue of freedom from ideology, to situate oneself 'beyond left and right', to declare that, finally, the tension arising from the discrepancy between human knowledge and the realm of the unknown is a thing of the past, is to reinscribe oneself more firmly than ever within the dialectic. Such convictions are representative of the most subtle and therefore most pernicious forms of false consciousness. In reflexive modernization, to reapply Lukács's words in a different historical context, 'immediacy is merely reinstated on a higher level'.[2] In the risk society nothing escapes human administration and human determination; the implication of 'reflexivity' is that all mediation has dissolved. For Beck it is the absolute itself, rather than the degree to which we fall short of the absolute, that is the problem. 'The sources of danger are no longer ignorance but knowledge' writes Beck; 'not a deficient but a perfected mastery over nature; not that which eludes the human grasp but the system of norms and objective constraints established with the industrial epoch.'[3]

The sociologist Karl Mannheim, writing over fifty years before Beck, along with the Frankfurt School theorists and the French post-structuralist Marxist tendency, anticipates the anxieties which Beck entertains towards ideological exceptionalism. As Mannheim's analysis of ideology makes clear, ideological exceptionalism is a problem which Beck, by detecting it in those theories of 'linear' modernization which he wishes to displace, simply replicates in his own work. In *Ideology and Utopia* Mannheim writes: 'As long as one does not call his own position into question but regards it as absolute, while interpreting his opponents' ideas as a mere function of the social positions they occupy, the decisive step forward has not been taken.'[4] In undermining the claims of the 'absolutists', reflexive modernization cements its own status as the crudest absolutism; the 'absolute' is reduced in stature to the merely existent, the world as it is, while being preserved *as* the absolute. Dialectical thinking, by contrast, retains an awareness that absolutism and relativism are by no means polarized, nor do they constitute absolute values in themselves; rather, such polarities are shown by mediation to be inseparable from each other and therefore, in their extreme forms, identical. In his reification essay, Lukács writes of the essentially static world constructed by 'relativism', despite its rhetoric of flux and 'eternal recurrence': 'Just as the relativists have only appeared to dissolve the world into movement, so too they have only appeared to exile the absolute from their systems.'[5] This sentence is at least as true of Beck and Giddens as it was of Nietzsche, about whom it was written.

This sense that the theory of reflexive modernization is susceptible to its own most elementary critique has led Scott Lash, one of its most prominent theorists, to declare that Giddens and Beck have taken reflexive modernization 'too far' in the direction of an 'all-conquering reflexivity'.[6] Beck's and Giddens's theories are characterized, he says, by 'uncomfortably strong veins of positivism' running through them; Lash is concerned, by his use of the term 'aesthetics', to argue for 'an excess of "flux", "contingency", "difference" and "complexity", that cannot be subsumed under the reflexive subject.' In this argument, intended to fill out an 'aesthetic dimension' to reflexive modernization, Lash is resisting what is, unfortunately, an inevitable implication of Beck's work, which is that there can be no aesthetic dimension as such to reflexive modernization. In a critical discussion of the risk society theory, this is precisely the conclusion drawn by Slavoj Žižek, who asks rhetorically, 'Is not the ultimate example of reflexivity in today's art the role of the *curator*?' Art in reflexive modernization, asserts Žižek, is defined purely by processes of selection rather than production:

> Today's art exhibitions display objects which, at least for the traditional approach, have nothing to do with art, up to human excrement and dead animals – so why is this to be perceived as art? *Because what we see is the curator's choice*. When we visit an exhibition today, we are thus not directly observing works of art – what we are observing is the curator's notion of what art is; in short, the ultimate artist is not the producer but the curator, his activity of selection.[7]

Žižek is using contemporary art's institutionalization of the readymade as a metaphor for reflexive modernization's belief that the modern world is as formed as it ever will be; all that can take place now is the continuing modification of these existing institutional forms. Not only is modern art produced for its 'exhibition value', rather than for any 'ritualistic' or symbolic purpose, as Benjamin wrote; the balance of this equation has shifted still further, such that the exhibition of an object is all that is needed to turn it into an artwork. This inference is perfectly consistent with aesthetic theories including Adorno's. If reification is no longer a problem, a possibility, or a reality in contemporary society, then the possibility of art – which, by (Adorno's) definition, constitutes a protest against reification – dissolves. Subjective expression in the face of a refractory, objectifying world is no longer a factor in the decision-making process of the artist. The 'aura' which Benjamin wrote about as a quality of the artwork itself, writes Adorno, is also 'whatever goes beyond its factual givenness, its content; one cannot abolish it and still want art.'[8] Thus a society in a state of reflexive modernization, in which no non-administered reality exists any longer – in which therefore no sublimity, no aura is possible – is also one in which art becomes untenable except as a purely institutionalized, instrumental or commercial pursuit.

In his article Lash distinguishes between the work of Beck and Giddens and that of Benjamin, Adorno and Derrida, on the basis of a distinction which Jürgen Habermas, among others, makes between symbol and allegory. Habermas identifies the symbol as 'Protestant in inspiration', while allegory is compatible with 'the Jewish unspeakability of the name of God'.[9] The work of the latter group of (Jewish) thinkers represents a quite different critique of modernity than that of Beck and Giddens. Adorno's 'negative dialectics', Derrida's *différance*, and Benjamin's interest in cabbalism attest to their respective commitment to 'that part of the object which has avoided subsumption by reflexivity' – the part, implies Lash, denoted by the 'aesthetic'.[10] Beck and Giddens are the latest in a positivistic tradition of sociology deriving from modernity's cognitive rather than aesthetic paradigms. For the 'hermeneutic' tradition represented by Benjamin, Adorno and Derrida, as well as by Sade, Baudelaire and Nietzsche, subsumption of the object by the subject – or vice versa – can only ever be partial. While cognition is a process of ordering the particular according to universal categories of knowledge ('objective universal validity'), aesthetic judgement is never reducible to such order. Concepts such as textuality, *différance* and excess, associated with such writers and developed in post-structuralist theory, are to some extent anticipated by Kant's theory of aesthetic judgement, which involves the subsumption of the particular object not by the universal but by a (subjective) particular – hence the Kantian paradox of 'subjective universal validity' referred to earlier. For all these writers, observes Lash, the object 'is never found in its pristine form as particular, but is always already partly universalized – as text or *écriture* – and hence is unsubsumable.'[11] That there is nothing outside of the text (*il n'y a pas de hors-texte*)[12] is a statement simultaneously of the ubiquity of reification and – *consequently* – of the impossibility of total reification, since the degree of correspondence between object and representation is never demonstrable; the extra-textual moment is the use value which textuality retains in residue. 'There is nothing outside of the text' affirms the metaphysical order of existence it is usually held to negate, inscribed within the concept of textuality itself; what is *hors-textuelle* is only accessible, although never completely so, through textuality.

Most decisive for Lash's critique, however, is his confrontation of reflexive modernization with the figure of Michel Foucault, whose work on the transformation of the disciplinary practices of power in late capitalism is apparently ignored – or at least sanitized, euphemized – by Beck.[13] Individualization, the obverse of Beck's globalization, far from being, as according to Simmel, the development and enlargement of a subjective sphere free from the influence of 'objective culture', is precisely the new mode of the disciplinary practices of power: 'What appears as the freedom of agency for the theory of reflexivity is just another means of control for Foucault, as the direct operation of power on the body has been displaced by its mediated operation on the body through the soul.'[14] Like Derrida's *différance* and Adorno's strategy of nonidentity thinking, Foucault's early attempts to pose limits to the 'imperialism' of reflexivity – by means of his celebration of Artaud's madness in *Madness and Civilization*, his professed laughter at Borges's 'Chinese Encyclopaedia' at the beginning of *The Order of Things*, even his insistence, in his most 'arid' and 'oppressive' text *The Archaeology of Knowledge*, upon the status of discourse as nothing more than an asset, 'finite, limited, desirable, useful – . . . an asset that is, by nature, the object of a struggle, a political struggle' – all these attempts draw on the Kantian faculty of aesthetic judgement, and posit a space, or an insubstantial sphere, at least, of non-reifiability.[15] It is an approach which reflexive modernization, with its model of modernity as a progressive, ultimately total and ultimately non-threatening colonization of what it is not, seems utterly oblivious to.

# 6

# The Aesthetics of Incomprehensibility

This obliviousness is most clearly discernible whenever Beck discusses literary texts. Walter Benjamin wrote that there are two ways to miss the point of Kafka's works: the natural (or psychoanalytical) interpretation, and the supernatural (or theological) one.[1] Benjamin is not explicit about the former; yet the natural and the supernatural interpretations are similarly flawed, he says, insofar as each misses what Benjamin calls 'the essential points'. The theological reading of Kafka involves taking *The Castle* as a representation of 'the powers above, the realm of grace', and *The Trial* as a depiction of 'the powers below, the realm of the courts and of damnation.' *America*, predictably enough, is taken to present 'earthly fate and its arduous demands', a realm which exists between the other two. Like the 'psychoanalytical' interpretation, which involves casting the central figures in Kafka's works (K., Karl Rossmann, Gregor Samsa, etc.) in a symbolically equivalent position within the Oedipal narrative, the 'theological' reading is mistaken insofar as it aims at a total interpretation of the work. Each inserts Kafka's texts – the themes of which it conceptualizes in extremely fixed terms (divine judgement, the symbolic order – legislated over by what Lacan calls the 'Name-of-the-Father') – into a pre-existing schema, the authority of which is external to and independent of them. Both reduce the texts in question to mere signifying systems; both mobilize a certain theoretical currency (psychoanalysis, theology), by means of which the text is forced into a relationship of equivalence with a divine or quasi-divine order of reality, a vision of the world as it is. In each case the exchange principle is paramount; an abstract value (Oedipus, religious eschatology) mediates two incomparable domains – Kafka's text on the one hand, and the order of signification on the other, with psychoanalysis and Judeo-Christian metaphysics as the brokering agent in each case.

Ulrich Beck's approach to Kafka is a combination of the psychological and the theological misinterpretations. Certainly he misses the point – so much so that in addressing the issue at all the sensation is like finding oneself trying to destone a cherry with a spade. The reflexive modernization thesis discovers a theology of relativism and pragmatism in Kafka's work, combined with a psychology of individualism and personal fulfilment. In Kafka's self-loathing, says Beck, 'it is possible to hear and experience an echo of the liberation from the yoke which the maintenance of the grand façade of the self has represented for its exponents to this day.'[2] In other words, the message of Kafka's works is simply that 'tradition' – as signified by the domineering father figures in the stories, the 'difficulties with women' suffered by his central characters, the pressure on his protagonists to marry – is incompatible with personal happiness, and with a world in which truth itself is entirely contingent; furthermore, Kafka teaches us that the destruction of tradition is necessary 'in order to discover the breadth of smallness, the joys of relativism, ambiguity, multiple egos, affirmed drives (which had previously bowed down to the rule of a superego).'[3]

Aware, perhaps, that there is little in the tone of the novels to support a reading of Kafka as a lesson in the joys of self-liberation and self-realization, Beck quotes from a passage in the diaries: 'My imperfection is . . . not congenital, not earned'; 'The reproaches lie around inside me . . .' – but he omits the following sentence: 'I, too, have my centre of gravity inside me from birth, and this not even the most foolish education could displace.'[4] The point of Kafka's 'self-loathing' is that it is no less painful or unconquerable on account of the fact that his failings are adventitious – quite the contrary. That his imperfection is 'not congenital', occurring despite rather than as a result of his personal qualities, makes it 'so much the more painful to bear'. Metaphysical order is incomprehensible, not disposable in Kafka; it is precisely the intractability of his works that renders them suggestive in terms of a Kantian formulation of aesthetic judgement. Another of Kafka's diary entries, dated 18 October 1921, reads: 'It is entirely conceivable that life's splendour forever lies in wait about each one of us in all its fullness, but veiled from view, deep down, invisible, far off. It *is* there, though, not hostile, not reluctant, not deaf. If you summon it by the right word, by its right name, it will come. This is the essence of magic, which does not create but summons.'[5] This aspect of Kafka, which animates Benjamin, is completely missed by Beck, for whom everything mysterious or invisible to man has simply dissolved. 'In the disintegration of identity, self, truth and reality,' writes Beck, 'the handcuffs and leg-irons with which people have imprisoned and mistreated themselves at the behest of outside powers also burst. One can sense something of the advantage that vagabonds or eccentrics, with their effervescent liveliness, have always had over the puffed-up ego-tyrants of the bourgeois world or the heroic self-asserters of the post-bourgeois world – at least in literature.'[6]

It is in this manoeuvre that the absolute, as Lukács says, is reinstated; man 'simply puts himself in the place of those transcendental forces he was supposed to explain, dissolve and systematically replace.'[7] For the theory of reflexive modernization, the kernel of humanity is unchanged by history, which, in the form of 'ideologies' and 'puffed-up ego-tyrants', comes and goes. The 'effervescent liveliness' of the vagabond is not, as it is for Hegel, a dialectical product of history (as in the Master–Slave narrative) but a biophilic subcurrent of it, a mediated essence, a universal constant, to be brought to realization by simply dismantling the layer of historically specific, outmoded 'ideologies'. Of these, the belief in a sphere beyond the immediate is the first to be cast into obsolescence. No one waits for Godot in Ulrich

Beck's world; reflexive modernization would simply relocate Samuel Beckett's Gogo and Didi to that sunny spot dreamt of by Gogo in the Pyrenees.[8]

For reflexive modernization, man – both species and individual – is the measure of all things. This relentless secularism, signified by the complementary concepts of 'globalization' and 'individualization', may be differentiated from any attempt such as Benjamin's to affirm the unknown, the inaccessible or the 'incomprehensible'. Individualization, says Beck, is a state to which all men and women in a global economy are 'condemned'. Individualization denotes not alienation or social disconnectedness, but the disappearance of ideological principles, the absence of metaphysical truths, and the obligation of individuals to construct new certainties – in terms of personal biography, identity, commitments and convictions. Decision-making, in reflexive modernization, is everything.

In this light, the attempt to preserve a sphere of 'non-reifiability' – a sphere which would by definition be impervious to decision-making as such – may appear to have something of a 'religious' character. The concept of reification indeed, like the aesthetic sphere itself, is most easily criticized along these lines. Momme Brodersen, following contemporaries of Benjamin such as Bertolt Brecht, all but dismisses Benjamin's Kafka essay as 'thoroughly mystical'.[9] Far from acknowledging the pertinence of such criticisms, however, or renouncing the 'metaphysical' aspect of his interpretation of Kafka as his relationship with the Frankfurt Institut für Sozialforschung strengthened, Benjamin later distanced himself only from what he calls its 'apologetic character'; his remark, in a letter to Gershom Scholem, to the effect that it is necessary to appreciate Kafka's work as a 'failure' if one is also to grasp its 'purity and beauty', is entirely commensurable with the earlier 'mystical' essay.[10]

For Benjamin the 'unfinished' status of Kafka's novels – or their quality as 'failures' – is the key to their great achievement. Kafka's works open up questions rather than foreclose them. That there is no solution to the motivating predicament of *The*

*Trial* is an artistic 'failure' which ensures that its success is located on a plane altogether removed from that of mere artistic coherence; artistic failure is the means by which the artwork manifests its truth content. Thus the – at least partial – negation of their status as artworks is among the achievements of Kafka's texts. The apparent meagreness of Kafka's ambition in avoiding any explicit reference to the metaphysical dimension is an important element of this. What Adorno calls the 'hermetic' quality of his works, at the purely textual level, lends them a metaphysical significance outside the familiar apparatus of literary 'symbolism'. Nowhere in Kafka, says Adorno, 'does there glimmer the aura of the infinite idea; nowhere does the horizon open. Each sentence is literal and each signifies. The two moments are not merged, as the symbol would have it, but yawn apart and out of the abyss between them blinds the glaring ray of fascination.'[11] This is what is meant by the 'fragmented' nature of art under capitalism insisted upon by Adorno, for whom every step toward the perfection of artworks 'is a step toward their self-alienation'.[12] Kafka forges a link between the thingness of the artwork and the unthought, a link from what merely exists to the indeterminable, bypassing all the well-trodden routes to transcendence. Kafka, says Benjamin, 'sacrificed truth for the sake of clinging to its transmissibility, its haggadic element.'[13] By this process, only, does he articulate the truth of a critical consciousness brought to bear on the existing world. 'Though apparently reduced to submission', concludes Benjamin, Kafka's writings 'unexpectedly raise a mighty paw against it.'

To talk about Kafka as exemplary of what Lash calls the 'aesthetic', and the way in which the aesthetic is occluded by certain currents in contemporary social theory, is perhaps dangerous. Kafka, one suspects, is a special case. The incomprehensibility which is a consistent element in his writing is peculiar to him; therefore to ground a theory of aesthetics on his work seems tendentious. Adorno says that anyone who has sensed Kafka's greatness knows how inappropriate is the term 'art' to describe it.[14] Yet it is for precisely this reason – his refusal of the artistic –

that Kafka (like Beckett, Schoenberg and Proust) is an important figure for an aesthetic theory (Adorno's) in which the concept of reification takes a central place. Uniquely of all human activities, art is conditioned by reification while at every point rebelling against it. Ever since its emancipation from a ritualistic context, which stripped it of its use value, art has straddled the border between pure expression and institutionalization. For Adorno, the moment of comprehension, the point at which an artwork is effectively exhausted, threatens always to tip the work into the latter category. 'Each sentence says "interpret me",' he writes of Kafka's work, 'and none will permit it . . . Among Kafka's presuppositions, not the least is that the contemplative relation between text and reader is shaken to its very roots.'[15] Kafka's works are about non-reifiability as much, and inasmuch, as they are about the condition of radical isolation in which all human judgements, including those of jurisdiction, are made. Benjamin is most explicit about this when he says: 'No other writer has obeyed the commandment "Thou shalt not make unto thee a graven image" so faithfully.'[16] Like Proust's narrator, whose literary ambitions in *Swann's Way* are frustrated by the steadfast refusal of the objects of his fascination to suggest some 'abstract truth',[17] or like Beckett, who 'returns us to the condition of particular objects, to their materiality, their extraordinary ordinariness',[18] Kafka refuses the symbolic transfiguration of immediacy into transcendence which, for Adorno, constitutes the reified practice of bourgeois art. Only by this refusal is the possibility of something other than what exists preserved. This paradoxical formulation, unacceptable both to theorists of the 'committed' artwork and bourgeois apologists for art's 'autonomy', is the reason for the hostile estimations of the concept of reification as idealist and politically reactionary on one hand, and as reductively materialist on the other.

*

# 7

# Ambiguity and Utopia

Reification – thingitude – is essential to all artworks, yet art reveals the concept of reification to be inherently ambiguous. The use value of the art object has atrophied with the decline of religion and the development of the 'cult of the individual' in the modern world. The 'aura' of art is associated no longer with ritual, but primarily with self-expression (of the artist) and sensory experience (of the viewer). The autonomous artwork hereby attains an 'absolute' value; its uniqueness becomes an expression of authenticity and 'non-reifiability' which translates with perfect ease into exchange value, while also rendering the concept of exchange value unstable. The artwork becomes the object of pure monetary speculation, completely fetishized to a degree that is expressed in the apparent freefall of the state of the art market. In the unique, 'non-reified' and 'non-reifiable' artwork we see the emergence of something close to an absolute commodity. Thus the artwork expresses in microcosm the truth that the end of reification is at the same time a condition of total reification, the precondition for the emergence of a society in which the sole items of desire and exchange are reified objects. The unique artwork is the ultimate object of fetishism; the cult of genius, the aura of individuality, the chimera of authenticity, all are attached to the autonomous artwork, which reveals itself to be the reliquary and vehicle of reified consciousness.

On the other hand, the *engagé*, commodified, or otherwise 'instrumental' artwork may also be read as a symbol of the artwork having lost its use value and been inserted into a system of exchange. The 'committed' artwork enters an economy in which its material essence becomes transferable against objectives, and objects, in the real world; thus the committed artwork is as 'reified' as the autonomous one, but only from the point of view of autonomous art. The committed artwork goes further in pointing up the concept of reification – insofar as it serves to justify 'autonomous' art practices – as *the reification of the concept*. The commodified artwork meanwhile – the pop record or the television sitcom – enters a different economy, that of the culture industry, in which its material essence is exchangeable against certain instrumental and ideological purposes. Given enough ideological–critical attention, the constituent elements of the commodified artwork may be 'read off', or exchanged, against the material objectives of the dominant power. Instrumentality in each case inserts the art object into a system of exchange; the committed and the commodified artwork have lost the authentic thingness of their specificity as artworks. The autonomous artwork, however, in claiming for its integrity a universal status, is no less reified, at least from the radical materialistic point of view of the 'committed' artist. The autonomous artwork attempts to exchange itself against the transcendent – conceived as a monad. Its presuppositions – the unified subject, the possibility of integrity, the oneness of God, the existence of 'will' independent of 'representation' – are evidence of a consciousness as steeped in reification as that of the *engagé* 'cultural producer'.

It is by means of these ambiguities that Adorno is able to make such surprising and paradoxical statements as the following: 'Art keeps itself alive through its social force of resistance; unless it reifies itself, it becomes a commodity.'[1] This radical ambiguity is that of the artwork itself, as soon as it is constituted in terms of use value and exchange value. Art is not simply the antithesis of 'commodification', nor of 'propaganda', nor of reification. For Adorno, the *categories* of committed, commodified and autonomous art are equally debased. The disinterested, 'aesthetic' contemplation of artworks exists on a continuum with the mythical fetishism of objects, from which it derives; thus the contemporary artwork is no more divorced from use value than it is reducible to it. Art cannot be circumscribed by the working week; at the same time it cannot be reduced to the status of a 'weekend pleasure', the antidote to routine, since this would be another institutionalization.[2] As Adorno observes in *Minima Moralia*, the figure of Nietzsche – a symbol of the 'complete' artistic temperament – is as unimaginable sitting at an office desk with a secretary in an anteroom as he is playing golf after work.[3]

Artworks, then, are neither about 'interest' (in the form of progressive or reactionary ideologies, for example), nor its renunciation, but the relation between the two.[4] It is this *relation* that constitutes the artwork's residue of 'incomprehensibility', which it is the task of the philosophy of aesthetics to understand – not in order to 'explain it away' but, in Adorno's words, 'to understand the incomprehensibility itself'.[5] Theoreticians of the 'committed' artwork such as Sartre and Brecht, as well as bourgeois theorists of the autonomous artwork such as Clive Bell and F. R. Leavis, have failed to appreciate the fact that the distinction itself is a product of the existing world and part of the existing conceptual structure of power; it has the function of embedding society within a familiar mental terrain in which choices are simple (and therefore, of course, ultimately undecidable): art or politics? social commitment or individual expression? As long as one recognizes the legitimacy of such oppositions, one is operating with entirely reified categories, and the development of a unified theory is impossible. Art, as anti-aesthetic movements such as Dada, Surrealism, Fluxus and the Situationist International were aware, is a byword for political absenteeism only in its reified, 'bourgeois' sense. Since meaning itself, the transition from signifier to signified, is exemplary of the ubiquity, and necessity, of reification in everyday life (Saussure's insistence upon the arbitrary structure of the sign elevates reification into the very process by which meaningful communication takes place), it follows that an aesthetic theory which takes reification as a central determining concept will validate artworks that interrogate the process of the creation of meaning. According to Adorno, Samuel Beckett's works – which, like Kafka's, have suffered from earnest attempts to read them as 'affirmative' – are neither void of meaning, nor steeped in it; rather they 'put meaning on trial; they unfold its history'.[6]

In so doing, writes Adorno, such works of art 'point to a practice from which they abstain: the creation of a just life.'[7] Works of art are condemned to reified existence by their 'thing-like' status – yet they also indicate the possibility of a world other than the existing one; they help to free empirical life, as he says in *Aesthetic Theory*, 'from that to which they are condemned by reified external experience'.[8] Thus two orders of existence are proposed: *the way things are*, which is by definition – under capitalism at least – discredited and reified; and an unknown future world of potentiality and 'justice', an unadministered world which is necessarily impossible and unimaginable under capitalism. Adorno's formulation of the relation between these two realms – a relation which art, embedded in the first, is nevertheless able to traverse – appears as a simple distinction analogous to that between *Realpolitik* and idealism, say, or realism and utopianism. Adorno's aesthetic theory suddenly looks less like a bourgeois or élitist defence of 'autonomous art' (as his work is most commonly caricatured), and more like a theory of the instrumentality of artworks in the service of revolutionary Marxism – instrumentality, however, in a somewhat rarefied sense. The artwork has a truly political function only by ignoring 'political' and partisan interests which, by their nature, concern the existing world; it is in this activity that the artwork is *inevitably* political, meaning that it sustains an indexical function in relation to an only theoretically or abstractly conceivable new world.

To use words such as 'ideal' or 'utopia' to denote this projected new world, however, is to risk losing it. 'The utopian moment in thinking is stronger', writes Adorno, 'the less it – this too a form of relapse – objectifies itself into a utopia and hence sabotages its realization.[9] Utopia, as he writes in his study of Hegel, is nothing other than 'the whole truth, which is still to be realized'; yet this same utopia is also 'the ray of light that reveals the whole to be untrue'.[10] The concept of utopia is hereby imbued with a dialectical – i.e. non-reified – character; furthermore, 'utopia', in this paradoxical formulation, *is* the possibility of non-reifiability. The relation between art and justice, say, is not simply an oppositional one, like that between pragmatism and idealism, or hope and fulfillment, or this world and the next, since for Adorno the two are inseparable. Utopia is not something achievable on the basis of a certain adaptation of the here and now. Utopia is achievable only as, and coterminous with, the *negation* of the here and now; thus the here and now is, for the time being at least (and the time being is all we have), indispensable to it. The positive consequences of this procedure, which Adorno calls 'negative dialectics', are inconceivable. Such an approach therefore demands a gesture of faith that is not only Kantian in its degree of conviction, since it takes place outside an economy of calculable means and ends, but appears almost religious in character. This post-Lukácsian concept of reification is one from which it is impossible absolutely to squeeze out the transcendent, in all its unknowability. The 'thoroughly mystical' Benjamin reads Kafka precisely because of his steadfast obedience to the second commandment – not to make for yourself graven images. Is reification, in fact, anything other than the thoroughly mystical concept of 'idolatry' by another name?

# 8

# Analogy of Religious and Commodity Fetishism

In Wim Wenders's documentary film *Buena Vista Social Club*, the principal singer in the group of elderly Cuban musicians,

Ibrahim Ferrer, introduces us to a statue of Saint Lazarus which he keeps as a fetish object on a shrine in his living room. He pays it tributes, in the form of flowers, perfume, pots of honey and rum, and every so often his wife bakes it a meringue. Ibrahim also shows us a staff with a carved head of the saint which was left to him by his mother when she died 58 years earlier, and to which, at the close of the film, Ibrahim attributes his good fortune – his lifelong freedom from material worries and his musical success.[1] The film as a whole is a hymn to communism; in the concluding sequence we see messages painted on the walls of Havana, such as 'ESTA REVOLUCION ES ETERNA' and 'CREYEMOS EN LOS SUEÑOS'.[2] Ibrahim's religious fetishism apparently enables him to avoid the fetishism of material objects. 'If we had followed the way of possessions, we'd have disappeared long ago' he says of his country. 'We Cubans are very fortunate; we have learned to resist both the good and the bad.'[3]

Whether or not one attributes credibility to claims that the Cuban revolution is an ongoing, 'eternal' one (in other words, that it is non-reified); whether or not Cuban communism has, in any authentic sense, avoided 'the way of possessions' of the capitalist West, this episode reveals a certain relation between religious and commodity 'fetishism' that demands some interrogation. Affirmation of the transcendent, a world beyond the immediate, in whatever form, implies at the same time an accommodation with the earthly domain, with the fact that all visible objects – to use an image I shall return to – 'are but as pasteboard masks'. Belief in the transcendent frees us from worry that the immediate world is all we have, and from the anxiety, therefore, that the immediate world is subject to reification. For the religious believer, the earthly sphere is already fallen and thus, compared to what it once was and what it will one day be again, utterly thing-like, a mere shadow of the world to come. The concept of reification itself, insofar as it pertains to commodity fetishism, is a thoroughly secular one, since it presupposes nothing beyond the earthly sphere; if it has traces of idealism, as Lukács's theory is sometimes said to, it is an idealism which relates strictly to this world. Thus religious belief – so often explicable, as with Ibrahim Ferrer, as a form of fetishization – promises freedom, if not from reification, then certainly from the anxiety towards it, which, as I have argued above, is inseparable from, although not coterminous with, the condition itself.

Marx's use of the term 'fetishism' in relation to commodification should, perhaps, be read in strictly metaphorical terms. Norman Geras has pointed out that the analogy between commodity fetishism and religious belief is 'inexact'. In the latter, he says, 'people bestow upon some entity an imaginary power'; in commodity fetishism, rather, the properties bestowed on the object are real and not imaginary, although these real properties are not natural to the object but social creations. 'They constitute real powers, uncontrolled by, indeed holding sway over, human beings; objective "forms of appearance" of the economic relationships definitive of capitalism.'[4] The social formation of religious belief, in other words, compared to that of commodity fetishism, is not necessarily particularly oppressive, and may function as a balm for the sufferings of the working classes. Marx's famous passage on religion at the opening of the *Critique of Hegel's Philosophy of Right* conveys his sympathetic awareness that religion, in certain conditions, has the quality of liberating men and women from their alienation, albeit in a 'fantastic' form:

> The state and this society produce religion, which is an inverted consciousness of the world, because they are an inverted world. Religion is that general theory of this world, its encyclopedic compendium, its logic in popular form, its spiritual [*spiritualistischer*] *point d'honneur*, its enthusiasm, its moral sanction, its solemn complement and its universal basis of consolation and justification. It is the fantastic [*phantastische*] realization of the human essence since the human essence has not acquired any true reality. The struggle against religion is therefore indirectly the struggle against that world whose spiritual aroma is religion.[5]

The inference is that in a reified world, no subjective response is more understandable and more rewarding – even, perhaps, more logically and politically defensible – than religion. For Marx the problem is not religion *per se*, but an 'inverted' social system which perpetuates suffering and exploitation. In a reified world, we might conclude, religious belief, as *the only possible* expression of 'the human essence', is positively mandatory. If 'false consciousness', as post-structuralist theorists have often contended, is an inevitable and universal condition of human life; if worldly existence is simply, as conceived in the sepulchral tones of nineteenth-century English poetry, a 'vale of tears';[6] if death (or reification), as Jonathan Dollimore argues, is the very precondition of human cultural production, of all philosophy and all literature;[7] if reflection is possible under capitalism only from the point of view of 'damaged life', as Adorno implies in the subtitle to his *Minima Moralia* – then this passage from Marx begins to look like an injunction, irrefutable and imperative, that we embrace religion as the only theoretical means of access to the universal – in the present or, indeed, in any *foreseeable* future.

Life as a 'vale of tears' is an image to which Marx himself has recourse, in the lines which follow on from the above. Religion, he says, is 'the sigh of the oppressed creature' and, in this respect only, 'the opium of the people'. Its 'abolition' represents a call for real happiness of the people to replace this 'illusory' happiness. 'To call on them to give up their illusions about their condition is to call on them to give up a condition that requires illusions. The criticism of religion is therefore in embryo the criticism of that vale of tears [*des Jammertales*] of which religion is the halo.'[8] The criticism of religion is pertinent to Marx's revolutionary politics only insofar as it is a criticism of the totality. Without this qualification, criticism in modernity threatens to replace the deluded happiness of the people with nothing more than a searing awareness of man's finitude. (The word translated into English in the passage above as 'abolition', significantly, is not *Abschaffung* but the Hegelian *Aufhebung*, a term which includes the senses of transcend, overcome, supersede, but also those of preserve, raise up.) The criticism of religion *as such* labours under the illusion that it abolishes a mediated existence to arrive at immediacy – the once and for all 'unrepeatable tearing of the veil' which Lukács warns against.[9] Liberation from God becomes, in effect, enslavement to an interminable struggle against reification. True emancipation is prohibited by what develops in its stead: a condition of morbid, existential contemplation, entirely removed from objective reality and therefore, as Lukács points out, able only to recognize it or to reject it.[10] This is the 'irrational chasm' which, according to Lukács, opens up between subject and object in bourgeois thought, the result of 'a theoretical approach based upon unmediated contemplation'; and he cites Fichte (along with Simmel) – who speaks of a *hiatus irrationalis*, a murky void between theory and practice – as exemplary of such thinking.[11] 'There is no being' declares Fichte in *The Vocation of Man*. 'I myself absolutely know not and am not. Pictures are: – they are the only things which exist, and they know of themselves after the fashion of pictures . . . I myself am one of these pictures.'[12]

Such melancholic self-absorption, as Fichte acknowledges, is the result of the systematization and therefore the alienation of knowledge, which, cut off from 'faith', is cut off also from reality and subjectivity. Knowledge has no positive content; rather, it only 'destroys and annihilates error'. It cannot give us truth, since in itself knowledge is utterly empty. Like the order of signification as conceptualized by Saussure, 'knowledge' for Fichte is a self-sustaining *system*, characterized primarily by internal coherence rather than any necessary correspondence to the world outside it. 'All knowledge is only pictures, representations; and there is always something wanting in it – that which corresponds to the representation. This want cannot be supplied by knowledge; a system of knowledge is necessarily a system of mere pictures, wholly without reality, significance or aim.'[13]

The figure of Captain Ahab in Herman Melville's *Moby-Dick* is a fictional representation of this modern bleakness, the personification of a misery caused directly by man's usurpation of the place of God. Ahab's desire to be revenged upon a 'dumb brute' who took off his leg is condemned by Starbuck, his chief mate, as blasphemous; indeed, his tormented pursuit of the whale is motivated by a thorough collapse of faith in the God-ordained world. In his cabin Ahab soliloquizes, simultaneously seizing responsibility for the administration of divine justice and upbraiding the very metaphysical order he wishes to displace: 'I now prophesy that I will dismember my dismemberer. Now, then, be the prophet and the fulfiller one. That's more than ye, ye great gods, ever were. I laugh and hoot at ye, ye cricket-players, ye pugilists, ye deaf Burkes and blinded Bendigoes!'[14] Ahab, furthermore, suffers from the anxiety towards reification like almost no other figure in modern literature. To Starbuck's accusation of blasphemy he responds with an articulation of disbelief in the very reality of the visible order of things:

> All visible objects, man, are but as pasteboard masks. But in each event – in the living act, the undoubted deed – there, some unknown but still reasoning thing puts forth the mouldings of its features from behind the unreasoning mask. If man will strike, strike through the mask! How can the prisoner reach outside except by thrusting through the wall? To me, the white whale is that wall, shoved near to me. Sometimes I think there's naught beyond.[15]

Discarding God without at the same time discarding 'man' necessarily ends in radical isolation, introspection, social fragmentation and this perception, experienced also by Fichte, that life is dissipating inevitably into mere form – or more accurately, that life is retreating to a private, rarefied and internal sphere *as against* mere form. The self as a monad, radically cut off from the world, is preserved in Fichte, as it is in Simmel, and rendered fictionally in the tragical, because unsustainable, hubris of Melville's Captain Ahab. Its end, paradoxically, is the restoration and enhancement of faith in God, who is in the process necessarily reconceptualized in even more rarefied and abstract terms.

Fichte concludes his account of 'the vocation of man' with

such a rediscovery and reconfiguration of his faith. The object in which he invests it is nothing more concrete than the Law of the spiritual world – 'the firm, immovable confidence of reason in a principle', he writes;[16] or, again, 'the One Eternal, Infinite Will' – an entity to which is attributed the creation of the world only in the 'finite reason' of our minds.[17] 'Sublime and Living Will!' he addresses this entity, in the sermonizing prose of the nineteenth-century English translation; 'named by no name, compassed by no thought! I may well raise my soul to Thee, for Thou and I are not divided. Thy voice sounds within me, mine resounds in Thee; and all my thoughts, if they be but good and true, live in Thee also.'[18] A greatly heightened sense of the second Commandment – not to make unto yourself graven images – clearly contributes to this re-imagination of God as 'a Will which operates purely as will; by itself and absolutely without any instrument or sensible material of its activity'.[19] A recovery of faith by such means offers the possibility of freedom from a perception of the world as one of pasteboard masks:

> The world on which but now I gazed with wonder passes away from before me and is withdrawn from my sight. With all the fulness of life, order, and increase which I beheld in it, it is yet but the curtain by which a world infinitely more perfect is concealed from me, and the germ from which that other world shall develop itself. My FAITH looks behind this veil, and cherishes and animates this germ. It sees nothing definite, but it awaits more than it can conceive here below, more than it will ever be able to conceive in all time.[20]

For Fichte we are embedded in finitude, yet the very certainty of that situation becomes a rationale for transcendence. The Eternal Will is lodged in our own being, reconfigured as the possibility of an autonomous existence. 'I become the sole source of my own being and its phenomena, and, henceforth, unconditioned by anything without me, I have life in myself. My will, directed by no foreign agency in the order of the supersensual world but by myself alone, is this source of true life, and of eternity.'[21] God becomes *that which is transcendent within man* – which is not the same as the abolition or the death of God.

In his writings on religion, Georg Simmel proposes a similar way of 'saving' God from the incursions of rationalism, in the form of a 'third view' between the idea of a real metaphysical sphere beyond mankind and the 'scientific' view of religious faith as a subjective fantasy. 'Perhaps this faith,' he says, 'this fact of spiritual nature, is itself a metaphysical phenomenon . . . When man looks up to a metaphysical-divine being, beyond all empirical detail, he is not only and always merely projecting his psychological emotions of fear and hope, exuberance and the need for redemption; he is also projecting that which is metaphysical within himself, those elements of his being that are beyond the empirical.'[22] Belief in religion, in other words, constitutes and confirms its real truth; disbelief, on the other hand, proves it to be a lie. The mere fact of a lapse of faith amounts to the death of the metaphysical faculty of the human soul. For Simmel, as for Fichte, the illusion itself is the truth; should the illusion founder, a real impoverishment in the spiritual life of human beings will have occurred. Nietzsche is right, therefore, to talk of the 'death' of God rather than, say, the lifting of the veil, or the 'awakening' of humanity from spiritual bondage, both of which imply a metaphysical, transhistorical level of truth that would presuppose the continuing existence of God.

Both Fichte and Simmel, however – and for Lukács the same applies to Nietzsche – fall short of the critique of the totality enjoined by historical materialism. Each levels his critique against religion qua religion, while the exploitative state of existing social relations, of which religion is an expression, is preserved. Each, in other words, takes religion on its own terms, rather than treating it as an expression of the totality – as, in Marx's words, the general theory of an inverted world, 'its logic in popular form'. The *Übermensch*, like Fichte's 'Eternal Will', merely displaces God, making man 'the measure of all things', and leaving the alienation between subject and object intact. Any accommodation with the reified world takes place in the individual conscience, which alone, says Fichte, 'is the root of all truth'. For such modern sensibilities the world is still a veneer of pasteboard, life a picnic *en costume*.[23] The entirely subjective response, which those of Fichte and Simmel remain, despite their codes of religiosity, fundamentally leaves the world as it is. Fichte claims to establish the unity of subject and object in the 'Sublime and Living Will', yet the exclusion of anything outside the individual from the 'transcendence' attained by his philosophy ensures its lapse into subjectivity, and thus its impotence regarding the objective world. 'For the individual,' says Lukács, 'reification and hence determinism . . . are irremovable. Every attempt to achieve "freedom" from such premises must fail, for "inner freedom" presupposes that the world cannot be changed.'[24] This is precisely what is meant by a remark in Kierkegaard's journal: 'A solitary person cannot help, or save, an age; he can only give expression to the fact that it is going under.'[25] The same applies to Simmel's sociological writings, as commentators on his work have noted – indeed Simmel notes it himself. All that is accomplished by a critical rationalistic approach to religion which seeks to defuse its metaphysical aspect, or to appropriate it on behalf of the human monad, is its neutralization as the embodiment of the 'human essence', its reduction to a means of personal spiritual gratification and the further fragmentation of social life. For religion to overcome alienation and atomization it must provide a transcendent experience and a genuine theory of the totality – just as, in order for philosophy to overcome reification, it is necessary that it 'relate to the whole of reality in a practical revolutionary way'.[26] In a reified society, religion offers more of a solution to human finitude than the critique of religion, which merely reproduces the individual as an isolated monad, operating within a meaningless, illusory world.

*

# 9

# The Desire for Transcendence

The capacity of religious belief for liberating men and women from their embeddedness in materiality may be represented from a Marxist-theoretical perspective, and contrary to the truth claims of religion itself, as its 'use value'. This use value of religion is dependent on the opacity of its illusion – on the seamlessness of its fetishistic character, on its success as a total ideology or metanarrative. Thus religion is in some sense the agent of a deconstruction of the opposition between use value and exchange value. At the moment in which its fetish quality is lost, religion loses its use value, whereupon, according to the Marxist analysis of the commodity, it becomes a fetish object, entered into an economy of possible world views, exchangeable with other religions, or art, or philosophy, and thereby severed from its role of liberating men and women from reification. Thus, the use of the term 'fetish' to describe African artworks, as Michel Leiris has pointed out, is incorrect; for such objects are not aesthetic but utilitarian, 'in that they fulfil a ritual function closely associated with everyday life'.[1]

Religion, in other words, is inseparable from its truth content, and continues in a decrepit condition once its truth content is removed. Like art, which for Hegel reached its apogee in the classical era, when the thing itself and its truth content were virtually indistinguishable, religion is obsolete as an embodiment of *Geist* – the complex and fascinating concept in which truth inheres in tandem with history. In the *Phenomenology of Spirit* Hegel describes classical Greece as an epoch in which 'absolute art' appears: spirit becomes 'not merely the substance born of the self, but . . ., in its representation as object, *this self*, not only to give birth to itself from its Notion, but to have its very Notion for its shape, so that the Notion and the work of art produced know each other as one and the same.'[2] In a reflective age, art, unsuited to reflexivity, is able to maintain a tangential relation with *Geist* only by its deterioration – in the form of abstraction or elaborate intellectualization. The only art which is any longer feasible is bad art, argues Hegel; just as the only religion still possible is bad religion, unless it confine itself to cultish eccentricity, thereby removing from itself all truth content in Hegel's sense.

Hegel is no aesthetician; his lectures on *Aesthetics* are misnamed as such. Art, like religion and philosophy, is for Hegel pertinent only as a vehicle for the representation of *Geist*, not as the locus of a form of pleasure or truth that is distinctive to it. As such, art is succeeded historically by religion, by which Hegel means Christianity, when it is no longer able to represent the products of the human mind, when truth itself, linked as always to human consciousness, goes beyond that which is able to be represented adequately in 'sensuous' form (as was the case with the gods of antiquity). 'The Christian view of truth is of this kind,' says Hegel; 'above all, the spirit of our world today, or, more particularly, of our religion and the development of our reason, appears as beyond the stage at which art is the supreme mode of our knowledge of the Absolute.'[3] The decisive development for the obsolescence of art and its replacement by religion is that of self-consciousness, at which point spirit seeks a more adequate expression than the art object. This higher medium is language, which, as he says in the *Phenomenology of Spirit*, renders 'an outer reality that is immediately self-conscious existence', and expresses therefore 'the soul existing as soul'.[4] Language makes possible a work of art that 'possesses immediately in its outer existence the pure activity' – self-consciousness – 'which, when it existed as a Thing', was in contrast to, and a contradiction of, the work of art. Language, therefore, is the mode in which Christianity finds its most appropriate realization. It is specifically in the Christian hymn, continues Hegel, that the inwardness of devotion 'has at the same time an outer existence.'

Religion in its turn is superseded by philosophy – in particular, by Hegel's brand of thinking pure spirit in the abstract, since for Hegel 'thinking is the essence and Concept of spirit' in its highest form.[5]

For Hegel therefore, reification is a phenomenon that arises, throughout history, when the *forms* of life are overtaken by life itself; reification is a material embodiment of belatedness, continually experienced and continually overcome, which pertains to the universal endeavour to express human consciousness at its most advanced stage. When art is severed from, because it is no longer adequate to, truth content, it becomes the vehicle for a form of pleasure that is specifically 'aesthetic'. The faculty of aesthetic judgement, as formulated by Kant, is wholly abstracted from 'spirit' in Hegel's sense; it is the product of an age in which art has lost its particular purpose: to express spirit in material or sensual form. In this development, art attains a false objectivity, 'external to the thing itself' and thus becomes reified; from this moment art requires engagement at the level of intellection – aesthetic rules and criteria which, however informal and subjectivized, presuppose a rupture between art and truth, a rupture which is both bridged and preserved by the category of the aesthetic.

Gillian Rose complains that Adorno 'misattributes' the concept of reification to Hegel; but it is to Hegel's critique of the Kantian delimitation of consciousness into separate spheres that Adorno is referring when he speaks of the concept of reification in Hegel's thought.[6] The faculty of judgement which constitutes our aesthetic relationship to works of art is the separation of those works from truth, as truth itself passes beyond the possibility of its concrete sensuous appearance. Hegel's explanation of this could not be plainer:

> It is not, as might be supposed, merely that the practising artist himself is infected by the loud voice of reflection all around him and by the opinions and judgements on art that have become customary everywhere, so that he is misled into introducing more thoughts into his work; the point is that our whole spiritual

> culture is of such a kind that he himself stands within the world of reflection and its relations, and could not by any act of will and decision abstract himself from it; nor could he by special education or removal from the relations of life contrive and organize a special solitude to replace what he has lost.[7]

With the loss of its truth content comes the 'death' of art, in the form of its intellectualization, as it turns from the simple *representation* of the immediate, sensuous world to a mode of reflection, contemplation of, and therefore the *transcendence* of immediacy. Likewise, the 'death of God', although announced by Nietzsche in far more declamatory tones than those in which Hegel explains the death of art, signifies the demise of religion as a truth-bearing enterprise, as human consciousness becomes capable of the high abstraction and concept-building possible in philosophy. As art and religion are disembedded from the realms of the sensuous and the linguistic respectively, however, they lose this capacity of genuinely liberating men from materiality, since they are debased through being forced to compete with each other in the cultural market place. It is only when art's sensuality is coterminous with the divine that it has the ability of taking men there; just as it is only when religion, which expresses the divine in linguistic form, *adequately* represents its truth as such, that it is capable of 'raising' men and women to transcendence. In the evolution of a specifically aesthetic form of pleasure – the self-sufficiency denoted by the 'autonomy of art' – or the evolution of a specifically religious 'way of life', delimited by rituals and symbolic forms, art and religion are, *as* 'art' and 'religion', debarred from transcendence and reembedded in materiality. The reification of art and religion, a symptom of their historical obsolescence, takes the form of their instrumentalization, their reduction to a mere use value. At this point they become 'cultural goods', writes Adorno, and 'are no longer taken quite seriously by anybody.'[8]

Adorno's early essay 'Theses Upon Art and Religion Today', written in English, is concerned with the Hegelian theme of the 'lost unity of art and religion'. The separation of these spheres dates from the dissolution of the 'archaic unity between imagery and concept', he writes – an event now obscured by centuries of history and culture. Since then, 'positive' religion also has 'lost its character of objective, all-comprising validity, its supra-individual binding force. It is no longer an unproblematic, *a priori* medium within which each person exists without questioning.'[9] This moment constitutes the dissolution of the unity between religion and philosophy, between the linguistic concept and the capacity of the human imagination; like the 'lost unity' of art and religion, it is a moment at which consciousness, spirit itself, consigns a certain mode of intellectually experiencing the world to obsolescence. Religion henceforth becomes, in effect, an idiosyncratic response, no longer an embodiment of *Geist* – which should by no means be understood as a purely idealist concept, but one which always, necessarily, inscribes consciousness within concrete material or intellectual practices.

It is impossible to separate this loss of truth of the immediacy of religion from the appearance of alienation in modernity, understood in the crudest Marxist terms to derive purely and simply from exploitation. 'Only a being with the existential structure of being-for-itself and being-beyond-itself can have the experience of alienation', writes Herbert Schnädelbach, in relation to Sartre. This fragmented 'existential structure', as Schnädelbach calls it, is precisely what is meant by the progression of human consciousness, of *Geist*, to the stage of reflection in modernity. The discrepancy between life and form, in other words, and the appearance of reification as a phenomenon and a concept in modern thought, is evidence not only of the foundations of capitalism in economic exploitation, but of the development of *an intellect capable of experiencing this exploitation subjectively*. Andrew Bowie, quoting the sentence of Schnädelbach's, appends the claim that 'only such a being can have aesthetic experience. Such experience depends upon the subject's ability to move beyond itself in ways which may transform aspects of its relationship to the world.'[10]

It is clear that aesthetic judgement, as it has been formulated by Kant, has the complexity of structure that renders it capable of expressing the alienation of the modern subject. For Andrew Bowie, as for Adorno, it is precisely the paradoxical nature of aesthetic judgement which, in a reified society, lends it the quality of embodying the spirit of a reflective age. Art, *as aesthetics*, is hereby rescued from its historical obsolescence and reconfigured in its Kantian form as Hegelian *Geist*. Art, as aesthetics, succeeds philosophy – which is why Adorno's aesthetic theory suffuses every sentence of his philosophical writings. 'The only solution to idealism' writes Robert Hullot-Kentor of Adorno's writing, 'is to fulfill it: to achieve the self-expression of the material.'[11] Thus Adorno's *Aesthetic Theory*, he says elsewhere, is oriented not to its readers but to the thing-in-itself.[12] Every sentence of that text, as Adorno made clear, was intended to contain in a concentrated and 'paratactical' form the whole work.

# 10

# Comment on Proust

In the last of Adorno's 'Theses Upon Art and Religion Today', he offers a model for the relation of art and religion based on Leibnitz's concept of the monad, to which Adorno compares the work of art. Each monad, according to Leibnitz, 'represents the universal within its own walls'; i.e. its own structure is exactly the same as the universal, although it has no immediate access to it, and makes no reference to it. Analogously, says Adorno, 'art cannot make concepts its "theme". The relationship of the work and the universal becomes the more profound the less the work copes explicitly with universalities, the more it becomes infatuated with its own detached world, its material, its problems, its consistency, its way of expression.' And Adorno mentions Proust, whose obsession with 'the concrete and the unique, with the taste of a madeleine or the colour of the shoes of a lady worn at a certain party' gives his work an 'instrumental' quality. *À la recherche du temps perdu* accomplishes 'the materialization of a truly theological idea, that of immortality.' Proust, claims Adorno, achieves exactly what has here been proposed as a conceivable objective of every artwork – the liberation from materiality, from reification. His novel 'undertook to brave death by breaking the power of oblivion engulfing every individual life'. It is Proust who, 'in a nonreligious world, took the phrase of immortality literally and tried to salvage life, as an image, from the throes of death. But he did so by giving himself up to the most futile, the most insignificant, the most fugitive traces of memory.'[1]

The relation between art and reality, and the purpose of the former regarding the latter, is a major preoccupation of Proust's novel. Art is described repeatedly, from Swann's perspective in particular, as the inheritor of the religious function of revealing another order of existence. The 'little phrase' of the composer Vinteuil, which Swann associates with his dawning love for Odette, belongs 'to an order of supernatural beings whom we have never seen, but whom, in spite of that, we recognize and acclaim with rapture when some explorer of the unseen contrives to coax one forth . . .'.[2] Just as Swann is tormented by uncertainty over the authenticity of the time he spends with Odette – whether it is artificial, 'invented for his special use . . ., with theatrical properties and pasteboard fruits', or 'a genuine hour of Odette's life'[3] – so too the narrator of the novel speaks of his childhood anxiety that reality should fail to correspond with the products of his imagination. His faith in the attainability of his desires is likened to the Christian faith in the promise of the life hereafter: 'During this month', he writes of a period spent dreaming in anticipation of a visit to the North of Italy, 'I never ceased to believe that [these visions of Florence, Venice, Pisa] corresponded to a reality independent of myself, and they made me conscious of as glorious a hope as could have been cherished by a Christian in the primitive age of faith on the eve of his entry into Paradise.'[4] Yet he finds that railway timetables and guide books minister more to his 'exaltation' than works on art – despite the fact that it is the aesthetic pleasures offered by these places that so excites his desire – since it is they which seem to promise the real gratification of his desire.

Proust's narrator writes always of the past as a time in which his 'faith' in the correspondence between imagination and reality was intact; the substance of his childhood love for Gilberte, of the same guileless order as Swann's love for Odette, is cast as a cherishable, long-abandoned delusion. Like religion, which, as in the passage above, is assumed by the narrator Marcel to be a relic of the past, the artistic imagination is pointed up as failing in its promise to deliver anything outside the systematic observance of its own formal conventions. Art, like love, vouchsafes a truth that is, in the final analysis, purely solipsistic: 'at the period when I was in love with Gilberte, I still believed that Love did really exist outside ourselves . . .'[5]

Swann is presented as a little more knowing than this, yet still capable, with the aid of Vinteuil's 'little phrase', of wilfully deceiving himself:

> He was well aware that his love was something that did not correspond to anything outside itself, verifiable by others beside him; he realised that Odette's qualities were not such as to justify his setting so high a value on the hours he spent in her company. And often, when the cold government of reason stood unchallenged in his mind, he would readily have ceased to sacrifice so many of his intellectual and social interests to this imaginary pleasure. But the little phrase, as soon as it struck his ear, had the power to liberate in him the space that was needed to contain it; the proportions of Swann's soul were altered; a margin was left for an enjoyment that corresponded no more than his love for Odette to any external object and yet was not, like his enjoyment of that love, purely individual, but assumed for him a sort of reality superior to that of concrete things.[6]

That his love for Odette is not warranted by its object is for Swann precisely the point; by such means it escapes the exchange economy. For Swann's aesthetic temperament the world is debased anyway, a creation of pasteboard; yet the little phrase consigns that world – which would seek to appropriate his love for Odette within its own pasteboard logic of material interests, 'those human considerations which affect all men alike' – to a sphere of irrelevance.

This ambiguity between, in Malcolm Bowie's words, 'art as supreme value and art as nullity',[7] between art as genuine transcendence and as vehicle of the most grotesque materialism, is replayed throughout this text. The artworks which Proust describes (many of them fictional) are nearly always inserted into highly formalized social contexts of performance and reception. Art in Proust, as Bowie says, is 'a weapon in the salon wars.'[8] Its use value – the glimpse it offers of the infinite, for example – is always debunked by exchange value; every sentence on art in *À la recherche du temps perdu* protests against the complacent belief that artworks transcend the fetishism of commodities. Swann, after all, is ultimately disappointed in his love for Odette, its validation by Vinteuil's 'little phrase' notwithstanding.

Swann is a highly reflective character; the possibility of love, in any straightforward sense, is inhibited by the fact of its intellectual mediation – by the feeling, albeit one that is agreeable to Swann, 'that he was leading the life of the class of men whose existence is coloured by a love-affair'.[9] In later life, Marcel has already suggested, we *come to the aid of* love; 'we falsify it by memory and suggestion. Recognizing one of its symptoms, we remember and re-create the rest'.[10] Love, unmediated by such strategies, is impossible for the *hônnete homme*. Analogously, how is it possible that art, which is always ultimately subordinated to the principles of exchange, should remain an unblemished mode of transport to the infinite, for a man of such acute worldliness and intellectual sophistication as Charles Swann?

Love and art in *Swann's Way* represent a correlation of worldly pursuits which awaken the desire for unknown delights, but fail to bring 'any precise gratification', at least in the immediate present.[11] The final pages of *Swann's Way* make this explicit, as Marcel walks through the Bois de Boulogne, unfavourably comparing the strollers around him with those spectacles of feminine beauty and style that had fascinated him in his youth, which had seemed to him to embody 'consistency, unity and life', and – obscurely – to justify his 'belief'. By contrast, the modern equivalents resist all attempts to invest them with meaning: 'they passed before me in a desultory, haphazard, meaningless fashion, containing in themselves no beauty which my eyes might have tried, as in the old days, to re-create. They were just women, in whose elegance I had no faith, and whose clothes seemed to me unimportant.'[12] This apparent yearning for meaning, however, is given a historical rationalization in the sentence immediately following, which altogether removes its conservative, nostalgic implications:

> But when a belief vanishes, there survives it – more and more vigorously so as to cloak the absence of the power, now lost to us, of imparting reality to new things – a fetishistic attachment to the old things which it did once animate, as if it was in them and not in ourselves that the divine spark resided, and as if our present incredulity had a contingent cause – the death of the gods.

'Belief' and the 'things which it animates' are here maintained in clear and irrevocable distinction. The desire to collapse them, to invest a particular social form with a particular order of weighty significance, is always belated, always a desire to *re*-invest. In a reflective age – in which, by definition, the disjunction between form and content is assured – the preservation of transcendence in art is possible only by the refusal of any claim to transcendence; and the same applies to love. Freedom from materiality is achievable not by any conscious self-elevation, but by affirmation of the ubiquity of materiality. Bret Easton Ellis's 'nihilistic' novel *American Psycho* achieves a level of transcendence that is utterly inaccessible to Douglas Coupland's God-retrieving *Girlfriend in a Coma*. 'Religious art today', says Adorno, 'is nothing but blasphemy.'[13] Proust materializes an aesthetic rupture between art and truth that has widened and deepened ever since. It is aesthetics, increasingly, that traverses the alienation between subject and object, and which does so precisely insofar as it maintains the distance between them. This paradoxical relation has further implications:

1. To try to strike through the mask is to recognize it, in all its pasteboard reality; to bestow reality upon it. Ahab hypostasizes the white whale, transforming it from a symbol of his alienation into a fetishized deity. Leaving the mask intact, conversely, demonstrates freedom from it, annihilating it all the more thoroughly.

2. Reality is no more or less truthful in its immediacy than in memory; experiences are embedded in time as well as in space. Recollection is impossible, except as the forcible wrenching of the past from out of the past, in the process of which it must lose either its charm or its truth.

3. Acknowledging the collapse of faith is itself an act of faith, and offers the only prospect of its preservation, and one's own salvation.

# 11

# Hierarchy of Mediation and Immediacy

Aesthetic judgement is not a qualitative *mode* but a morphological *structure* of appreciation. The appearance of alienated consciousness, a disjunction between subject and object, as Hegel was aware, is a development which demands and presupposes a reflexive vehicle of representation. The form-content relation specific to modern 'aesthetic' experience is far more appropriate to this condition than Hegel acknowledged. Aesthetics is a structural complexification of religion, its reconstitution in a reflective age.[1] Form, writes Adorno in *Aesthetic Theory*, 'secularizes the theological model of the world as an image made in God's likeness, though not as an act of creation but as the objectivation of the human comportment that imitates creation; not *creatio ex nihilo* but creation out of the created.'[2] Form, that is to say, inherits the aspiration to transcendence of the religious sensibility, but invested with knowledge of its unattainability, and of its fundamentally aspirational nature. The hubristic impulse embodied in Captain Ahab, which finds unbearable the discrepancy between appearance and reality and craves its collapse, is transformed, in the aesthetic sensibility, into an experience of pleasure deriving from the intellectual apprehension of truth.

Form does not put itself in the place of content; the aspiration to transcendence is constitutive of the aesthetic, but is consumed by it. Nor does form reside in a merely subsidiary relation to content, a relation of substitution or equivalence (as in traditional, pre-symbolic or pre-artistic religious iconography); the aesthetic relation, rather, is a dynamic one which, in spanning the gap between Kant's formalistic theory of art and Hegel's spiritual–historical one, attains a dialectical structure. Convergence of subject and object, as said earlier, is imputed by aesthetic judgements, not *postulated* by them – and the historical realization of such convergence is progressively less assured. 'What promises to emancipate and thus strengthen the subject', writes Adorno of art's bid for transcendence, 'weakens it at the same time through its isolation'.[3] The truth *content* of art is non-dissociable from its paradoxical *structure* of reaching out for truth while being unable to secure it; this is the very essence of art's truth content in modernity. Form itself represents a commitment to mediation over immediacy, says Adorno,[4] meaning that in artworks the world is revealed as dialectically suffused by representation – a truth which is confirmed by the fact of its representation as the truth content of *art*. Art and aesthetics are the bearers and fulfillers of the truth that mediation, rather than immediacy, is the bearer of truth. Thus, it makes no sense to talk of the unity of subject and object, or the recovery of a condition of immediacy as the goal of art or of aesthetics – except, paradoxically, as the immediacy of the mediated, the subjective coherence of the objectively or 'spiritually' constituted. 'Immediacy itself is essentially mediated', quotes Adorno from Hegel's *Lectures on the Philosophy of Religion*;[5] and from the *Logic* the following: 'Immediacy of knowledge is so far from excluding mediation, that the two things are linked together – immediate knowledge being actually the product and the result of mediated knowledge.'[6] What this means in relation to subjectivity, say, may be illustrated by considering a distinction which Hannah Arendt draws between solitude and loneliness in *The Origins of Totalitarianism*.

Just as for Andrew Bowie the possibility of aesthetic experience emerges out of a subjectivity that is in some sense fragmented – split, in Schnädelbach's words, into 'being-for-itself' and 'being-beyond-itself' – so Arendt writes of the experience of solitude, distinct from that of loneliness, as a product of the modern divided self. In solitude, she writes,

> I am 'by myself', together with my self, and therefore two-in-one, whereas in loneliness I am actually one, deserted by all others. All thinking, strictly speaking, is done in solitude, and is a dialogue between me and myself; but this dialogue of the two-in-one does not lose contact with the world of my fellow-men because they are represented in the self with whom I lead the dialogue of thought. The problem of solitude is that this two-in-one needs the others in order to become one again: one unchangeable individual whose identity can never be mistaken for any other.[7]

Arendt distinguishes these experiences – loneliness and solitude – in terms of their truth value; yet this distinction alludes as much to their respective attitudes towards truth as it does to the significance of their insights. Solitude becomes loneliness when the solitary individual, convinced of the corrosive effect of the world upon his thought, isolates himself, thirsting for the authenticity which he or she locates in the possibility of an immediate existence. The lonely individual is somebody trapped within the remorselessness of pure logical reasoning, as far removed from experience as it is from thinking, since its concern can only be with what is self-evident. The 'truths' of the thought processes of loneliness, therefore, are wholly empty, since they *reveal* nothing. Arendt quotes Luther: 'A lonely man always deduces one thing from the other and thinks everything to the worst.' And she comments: 'The famous extremism of totalitarian movements, far from having anything to do with true radicalism, consists indeed in this "thinking everything to the worst," in this deducing process which always arrives at the worst possible conclusions.'[8] Thus she describes a situation in which loneliness results not in the isolation of individuals within selfhood, but in the loss of the self, which is 'confirmed in its identity only by the trusting and trustworthy company of equals'.

Such loneliness, writes Arendt, has become 'an everyday experience of the evergrowing masses of our century'.[9] It is also the process by which totalitarianism organizes the interiorities of men and women. Totalitarianism exerts 'an inner coercion whose only content is the strict avoidance of contradictions that seems to confirm a man's identity outside all relationships with others.' This insistence upon consistency, says Arendt, has the effect of expelling truth content from thought itself; by such means totalitarianism denies to the great majority of men and women the dialectical experience of solitude, embedding them, rather, in a condition of isolated loneliness. This, then, is what is meant by alienation, and it is not, for Arendt, the effect of an excessively mediated society, as in the jaded 'apathy' often attributed to the 'abundance' and 'superfluity' of Western economies, but of an *insufficiently* mediated one – a diagnosis which nonetheless applies to just those same 'decadent' Western societies. Alienation, in the form of loneliness, is regression and failure, not progress 'gone too far' or an inevitable side-effect of the success-story of modernity, but a retreat from, or a means of containing and delimiting, the human potential of modern societies.

The French sociologist Joseph Gabel uses the term 'morbid rationalism', derived from the work of Eugène Minkowski, to describe this reified consciousness.[10] Gabel's book *La fausse conscience* (translated into English as *False Consciousness*), an attempt to analyse social conditions by synthesizing the tools of clinical pathology with those of Marxist social theory, makes explicit the link between the *immediacy* of delirious states of consciousness and their *falsity*. For Gabel the phenomenon of schizophrenia is a model for the constitition of reified consciousness itself. Gabel identifies 'delirium' – like alienation for Schnädelbach, solitude for Arendt, and aesthetic judgement for Andrew Bowie – as an experience which is definitive of the modern reflective subject. 'Man alone', he writes, 'is capable of having states of delirium, just as he is the only being for whom authentic consciousness – which is the result of a dialectical transcendence over false consciousness – is not . . . an *immediate given*, but a *conquest*, achieved only gradually in the process of individual maturation.'[11] Gabel's evaluation of schizophrenia as reified consciousness is at odds with the more recently emergent tradition which associates a 'schizophrenic' existence with the information-overload characteristic of postmodern subjectivity, which privileges 'schizophrenia' as the inevitable response of the contemporary subject to the disappearance of reality in postmodernity, and which urges the subject into a 'fatally strategic' embrace of his or her alienation in order to outpace the irresistable reifying forces of capitalism. Fredric Jameson has referred to schizophrenia as 'the terrifying rush of the non-identical', implying, like Gilles Deleuze and Félix Guattari, that the schizophrenic, for all his or her confusion, has access to a truth (that of capitalism, in particular) that is obscured to conventional consciousness by 'the bourgeois reality principle'.[12] Jean Baudrillard, pursuing similar lines, writes:

> The schizo is bereft of every scene, open to everything in spite of himself, living in the greatest confusion . . . What characterizes him is less the loss of the real, the light years of estrangement from the real, the pathos of distance and radical separation, as is commonly said; but, very much to the contrary, the absolute proximity, the total instantaneity of things, the feeling of no defense, no retreat. It is the end of interiority and intimacy, the overexposure and transparence of the world which traverses him without obstacle. He can no longer produce the limits of his own being, can no longer play nor stage himself, can no longer produce himself as a mirror. He is now only a pure screen, a switching centre for all the networks of influence.[13]

For Baudrillard this situation is inevitable, and he presents it in a tone of utter neutrality. What he calls here the 'ecstasy of communication' brings about a reversion to immediate existence, the effect of a progressive erosion of the barrier separating the bourgeois subject from the world around her. Like Georg Simmel, Baudrillard maintains a fixed conception of the relation between subject and object even in its dissolution; he writes of 'this forced extroversion of all interiority, this forced injection of all exteriority that the categorical imperative of communication literally signifies'.[14] Subjectivity in other words, a once pristine domain, *has been colonized* by objective culture, and this process is irrevocable; to cling onto one's interiority is to clutch for something that has already vanished. Thus for Baudrillard the 'schizophrenic', to whom words and images no longer signify, is emphatically not in a condition of 'false consciousness', still less of 'reification'; this category, in so far as it may be applied at all, pertains rather to the claim to autonomy of the modern anxiety-ridden bourgeois subject.

For Gabel on the contrary, schizophrenia is a form of false consciousness predominantly characterized by the absence of 'dialectical' thinking and by subjective immersion in an 'egocentric' moral universe: 'The conceptual aparatus of ideologies is formed in an egocentric way: the presence of a privileged system in the field of consciousness encourages anti-dialectical identification at the expense of intuition about differences, and this by virtue of a mechanism close to the logic of schizophrenics.'[15] His perspective here is similar to that of Arendt's in *The Origins of Totalitarianism*. For Arendt, totalitarianism aims not to instill convictions in the population, but to destroy the possibility of their formation by radically isolating the individual from the world. Society follows a purely 'objective' logic, impervious to the claims of justice, of merit, even of rationality.[16] According to this analysis the National Lottery, for example, is a quasi-totalitarian institution which removes all rationality from the world and thus discourages, even prohibits, the formation of a politically engaged working class, a population capable of viewing itself in non-egocentric, historical terms. Nature, in the form of pure chance, is given total sovereignty over the fortunes of men and women – just as during the Third Reich nature, in the form of racial origin, determined whether people were participants in or victims of the regime. 'It could be you!' is an ideological sentiment completely of a kind with the insistence, in Himmler's orations, upon the 'chosenness' of the Nazi operatives, who were encouraged to consider themselves involved in 'a great task that occurs once in two thousand years'.[17]

Under the title 'The Plot to Make Us Stupid', David Runciman writes of the incompatibility of the ostensibly noble aims of national lotteries with their demeaning effect at the level of consciousness:

> Alone among government sources of income, the money raised by the Lottery is set aside to further the moral life of the nation, as it might be called, in some broad or classical sense (the sense in which artistic and athletic achievements are considered also as moral ones). However, alone among government sources of income, the money to pay for these improvements is raised by fostering ignorance, superstition and fear.[18]

National lotteries depend for their operation on false consciousness; on the belief, co-existing with the sense of fairness deriving from chance, firstly that sequences of numbers chosen by people actually 'belong' to them – a fetishistic relation which is essential to the conviction that a week's game must not pass without participation – and secondly, that some sequences of numbers (eg. 'random-looking' sequences) are more likely to come up than others (eg. consecutive sequences). These beliefs are incompatible with the supposedly egalitarian idea of chance. The National Lottery is ideologically incoherent; and for Gabel the same incoherence is the dominant intellectual characteristic of racist consciousness, the epitome of reified thought.

Racist false consciousness 'considers as ahistorical and "natural" racial peculiarities of historical origin' (such as the keenness of Jews for money, or the partiality of Scots for alcohol, or – Frantz Fanon's example – the criminality of the Algerian,[19] each of which is explicable as a historical phenomenon which disappears once historical conditions change). Racist ideology, meanwhile elevates upon this false consciousness 'a pseudo-history which, instead of explaining the Jew through history, claims to explain History through the Jew.'[20] Racism is an example of a non-dialectical consciousness adopted as a source of reassurance in the absence of any apparent logical coherence to the world; similarly the National Lottery represents a psychological reversion to faith in a form of immediacy which is autonomous of human society – a reversion, however, that has a sense of purpose *subjectively* mapped upon it; this constitutes its 'schizophrenic' nature. Freud writes that in schizophrenia, words undergo the same processes of displacement and condensation which, during sleep, convert the latent dream-thoughts into manifest dream content. 'The process may go so far that a single word, if it is specially suitable on account of its numerous connections, takes over the representation of a whole train of thought.'[21] For Gabel the same holds true of the reified mental constitution. The schizophrenic thought process has an 'identificatory basis', meaning 'a pathological preponderance of the function of identification';[22] it pursues connections at the level of immediate correspondence rather than historical causation, constituting a form of 'morbid rationalism'. It thus denotes a mindset equivalent to that of

Arendt's lonely philosopher, or the subject of a totalitarian regime: 'thought enclosed within itself, dogmatic, detached from reality, unchanged by experience.'[23] And both Arendt and Gabel identify this situation as a characteristic ideological objective of modern governments.

In *Anti-Oedipus* Deleuze and Guattari also describe the generalized consciousness of late capitalism as 'schizophrenic'. Yet the emphasis of *Anti-Oedipus* is quite different to that of Gabel's work; the critical procedure of 'de-territorialization' or 'schizo-analysis', for Deleuze and Guattari, is a process of breaking through the totality of reified consciousness to arrive at the position of the 'desiring subject'. It is on this basis that they rate the writings of Proust and Kafka, amongst others, so highly. 'If schizophrenia is the universal,' they write, 'the great artist is indeed the one who scales the schizophrenic wall and reaches the land of the unknown, where he no longer belongs to any time, any milieu, any school.'[24] *À la recherche du temps perdu* is 'a great enterprise of schizoanalysis: all the planes are traversed until their molecular line of escape is reached, their schizophrenic break-through . . .'[25] The global meaning of Proust, the 'Whole', over and beyond its 'rhizomatic lines', is merely 'a product, produced as nothing more than a part alongside other parts, which it neither unifies nor totalizes . . .'[26] Meanwhile Deleuze and Guattari, like Ulrich Beck, read Kafka as a writer of liberation, 'an author who laughs with a profound joy, a *joie de vivre*' and whose reputation as an artist of melancholy preoccupations and solitude is merely the result of 'stupid' and 'deformed' readings of his work which have misunderstood his 'clownish declarations' of impotence and culpability.[27] In Kafka, justice is revealed as nothing other than 'desire', the 'polyvocality' of which is the real concern of his writings.

These literary interpretations seem to accord with Deleuze and Guattari's rejection of the dialectic:

> We no longer believe in the myth of the existence of fragments that, like pieces of an antique statue, are merely waiting for the

> last one to be turned up, so that they may all be glued back together to create a unity that is precisely the same as the original unity. We no longer believe in a primordial unity that once existed, or in a final totality that awaits us at some future date . . . We believe only in totalities that are peripheral. And if we discover such a totality alongside various separate parts, it is a whole *of* these particular parts but does not totalize them; it is a unity *of* all of these particular parts but does not unify them; rather, it is added to them as a new part fabricated separately.[28]

Such a notion of immediate, 'molecular' truth is opposed, rhetorically at least, to the close relation between truth and mediation presupposed in the concept of *Geist* – 'the most sublime Notion' says Hegel, 'and the one which belongs to the modern age and its religion'[29] – in which subject and object, fragment and whole, effectively converge. In a few fascinating paragraphs in the Preface to the *Phenomenology of Spirit* Hegel explains this relationship, and the nature of mediation itself:

> Of the Absolute it must be said that it is essentially a result, that only in the end is it what it truly is; *and that precisely in this consists its nature*, viz. *to be actual, subject, the spontaneous becoming of itself* . . . The beginning, the principle, or the Absolute, as at first immediately enunciated, is only the universal. Just as when I say '*all* animals', this expression cannot pass for a zoology, so it is equally plain that the words, 'the Divine', 'the Absolute', 'the Eternal', etc., *do not express what is contained in them*; and only such words, in fact, do express the intuition as something immediate.[30]

In the light of Hegel's philosophy of history, it becomes apparent that there exists a form of 'inverse' fetishism, which retreats in horror from terms such as 'Absolute'; furthermore, that this movement of retreat itself constitutes the truly neurotic, truly fetishizing, truly reified consciousness. The idea of the Absolute as 'a primordial unity that once existed' or 'a final totality that awaits us at some future date' is not a Hegelian one, despite received wisdom to the contrary. In Hegelian *Geist*, the unity of subject and object is not an ultimate end of knowledge, but a methodological principle, etched into every moment in history. There is no Kantian separation in Hegel between, for example, noumena and phenomena, or between rationality and the real, or between science and aesthetics, or between the fragment and the whole, or even between mediation and immediacy. 'In Kant,' writes Adorno in a crucial essay on the concept of mediation in Hegel, 'critique remains a critique of reason; in Hegel, who criticizes the Kantian separation of reason from reality, the critique of reason is simultaneously a critique of the real.'[31] Such an idea is also presupposed in Lukács's essay on reification; indeed, Lukács alludes implicitly to the passage from Hegel quoted above, *preempting* Deleuze and Guattari's objection to the dialectical theory of history fifty years later. The whole is not the sum of its parts; nor is it simply *more* than the sum of its parts, a *Gestalt*. Rather, 'the essence of the dialectical method lies in the fact that in every aspect correctly grasped by the dialectic the whole totality is comprehended and that the whole method can be unravelled from every single aspect.'[32] For Lukács, Hegel's philosophical system makes possible the *rejection* of the idea of knowledge as 'infinite progression' (or, conversely, infinite regression). 'The developing tendencies of history', he says a few pages later, 'constitute a higher reality than the empirical facts'[33] – yet this is neither a movement away from, nor one towards, immediacy. The concept of mediation in Hegel is not the conventional one of a *compromise* between two extremes, a third way that 'reconciles' two incompatible principles. Mediation for Hegel, as Robert Hullot-Kentor points out, is itself a route of extremes;[34] mediation produces the unity of subject and object, of mediation and immediacy, being and becoming, contemplation and action, as a unity of *polarities*. The misnamed dialectical 'synthesis' takes place at the moment that a concept attains its most perfect realization, the moment *at which it becomes its own opposite*. Whereas mediation as compromise affirms that which it 'sublates', since it assumes, as a point of departure, the pre-existence of the world as it is, Hegelian mediation is a dynamic dispensation which presupposes the co-existence – even the *identity* – of the world as it is and the world as other. Mediation is simultaneously mediation and immediacy, just as contemplation, for Adorno, is simultaneously action and contemplation. The attempt to maintain them in opposition – to privilege action over contemplation, for example – is the truly contemplative procedure, the product of a reified consciousness which attributes reality, precisely, to the conceptual world as given.[35] Likewise, what is immediate, in-itself – *le monde comme donné*, as Lucien Goldmann says – is accessible only in the process of its mediation; only in its mediation, in fact, does the mediated achieve immediacy. Thought is not only necessary to action; in a reified world, thought *constitutes* action, more so than any mere action undertaken on the basis of the world as given.

From this perspective Hegel is no idealist; nor is his theory of history a 'monumental' or totalitarian one. It makes no sense, therefore, to insist on the reifying violence of such 'monumental' terms as 'Absolute' or 'universal' *in opposition* to Hegel, or to discard the dialectic on this basis, since for Hegel absolute knowledge is a hypothesis, projected into a receding future; its importance is methodological and political as much as (or more than) it is scientific.

'Hitler got the fascists sexually aroused' write Deleuze and Guattari. 'A revolutionary machine is nothing if it does not acquire at least as much force as these coercive machines have for producing breaks and mobilizing flows.'[36] On the contrary; the true purpose of a revolutionary 'machine' is to *mediate* the immediate reality which is produced by such 'coercive machines', not to compete *in terms* of immediacy. Lukács talks not of 'freedom' or 'liberation' from reification, but of a real situation in which reification has been 'overcome'. Overcoming reification is not a matter of penetrating through the 'layers' of mediation, of 'false consciousness', but of precisely *mediating* 'immediate' reality, which is untrue. The problem arises when the logic of mediation is equated with the logic of reification, as it is in Deleuze and Guattari; in fact these logics should be counterposed: the critique of reification is always a critique of the 'logic of mediation' itself.

Thus Deleuze and Guattari are wrong to contrast Proust to Hegel as, say, the rhizomatic to the monumental, the materialistic to the totalitarian, the immediate to the metaphysics of mediation. The global significance of *À la recherche du temps perdu* is unnarrated; in this way the text exceeds its own materiality, just as Swann's behaviour exceeds rationalistic explanation – yet this is not a dissolution of monumental rationality but a situation, precisely, of the dialectical mediation of material reality. In the gap between *Du côté de chez Swann*, in which Swann finally conquers and disposes of his love for Odette, and *À l'ombre des jeunes filles en fleurs* – he marries her! It is the mediatedness of marriage, not the immediacy of first love, which successfully transcends materiality. Proust's narrator tells us: 'It is because they entail the sacrifice of a more or less advantageous position to a purely private happiness that, as a general rule, ignominious marriages are the most estimable of all.'[37] In marrying her, Swann successfully mediates his ailing love for Odette; by this means he creates 'a supplementary person, distinct from the person the world knows by the same name'.[38] This rejection of the estimation of the world is his great triumph, and that of Proust's enterprise; it is why the valuation of art and aesthetic judgement throughout *À la recherche du temps perdu* subsists, contrary to all the evidence presented throughout the text of its obsolescence. Proust values art despite, *and in so far as*, he refuses its claims to significance. This is not a fragment to place alongside other fragments, but a whole which is implicit in every sentence of *À la recherche du temps perdu*.

*

# 12

# The Virtue of Obsolescence

Adorno says of Hegel that the fascination of reading him in the present is due to the following paradox: on one hand he has been rendered obsolete by science and scholarship; absolute knowledge has not, after all, been attained, nor has humanity shown much progress in replacing superstition by rationality. On the other hand such facts make Hegel more timely and more necessary than ever in opposition to them.[1] Hegel is a radical force to the precise degree that his theory has been discredited by history; his obsolescence is the very source of his value. Something similar is true, I want to argue, of the concept of reification as it is expanded on by Lukács in *History and Class Consciousness*.

The work of Jean Baudrillard illustrates both why reification has been rendered anachronistic and why the concept retains critical significance in the face of that apparent antiquation. The classic 'high postmodernist' diagnosis, as put forward in Baudrillard's most influential works – that reality suffers a contamination effect by the process of mediatization, that as a consequence the reality principle itself has become obsolete, that reality no longer functions according to a 'spatial' model of truth and appearance – has been updated with characteristic subtlety in Baudrillard's book *The Perfect Crime*. Reality, he writes, has begun to collude with those who deny its existence, in so doing taking revenge upon them 'by paradoxically proving them right. When the most cynical, most provocative hypothesis is verified, the trick really is a low one; you are disarmed by the lamentable confirmation of your words by an unscrupulous reality.'[2]

The reason for the obsolescence of reification is that reality, by abandoning the pretence (or the belief) that it exists in distinction from representation, confirms its truth, thereby destroying its critical fulcrum. As Baudrillard observes, 'a theory which is verified is no longer a theory'; the coincidence of idea and reality amounts to the 'death throes of the concept'[3] – and reification, more than any other theory, is dependent on the concept. The intentionally perplexing message of Baudrillard's analysis is that this prevalent unreality is a real state of affairs in which individuals are more politically disfranchised than ever. In embracing its own constructed character, reality destroys even the possibility of its critical analysis. The 'unconditional realization of all ideas', writes Baudrillard, is where hell begins, what hell is;[4] the allusion, once more, is to Hannah Arendt's theory of totalitarianism, which provides an analogy to the idea of total reification as total administration.

Perfect totalitarianism implies that no distinction between essence and action – or being and becoming – would be either possible or necessary. Under perfect totalitarianism, writes Arendt, 'all men have become One Man'; 'every act is the execution of a death sentence which Nature or History has already pronounced'.[5] Fear increases under real totalitarian governments, yet it ceases to offer any guide as to how to behave; terror 'chooses its victims without reference to individual actions or thoughts, exclusively in accordance with the objective necessity of the natural or historical process.' The inhabitants of totalitarian regimes are 'thrown into and caught in the process of nature or history for the sake of accelerating its movement; as such, they can only be executioners or victims of its inherent law.'[6] Perfect totalitarian regimes are societies of *pure immediacy*, in other words, whose *essence* is terror. This is the dystopian vision behind what Baudrillard calls 'the unconditional realization of all ideas'; it denotes a correspondence between subject and object, the collapse of all mediation into immediacy, and the conflation of future and past into a whirlwind present that is simultaneously the end and the origin of history. The one thing that can be said for both victims and executioners of totalitarianism is that they are free of the sense, supposedly pervasive in 'late modern' societies, that their self-identities are being eroded by 'objective culture'; that they suffer from a disjunction between interior being and exterior determination; that life has become a 'dull reflection of itself'. Worryingly and deleteriously for the theory of reification, the absence of anxiety towards reification is common to the ideal totalitarian state and the 'non-reified' world dreamed of by romantic theoreticians. With the decline of transcendental 'metanarratives', which enable categorical concepts such as commodification and reification to be applied to society from above – from a position not itself affected by this anxiety – those concepts themselves fall into abeyance.

For Arendt, however, no such regime has ever existed in a pure state; indeed, she hints that attempts to create such societies are self-defeating, necessarily undermining themselves by their very principles of operation. The terror of totalitarian regimes stems from their failure to achieve the correlation between individual and society implied above. Perfect totalitarianism would no longer be totalitarian in quite the same way, since the tension (between individual and society, subject and object) necessary to *perceive* it would no longer exist. How could one distinguish between total individual fulfilment and total individual oppression in a society in which the ends of individuals were by definition those of the collectivity? Similarly, an age of total reification, as I have said before, would imply no corrosion of or restriction upon individual freedom, since the constitution of an individual under such conditions would be quite different. If one feels threatened by reification, it is proof of one's transcendence of material reality, of the present impossibility of total reification, and of the continuing utility, therefore, of the *theory* of reification. In the absence of any such feeling, however, it is debatable whether the phenomenon itself could be said to have any substance at all.

By merely proposing that a condition of 'total administration' has been attained, reflexive modernization *verifies* the theory of reification with an effect that is more nihilistic than the thought of the most extreme postmodernist. Ulrich Beck and

Jean Baudrillard share far more than either would care to admit. Periodizing even more recklessly, Arthur Kroker has suggested that the phase of simulation, which long ago succeeded the ages of alienation and reification, has itself been replaced by a phase of 'cynical power' in which power appears 'as an empty sign of its own disappearance':

> Self-referential, random in its movements, always internally contradictory because always flipping the fabled so-called opposites of modernist culture [self and other, nature and culture, essence and experience], cynical power is hegemonic ideology today. It's what the British social theorist, Anthony Giddens, has reverentially described as the 'third way' of 'reflexive modernization.' The 'third way' – that's cynical power as the political form of micro-fascism at the millennium.[7]

Yet, in crediting this situation with the status of a new phase in history, Kroker – for all the criticism implied in his disparaging tone – recognizes and *substantiates* the account of the world offered by Giddens and Baudrillard. Each of these writers looks upon his own theory with the benevolence of the indulgent patriarch upon his offspring; each fails to acknowledge the thoroughgoing implication of his 'theory' in a situation in which he has declined to intervene politically. Giddens's 'third way' – like Beck's theory of reflexive modernization, Baudrillard's theory of simulation and Kroker's model of 'virtualization' – should be criticized as utterly unhistorical. Baudrillard, Beck, Giddens and Kroker illustrate Hegel's importance for Adorno by default. Each puts forward a highly relevant *description* of the present situation – yet each thereby ensures its craven complicity with it, and thus its own *critical* superfluousness.

The idea that we live in a completely reified society is as untenable as the idea that the 'age' of reification has come to an end, which, in any case, is the same thing. Again, it is possible to talk about this by way of analogy. Consider first the concept of monopoly; how is it possible to distinguish between a hypothetical total monopoly (in which a single, diversified company owns everything and completely dominates every market, effectively competing with itself through each individual outlet) and total, atomised (and therefore regulated) competition? The idea of monopoly is dependent upon its non-realization – upon the presence of some smaller company to monopolize *against*. One could speculate further therefore: it is the degree to which corporations *fall short of* cultural and economic domination, as much as the converse, that excites anger against them. In the outcry against the colonizing tendencies of large companies such as McDonald's or Starbucks, the idea of the large corporation is itself a reification: 'It's sort of an illusion of choice that is being offered, rather than real choice . . . They are offering a higher level of beverage, but there is something slightly sinister about it, because they offer a simulacrum of choice, a simulacrum of domesticity and intimacy – but you really are just being manipulated by a large corporation.'[8] What does it mean to talk about a 'simulacrum of choice' rather than, say, 'real choice'? What does it mean to be 'manipulated by a large corporation'? The story is told of an independent coffee shop in Toronto – Dooley's – which resisted the hostile overtures of Starbucks, 'and won'. As a result of a furious local campaign by its regular customers, Starbucks now 'sublets the outlet to the original Dooley's'.[9] Is this really a triumph for independence, or is it rather the inherent logic of consumer capitalism carried a stage further, in the direction of a pernicious, benevolent pluralism? By articulating their hostility to certain capitalist enterprises in these subjectivist (and totalizing) terms, 'activists' affirm the dependence of their campaigns on a fetishistic conception of their antagonist. By speaking of the inherent evil of 'global capital', for example, they contribute to the reifying effects of capitalism, further precluding any true analysis of the totality.

A second analogy is that of the perfect crime – a 'purer' metaphor than that of monopoly perhaps, which has a theoretical link with the concept of reification – although Jean Baudrillard's book *The Perfect Crime*, which addresses the relation between reality and representation, is germane. Contrary to Baudrillard's suggestion that the perfect crime, 'the murder of reality', has 'always-already' been perpetrated – that this 'perfect crime' is a first principle of human existence itself – the concept of the perfect crime is an ahistorical abstraction.[10] The perfect (or unsolvable) crime takes two possible forms: (i) the crime which has no motive (as in Dostoevsky's *Crime and Punishment*, in which Raskolnikov murders for the sake of sensory and intellectual titillation), and (ii) the crime which has no perpetrator (as in Edgar Allan Poe's *The Murders in the Rue Morgue*, in which the 'murderer' turns out to be an unreasoning orang-utan). Ever since the Loeb-Leopold case of the 1920s, however – indeed, ever since *Crime and Punishment* – the appeal of committing a 'motiveless crime' has itself been considered among the list of possible criminal motives. Thus we read in a report on the impact of a recent case in Italy: 'Hints were dropped by the investigators that the two young academics had been intellectually fascinated by the concept of a "perfect crime".'[11] The concept of the motiveless crime, like the concept of the reified (or unreified) object, has no correspondence in historical reality, since reflection will in time generate a motive precisely out of the absence of motive. Secondly, a crime without a perpetrator is simply not a crime – merely, at most, a 'crime effect'. The 'murder of reality' is an illusion which stems not from an excess of mediation but from the failure to mediate reality; the 'death' of reality is effected by a reversion to the most immediate state of the contemporary world, a product of the inverted 'logic' of mediation and of the anxiety of reification which results from it. Baudrillard's book, correctly and inevitably, is an indictment of itself as the real perpetrator of this state of affairs. The idea underlying the book, the author hints, is itself the murder weapon; in this way Baudrillard confirms how little the concept of 'the perfect crime' has to offer in the way of concrete political analysis.[12]

A final analogy to the idea of total reification is that of the perfect work of art. Giorgio Agamben, after Jean Paulhan, distinguishes between two types of artist, the Rhetorician and the Terrorist, each of whom is on a quest for a different conception of the perfect artwork. The Rhetorician is the sophisticate of aesthetic modernity, a disparager of meaning, who seeks to 'dissolve all meaning into form and make form the sole law of literature'. The Terrorist, on the other hand, wishes to destroy art, paradoxically by creating a perfect artwork that would annhiliate all form; his dream is 'of a language that would be nothing but meaning, of a thought in whose flame the sign would be fully consumed, putting the writer face to face with the Absolute.'[13] Each is contemptuous of the naivety of the other. Thus the Terrorist flees from the pure form of the Rhetorician; but his quest for pure meaning can result only in the further encapsulation of his work within pure form. In the pursuit of the perfect artwork one becomes, inevitably, merely a man or woman 'of taste' – a category as far removed from genius as the philistine, perhaps *infinitely* more so. 'If the man of taste thinks about himself for a moment,' writes Agamben, 'he must notice not only that he has become indifferent to the work of art, but that the more his taste is purified, the more his soul is spontaneously attracted by everything that good taste cannot but condemn, as though good taste carried within itself a tendency to pervert itself into its opposite.'[14] Genius and good taste are not only distinct qualities; they are incompatible within the same brain. The perfect work of art, a conception that arises along with the idea of 'taste' itself, is a nothing. The genius is the person who discounts the values of taste, consigns them to their proper place, which is the sphere of irrelevance. Flaubert writes – and Agamben quotes – the following: 'Les chef-d'oeuvres sont bêtes; ils ont la mine tranquille comme les productions mêmes de la nature, comme les grands animaux et les montagnes' ('Masterpieces are stupid: they have placid faces like the very products of nature, like big animals and mountains').[15] The urge for the 'perfect' artwork may be motivated by disgust with the 'imperfect' one, or with the form/content relation itself, just as the urge for a non-reified existence springs from disgust with the 'reified' world; yet that movement of revulsion takes with it something of what it is repelled by. The result of the artistic pursuit of pure meaning, in other words, can be nothing other than an artefact of pure and characterless aesthetic form.

The implication of all this is not only that the category of reification is embedded in history, but that the *anxiety* towards reification is its dominant contemporary cultural form. All the signs are that the overriding characteristic of contemporary consciousness is precisely *the fear of reification*. In all its abstraction, reification has become the dominant evil – and thereby its own reified form. A similar point is made by Julian Stallabrass in a critique of what he calls provocatively 'high art lite'. Young British artists' use of 'theory', he writes, is made 'only in the service of the work's autonomy.'[16] Indeterminacy, deconstruction, and so on, become 'linked and serviceable tools for saying everything and nothing, for stamping a work with the mark of value, while never being reductive, never subjecting discourse to closure, never trampling over anyone's subjectivity, never completing a thought' – all of which procedures might be seen as instances of reification. Strategies of resistance to reification, when severed from their ends, become ends in themselves and hence utterly meaningless – a decadent version of the very reification they mean to oppose, to paraphrase Lukács.[17]

Perhaps this unmanageability of the concept of reification, however, is due to its unwieldy abstraction. Far from becoming itself reified, the concept may be criticized for a tendency towards expansion, a tendency to become what Hegel calls a 'bad infinity'. Better, say some commentators, to use more concrete, specific terms such as commodification, racism, essentialism, objectification. Edward Said has written of how reification – in Lukács, at least – becomes 'too inclusive, too ceaselessly active and expanding a habit of mind' – at which point it becomes a 'theoretical parody' of the situation it was formulated to overcome.[18] Gillian Rose, in writing of Adorno's 'obsession' with the concept, intends much the same cautionary note; yet, of the four major theorists discussed by Rose, only Adorno, she claims, is concerned with 'the way a relation between men appears in the form of a natural property of a thing'. Lukács, despite his pioneering theorization of the term, was interested primarily in 'alienation', Benjamin in commodity fetishism, and Simmel in a project of theoretical 'syncretism' which, claims Rose, was a factor in the later unwieldy development of the concept of reification.[19]

My intention here has been to stress that, on the contrary, it is the abstraction and ambiguity of the concept that permit its retention as a universal critique at precisely the point at which totalizing narratives seem untenable. In a situation where the political establishment is conspicuously anti-racist and highly 'tolerant', for example, the concept of reification throws up even that tolerance as potentially repressive and degrading. The statement that Stephen Lawrence was killed 'for no other reason than [that] he was born black', and, further, that this is 'a sign of how far we still have to go' is a confection which should be rejected in its entirety.[20] The concept of reification implicates both racism and the liberal, hate-fuelled response to racism, which halts its inquiry into the source of such evil with the successful prosecution of the perpetrators; which elevates 'racist consciousness' into a self-sufficient, primary cause. In a situation in which politics is taken to be 'all spin and no substance', meanwhile – that is to say, where the operation of ideology is apparently visible as never before – the concept of reification points up even the notion of spin as an ideological chimera, a falsehood in which ideology itself is reified, made containable. 'Spin' presupposes a spatial model of truth *beneath* or *mediated by* appearance, a distinction between a 'spun' and an 'unspun' world. The concept of spin lends support to the idea of an untarnished domain of politics outside 'vested interests'; it sustains the logic according to which mediation is a progression away from, rather than towards truth; 'spin' is an ideological confection which should be subjected to intense critical scrutiny.[21]

The urgent need, then, is for political critique at every stage to *mediate* contemporary, 'immediate' reality. Contrary to almost all received opinion, we are living not in a more mediated society than ever before, but a less mediated one. Reality is increasingly what it appears to be, just as political agendas are increasingly what they are professed to be – yet this is evidence not of the overcoming of reification but of its proliferation, of a model of truth based not on revelation and mediation but on consistency and immediacy.

Proust's narrator observes that the great work of art does not generally seek an audience among those few of its contemporaries capable of understanding it, or that, appearing 'ahead of its time', the work finds such an audience only 'in posterity'. Rather, the work of genius *creates*, not merely its own posterity, but posterity itself, by actively 'fashioning and enlarging' its audience. Thus it is essential that the artist should launch his or her work 'boldly into the distant future', rather than addressing, or reflecting, its present.[22] Likewise, history is not the discovery of truth, but its generation; not the search for or reflection of truth, but its *revelation* – which consists not of the unveiling but the production of truth. The present needs to be viewed dialectically rather than contemplatively, with a methodological insistence on the immediate as embedded in a wider totality, rather than as the summation and end-point of history; as a mediation of past and future, rather than the triumphant culmination of a forgettable past, or the prelude to a foreseeable (or even an unforeseeable) future.

Understandably, the concept of 'totality' sounds anachronistic in the contemporary climate. Proustian 'aesthetics', like the philosophy of history, has a reputation as a product of class privilege, socio-cultural discrimination and Eurocentrism. Multicultural society is by nature inhospitable to any talk of universal values. Difference, rather, has been the political watchword of late modernity, and the means with which, by common consent, society has surmounted the ideological horrors of the first half of the twentieth century. Yet, privileging difference over universality has meant acceding in the diagnosis of the end of history – history viewed, that is to say, in the maligned terms of the

'Enlightenment', as the aspiration to universality. Difference implies a synchronic rather than diachronic perspective, a paradigm framed in spatial rather than temporal terms and thus a rejection of the 'grand narrative' of history itself. Is it possible to reconcile the fact of the pluralization of values in contemporary society and the postmodern critique of universality, in the name of heterogeneity, with the need for a critical practice which refuses, as a working principle, the epistemological basis of the world as it is?

In his essay on reification Lukács writes that there is no need for the relation to totality implied in the concept of reification to become 'explicit'; only that there be an 'aspiration towards totality'.[23] Lukács is unnecessarily apologetic here, since the category of totality is *by definition* one of aspiration – one cannot achieve (reify) 'totality' without losing its universal quality. This, rather than the death of 'metanarratives' such as rationality or historical progress, is the proper lesson of late twentieth-century critical thought, and of Lukács's theory of reification itself. To discard the commitment to totality on the basis of its non-realizability – to discard the possibility of meaning on the basis of Derrida's theory of the 'endless deferral' of the signified, for example – is to discard the concept of aspiration *per se*, and thus all possibility of intervening in political reality. The postmodern suspicion of theories of totality has had the effect of crystallizing a widespread although tacitly held belief in the end of history, even among those for whom Francis Fukuyama's 'end of history' thesis is a postmodern joke.[24] The ironic effect of Fukuyama's essay has been that this evident belief in the end of history *on the left* has remained unstated as such.

On the other hand, the concept of reification is unsustainable in the way it was formulated by Lukács. History since *History and Class Consciousness* has, after all, failed to justify Lukács's faith in the working class as the truth-bearing subject-object of history. 'Reification and the Consciousness of the Proletariat' was written with a certain 'implacable rigour', like that which Adorno attributes to the species of bourgeois cultural criticism which fails to recognize its own implication in the culture it criticizes. Such criticism succumbs to its own critique by failing to abstract from the categories it is using. Similarly, the concept of reification must acknowledge that it, too, is implicated in its own critique, by incorporating the concept of anxiety.

Discarding the concept of reification, on the other hand, betrays an acceptance that the process of reification has reached the stage, anticipated (but only anticipated) by Adorno, of 'absorb[ing] the mind completely'.[25] This, as I have sought to show in the preceding discussion, is irrational and defeatist; it suggests a reified notion of reification, and implies that meaning itself, the very basis of thought and action, is at a point of collapse. With the end of history, the *concept*, which is an entity condemned to reification, becomes either an empty, characterless vessel or the thing itself. This fact demands that the concept of reification be remobilized as a means of saving, precisely, the concept, together with meaning, history, the unimaginable future, and the continuing possibility of intervention in the present.

# PART THREE

# Redemption

*In the mirror I saw ME, of course, only better: more 'me' than before. And I had the strangest sensation: I was wearing, I had no other words for it, I was wearing THE SHIRT ITSELF and THE JACKET ITSELF: And in them, I was MYself . . .*

Wim Wenders[1]

# 1

# The Pleasure Tendency

A sense of guilt has attended me these last few years, rarely conscious or acknowledged, but reawakened whenever my vision, or my fingers, should happen to encounter, along the rows of bookshelves in my study, a small thin pamphlet which I acquired shortly after its publication in 1984. It is not the means by which I acquired the book that troubles my conscience, but the mere fact of its acquisition, which directly flouts a prohibition imposed by the text itself. Inside the front cover a codicil appears explicitly forbidding the reader from taking possession of it: '*PASS IT ON. This book is free and NOT INTENDED FOR PERSONAL POSSESSION. If you find it on a friend's shelves, take it; it's as much yours as theirs.*'

Ever since, I have suffered not only a fear of the book's loss, but a persistent sense that, in my attitude towards it, I have violated the spirit in which it was produced and distributed; that I have succumbed to the 'petty bourgeois' consciousness targeted in the book itself; that I am contributing to the 'problem' more than to the 'solution'; and that, for all my supposed sympathy with the ultra-left position advanced in the text, mine is marked down as a regressive or reactionary spirit by a fetishistic attachment to the book as thing, an object rather than a process. In the early years of my custodianship of the book it languished at the back of my shelves, hidden behind an innocuous thriller for fear

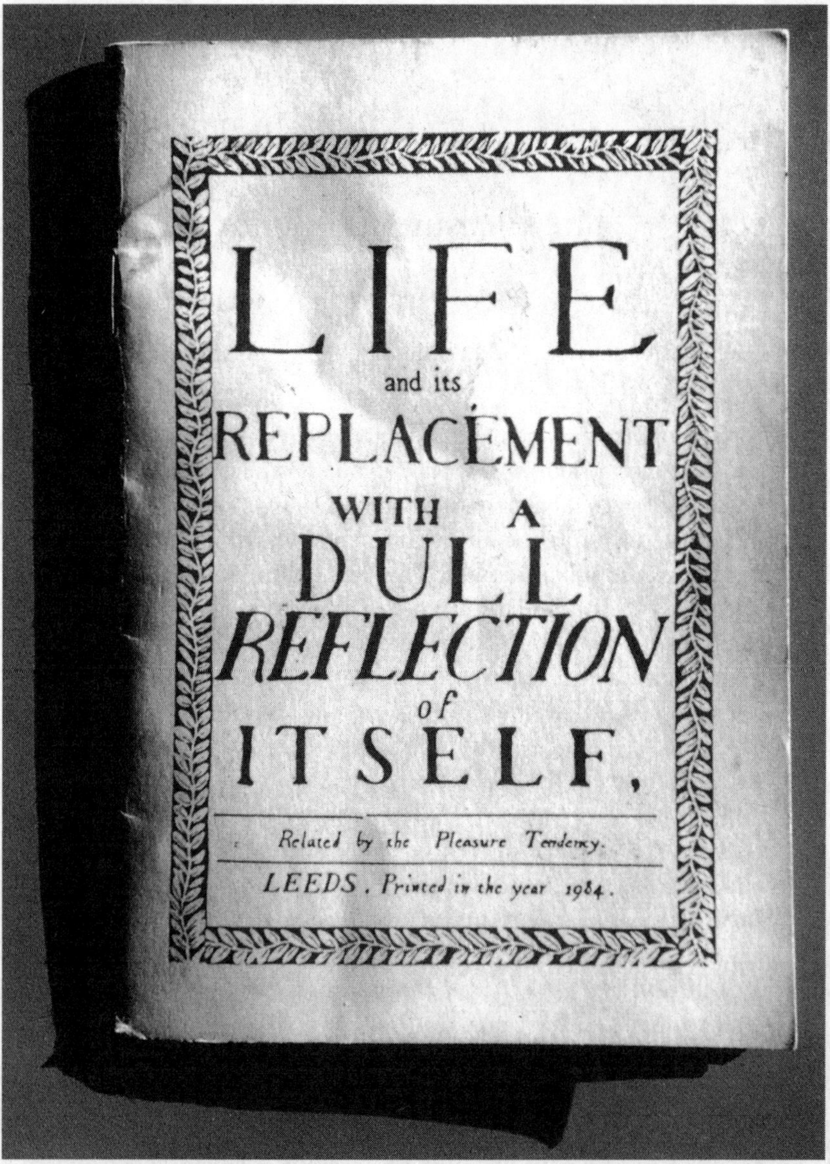
LIFE
and its
REPLACEMENT
WITH A
DULL
REFLECTION
of
ITSELF,
Related by the Pleasure Tendency.
LEEDS. Printed in the year 1984.

that a visiting acquaintance might find it and, incited by the codicil, lay claim to it. Once I even transcribed the whole text onto my computer's hard drive in an attempt to preserve its essence against the risks attending its material existence; but the machine has long since broken down and been thrown away, while the book remains in my possession, as fragile and mysterious as ever.

I first saw 'my' copy of the book as it was passed around a table in The Metropolitan, a public house on London's Farringdon Road, on a summer evening in 1984, one month after the publication date which appears in the front. In a tiny room upstairs, Conflict, a well-known anarchist punk group, were going onstage, performing that night under a pseudonym, 'Increase the Pressure'. As the book circulated the table, the codicil was pointed out to each reader, the effect of which was as if a curse had been pronounced on the book itself. One or two paragraphs were glanced at, but nobody held onto it for more than a few moments, and presently everyone departed to watch the band, leaving me alone with my prize, which I pocketed before also going upstairs.

The book is entitled *Life and its Replacement with a Dull Reflection of Itself*, and its authorship is attributed to the 'Pleasure Tendency', whose 'preliminary theses' the book claims to put forward. It is, as might be imagined from the title, a manifesto for living in, or in spite of, an age of increasing, almost total reification. The author or authors are unapologetic in their critique of the 'modern', a term that is used almost interchangeably with the 'Economy'. The text opposes every dissipation of 'life itself' into its cultural 'forms', epitomized by commodities, money, and the infrastructure of official institutions; indeed commodification is described as 'the main way that life has been falsified', and a 'cancer' that has spread throughout work and leisure, and which has even begun to encroach on 'love, the emotions and nature'.[2] To publish or distribute the text commercially – no matter how low the price, or unconventional the purveyor – would have rendered spurious the extreme positions advocated within it; one stated intention for the book is that it be 'kept away from both alternative and official hands for as long as possible'.[3] Refusing to offer it at a price also testifies to a desire to imbue the book with a quality that is beyond merely economic value, as the theses themselves make clear: 'We would point out the special joy one may feel upon finding something that another has lost, or on possessing something stolen. Here, the object stands (or falls) to us as it were on its own merits and qualities, stripped of the pseudo-quality of price.'[4] In fact, as my (no doubt perverse) attachment to the book demonstrates, such unpriceable objects can easily become 'totally' fetishized; their value escalates, like that of unique artworks under capitalism, to the level of absolute commodities, their use value being thereby obliterated altogether.

Certainly, the ownership-codicil may be seen as having prevented rather than facilitated the book's open discussion among theorist or activist circles. Had the book been published and sold in bookshops it might even have had some intellectual or political impact. No doubt the few copies that were printed have long disappeared into the private libraries of individuals motivated, like myself, by a form of archive fever – or, more likely, were swept up and destroyed near the point of distribution, having been used as beer mats or scribbled over with telephone numbers. Twice, in September 1984 and October 1986, copies were deposited with the British Library in London, an act which seems to amount to another violation of the book's own zealous prohibition on ownership, and its hostility to 'official' institutions.

Nevertheless, it is difficult to see the book as anything other than extremely successful on its own terms; it is this consistency that makes the text fascinating and exemplary as an unstinting critique of reification. Despite claiming to operate purely on the level of theory, *Life and its Replacement with a Dull Reflection of Itself* seems on a first reading to have little of the reflexivity or the philosophical circumspection which characterize other treatments of the theme of reification; indeed the book is quite unambivalent as to the malignity of the phenomenon, the possibility of its dissolution, and its effective simultaneity with, variously, commodification, representation, mediation, capitalism, culture and modernity – all claims which are treated with caution and even scepticism in most of the recent literature.

Theory is justified in the book on the grounds that it is only ever 'a hypothesis, never fully proven, always open to debate', and is thereby located in opposition to ideology – 'a constraint, in which people are fitted to ideas'.[5] Like Georg Simmel's quest in *The Philosophy of Money* for a 'science of a more fundamental nature', the goal of which would be to think 'without preconditions' – or like that most forceful apologia for theory in modern writing, Adorno's essay 'Resignation' – the defence of theory in the Pleasure Tendency theses is organized around the concept of reification; indeed this is true of the book as a whole.[6] Theory permits one to think outside the purely reified categories within which, alone, action is possible. It enables us to transcend the binary, economistic relation between self and other; it offers another view of life than the prevailing, commonsensical one. It is for this reason that, despite its sustained critique of Christianity and organized religion, *Life and its Replacement with a Dull Reflection of Itself* cannot be described as a materialist or secular text; for at every point it affirms the possibility, even the inevitability, of something which doesn't exist.

The book opens with a section, entitled 'That Which Cannot be Said', which is concerned with the question of what the future will be like; it is with iteration, we are told in explanation of the heading, that 'falsification' begins.[7] Thus, only clues may be offered as to how this future will be. A time is anticipated

> when merely taking a walk outside tickles the pleasure centre. When the deluge of falsified experience recedes, when the few books which are still read are those which stimulate debate, enhance learning and inspire action. When all life is lived intensely, or passes exactly as one would wish. When the parasite Art is no more.[8]

Throughout the book, as here, representation and mediation are equated with falsification; representation is talked of as anathema ('once represented, something is dead').[9] The text is thus susceptible to a basic deconstructive reading which – as in the critique of the speech/writing opposition undertaken in Derrida's 'Plato's Pharmacy' or *Of Grammatology* – would seek to show how the hostility towards representation, and the privileging of the 'natural', presuppose a metaphysical logic which the necessity of writing has always already disrupted. There is no Eden preceding or violated by representation. Signification itself is the moment of violence which precedes and underpins all claims to truth, schemes for perpetual peace, or moments of transcendence. The deconstructive critique would thereby show up the utopian vision of the Pleasure Tendency theses to be constituted by such violence, and inseparable from it. The end of violence, the projection of a world free of 'parasites' or 'falsification', the longed-for moment at which the Economy is 'surpassed' – these Messianic anticipations perpetuate a foundationalist illusion, and are inseparable from the very violence which they anathematize.

Yet all of this, arguably, is presupposed in the hyperbole with which the text performs its social critique. *Life and its Replacement with a Dull Reflection of Itself* – very like Valerie Solanas's *SCUM Manifesto* in this respect[10] – *quotes* the ultra-leftist discourse it adopts, evacuating its own 'metaphysical' terrain in the very moment that it marks it out. This discursive lack of innocence extends through the book's representation of the range of recognizable political identifications. In the end, every external subject position is left untenable by the Pleasure Tendency theses. 'Anarchists', 'Communists' and 'Socialists' are all criticized explicitly.[11] Contemporary femininity is dismissed as a violation, in some unspecified sense, of 'the essence of womanhood'.[12] The Greenham Common anti-nuclear protesters are attacked as 'the female face of authority' and 'a willing army of dupes'.[13] Anti-racism is denounced as part of a 'progressive' agenda whiningly fixated upon 'the fringes of normal society'.[14] Liberal causes are characterized as 'Issues' – artificially-nurtured Social

Problems by means of which people are bestowed a pre-packaged identity, and diverted from the singular task of 'superseding the Economy'.[15] Positive identity is itself a form of commodification, a symptom of the process by which Economic Organization 'creeps nearer and nearer to the soul itself.'[16] There is no site of stable identification prescribed in the whole book – yet the critique of identity, like the hostility towards 'officialese', representation and every conceivable institution, is articulated throughout with a certitude that invites speculation about its subjective political allegiances.

In fact, it is the absence of positive identification which bespeaks the true subject position of the text, and which is symptomatic, I would claim, of the immense social and political significance of anxiety *per se* in the present moment. Despite its anonymity, not to mention its studied tone of objectivity and incorruptibility, *Life and its Replacement with a Dull Reflection of Itself* is an expression of primarily subjective dissatisfaction, the pathos of which is most acute in the dreamlike speculations about the future and the descriptions of moments of pleasure seized from the interstices of a life of 'drudgery'.[17] At times a certain vulnerability and bewilderment emerges from the furious polemic – usually at moments when the theses turn their attention to the question of what lies behind the veneer, at which point the unnameability and intangibility of its antagonists draws forth a howl of impotence: 'We punch into thin air. Who is to blame? Where do we strike first? It's no accident that no one has come up with the right answer . . . Not quite comprehending, we are like the fly caught up in the spider's web who wriggles and wriggles . . .'[18] The one position that is maintained intact by the text, represented without ambiguity or any hint of deflating pastiche, is that which is imputable from this expression of subjective anxiety. Suddenly it becomes apparent that the freedom of the text from 'reflexivity' or 'circumspection' is a rhetorical illusion. Instead the reflexivity, self-doubt and circumspection of the Pleasure Tendency theses is the most convincing and forceful thematic of the book as a whole.

While seeming initially vulnerable to a deconstructive critique, *Life and its Replacement with a Dull Reflection of Itself* manifests a supreme indifference to that critique, an indifference which in effect overcomes it. The vehicle of this transporting indifference is the *consciousness* of the subject of late capitalism itself, an irrefutable entity which simply cannot be deconstructed; its continuing operation – notwithstanding the logic which suggests that transcendence is a metaphysical illusion – may be traced through innumerable works of art and literature. Once the theme of anxiety is introduced in the Pleasure Tendency theses, they return to it repeatedly, as to a motif which presupposes and establishes consciousness as a third term *mediating* the relationship between self and other. Consciousness is distinct from both subject and object, and yet, in the moment of overcoming, promises to absorb and transform both. Consider the following proposition, from the opening section of the book:

> The defenders of the old illusions are only cleverer than their predecessors. Like proprietors of a giant theatre, their show may come ever closer to what the audience are feeling, but the separation between the two only gets greater because of it. Only the *form* of the relationship between life and its representation is left to be apprehended by the senses.[19]

What is signalled here – in the gap between subject and object, between perception and phenomenon – is precisely the anxiety towards the disjunction, a feeling which, as Kierkegaard, Freud and Sartre all make clear in their definitions of anxiety, is distinguished (from *fear*, for example) by having *no identifiable object*. Anxiety lies outside the economy of subject and object; it therefore looks forward – merely by its existence, its identifiability, by one's experience of it – to a nullification of that economy. This becomes clear in the proposition which immediately follows: 'The observer can see less and less to complain about. All he feels is the agony as the gulf within him widens.'[20] Here the anxiety towards reification is expressed in concentrated form; it is the feeling observable in Melville's Captain Ahab fulminating against the gods, in Proust's childhood narrator interrogating phenomena for their aesthetic significance, in Swann's torment over the authenticity of his relationship with Odette, and in Fichte's solipsistic retreat into a picture-book reality in *The Vocation of Man*. It is to this anxiety, furthermore, that the Pleasure Tendency theses look for a remedy: 'The almost illegal dissatisfaction that the ordinary, fairly well-off person feels – which is kept a public secret – must also be a force which will carry humanity to its next stage.[21] Indeed, the book's definition of the Pleasure Tendency as 'civilization dreaming', which appears as a slogan on the back cover, further implies that the solution is to be found, in the first instance at least, in consciousness. In a section entitled 'Civilization' we read: 'We can only dream and plan for a tomorrow of wide, quiet streets, magnificent buildings, civilization in a thousand diverse ways.'[22] One would be right to see an implicit conservatism beneath the iconoclasm; *Life and its Replacement with a Dull Reflection of Itself*, for all its counter-cultural baggage (the anonymity, the manifestive tone, the unorthodox distribution), is 'Eurocentric' and certainly nostalgic in places.[23] What is more interesting, however, is to see this text primarily as an articulation of mainstream, 'petty bourgeois' anxieties, but in a counter-cultural register which is unaccustomed to them and which, in turning towards them, exhibits its own anachronism. The Pleasure Tendency theses offer no practical recommendations for overcoming reification, but they dramatize the degree to which a highly theoretical, even recondite social critique has become a generalized social anxiety.

I shall discuss Kierkegaard's theory of anxiety in a later section, but it is worth briefly elaborating the best-known aspect of his definition of anxiety here: the distinction between anxiety and fear. Fear, says Kierkegaard, refers to 'something definite', whereas anxiety relates to the freedom of the individual; anxiety is 'freedom's actuality as the possibility of possibility'.[24] Sartre explains this in *Being and Nothingness* as follows: 'A situation provokes fear if there is a possibility of my life being changed from without; my being provokes anxiety to the extent that I distrust myself and my own reactions in that situation.'[25] Sartre's example is vertigo, which he says is a kind of anxiety 'to the extent that I am afraid not of falling over the precipice, but of throwing myself over.' Human anxiety is a symptom of the freedom of individuals; it is thus a form of religious – or *pre*-religious – experience in itself, a tension arising from the perception of the impossibility of the 'state of fulfillment and perfection' which the soul *nevertheless* feels to be always imminent.[26] Anxiety signifies a superfluity, an excess of individuality, in which the subjective response is far from predetermined by external circumstance; it is thus akin to what Derrida sometimes calls a situation of undecidability – yet the very existence of anxiety is also a testament to the non-deconstructibility of consciousness itself. Anxiety implies freedom, individuality. It is because we are free beings – indeterminable, in the final analysis, by objective social processes, and able to confound those processes – that we experience anxiety. For Kierkegaard this is as much as to say that the religious instinct, the capacity for transcendence, is a quality of humanity, something that exists within us, rather than a superstition which may be educated out of us, or, conversely, the intimation of a being which is by definition beyond our reach.

A political context for this 'religious' model of imminent (and immanent) possibility may be found in Frantz Fanon's insistence that consciousness is 'a process of transcendence', and his suggestive conception of 'man' as 'a yes that vibrates to cosmic harmonies.'[27] This is a premise of Fanon's work, rather than its culmination – it emerges out of the fugue of assertion and polemic in the first few pages of his first book *Black Skin White Masks* – and it tells us a lot about the nature of the reification from which Fanon wants to free colonial society. The reified, Manichaeistic relationships between black and white and between men and women in a broken world are solvable, he implies, only alongside the anxiety which constitutes and determines them. This complex arises with the forgetting of the fact that God is a being whose existence is inseparable from 'man' – that God, in Simmel's phrase, implies nothing less – or nothing more – than the 'state of fulfillment and perfection' of man. Anxiety is an expression of dissatisfaction born of the *economy* of self and other, which sees black and white – and, more fundamentally, man and God – as perpetually ranged against each other: 'Uprooted, pursued, baffled,' writes Fanon, 'doomed to watch the dissolution of the truths that he has worked out for himself one after another, [man] has to give up projecting onto the world *an antinomy that co-exists with him*.'[28] With the acceptance of that antinomy, in other words, the predominance of the objective world ceases to detract from the self; objective culture becomes instead the vehicle and opportunity for the self's augmentation and completion. The tragic destiny of modern man – his continual diminution with the progress of modernity and the retreat of the gods – is overturned to become instead the journey towards realization and wholeness.

# 2

# Reification as Cultural Anxiety

The correlation between the anxiety towards reification and the knowledge that human beings inhabit a finite world, its bounds determined by the limits of visibility, may easily be reconstructed. 'As the gods are pulled down from heaven' writes René Girard, 'the sacred flows over the earth; it separates the individual from all earthly goods; it creates a gulf between him and the world of *ici-bas* far greater than that which used to separate him from the *au-delà*. The earth's surface where Others live becomes an inaccessible paradise.'[1] The 'death of God' is not simply a moment of demystification, but the inauguration of an experience of alienation between self and other, as humanity itself is elevated into the space formerly occupied by the divine. From this moment on, the human individual projects everything which detracts from the perfectibility of the self onto everything other than the self – the world, progress, or modernity – rather than seeing this idea of perfectibility in relation to the promise of a world to come. This gulf which opens up between self and world inaugurates the anxiety towards reification.

In the course of this work I have sought to uncover a vital distinction between dualistic or 'secular' models of thought – which deny, as a foundational principle, the existence of anything beyond the immediate relation of self and other, of interiority and exteriority, of man and nature – and a triadic, dialectical or 'religious' model, according to which self and other are mediated by a third order of existence which transcends and successfully *synthesizes* both. The first is the dominant model of contemporary critical, philosophical and political thought, even when (as in post-structuralism and postcolonialism) it seeks to 'deconstruct' such binary, oppositional models; the second is the structure common to Christian, Hegelian and Marxist metaphysics, in which the anxiety generated by the economy of self and other is effectively absorbed by a significant third term: Jesus Christ, absolute knowledge, or the coming proletarian revolution. It is my contention that what is *essential* in such philosophies – the third, mediating term – is by no means obsolete; on the contrary, this third term has the greatest need of being rediscovered and/or reinvented in the present time. Indeed, the direction of the argument to be pursued here is that this triangular structure already – even *always already* – exists; that its continuation is implied in the very anxiety towards reification which I have been tracing in this book; that a transcendent third term has as much potential to make sense of modern life as its predecessors did in the past; that the failure to mediate self and other may be attributed to a cross-cultural *determination* upon a dualistic, secular metaphysic, rather than to the extinction of 'transcendence' in 'actuality'.

This is the great insight of Girard's classic study *Deceit, Desire and the Novel*, where metaphysical desire is seen to persist despite the disintegration of religious belief. 'Denial of God does not eliminate transcendency' he writes, 'but diverts it from the *au-delà* to the *en-deçà*. The imitation of Christ becomes the imitation of one's neighbour.' Thus 'envy, jealousy, and impotent hatred' towards one's peers take the place of the yearning for a relationship with God.[2] It is exactly this frustrated yearning that, analogously, lies behind the anxiety towards reification. Were we able to recover or reinvent the relationship with God, this anxiety would be radically contained, even obliterated, along with reification itself.

For Marcel Proust this triangular structure is found in the realm of aesthetic perception, a mode of thought that is not restricted to the appreciation of artworks; indeed, artworks are often presented in *À la recherche du temps perdu* as inimical to aesthetic appreciation, since they all too readily become part of the objective world – hence the sustained critique of artworks as 'elevated' but empty commodities throughout the book. For Proust the aesthetic represents a whole approach to life, comparable in weight and significance to religious belief. In 'Place-Names: The Name' he writes of aesthetic perception explicitly as a form of belief, and of the decline of this mode of perception specifically in terms of a lapse of faith. As he walks through the Bois de Boulogne, Marcel the narrator reflects:

> The idea of perfection which I had within me I had bestowed, in that other time, upon the height of a victoria, upon the raking thinness of those horses, frenzied and light as wasps on the wing . . . Alas! there was nothing now but motor-cars driven each by a moustached mechanic, with a tall footman towering by his side . . . And seeing all these new components of the spectacle, I had no longer a belief to infuse into them to give them consistency, unity and life; they passed before me in a desultory, haphazard, meaningless fashion, containing in themselves no beauty which my eyes might have tried, as in the old days, to recreate.[3]

Here the aesthetic as a transcendent possibility mediating and transforming subject and object has itself become lost to consciousness. Art is an activity which depends on belief to sustain it – the belief that objects of artistic production have meaning, truth content – and belief, as I have already pointed out, is a transforming mechanism, neither purely subjective (restricted to interiority) nor purely objective (restricted to the world). Belief is simultaneously a mode of perception and of creativity, and, like aesthetic judgement, it may be neither administered nor enforced, neither ratified nor refuted.

Proust, like Girard, is aware of the inverse correlation between belief and reification – this is the significance of his reference to the 'fetishism' which survives the departure of belief, quoted earlier.[4] With the loss of the intimacy between art and truth comes the degeneration into aestheticism, into Art, or *l'art pour l'art* – a deeply anxious state of mind. The unknown but transcendent God who gives sense to life is abruptly, fatefully contained within a dead form. The anxiety towards reification – the anxiety which, incidentally, activates its theorization – arises from a secularism which sees the world in terms of a closed, *economic* relationship between self and other, according to which the alluring and seductive other is perpetually obscured by the unsatisfactory here and now. Yet the process of *theorizing* the situation of reification as such constitutes an expansion of consciousness, such that this secularism is replaced by a triangular structure and a transcendent third term that casts *everything that exists* – all theories of reification, among other things – into doubt.

We can see, again, just why the period during which Lukács was able to develop his theory of reification was so momentary – why the theory itself, as he formulated it in *History and Class Consciousness*, demanded its almost immediate repudiation. For as soon as one attains the enlarged perspective which must inform a theory of reification, one is no longer troubled by the phenomenon; the anxiety dissolves as it comes into relief as *itself* an effect of reified consciousness. Reification is the product of a dualistic philosophy for which every success in the objective world has a corresponding effect of detraction in the subjective one. With the rejection of this dualism, both the anxiety towards reification and, consequently, the theory itself become purely and simply obsolete.

In their book *The Social Construction of Reality*, an extraordinarily forthright title which accurately reflects the manifest humanism of the text itself, Peter Berger and Thomas Luckmann take a less reflexive (less dialectical) view of the concept. Reification, they write,

> is the apprehension of the products of human activity as if they were something other than human products – such as facts of nature, results of cosmic laws, or manifestations of divine will. Reification implies that man is capable of forgetting his own authorship of the human world, and, further, that the dialectic between man, the producer, and his products is lost to consciousness.[5]

Berger and Luckmann acknowledge that reification is 'a modality of consciousness'. In their lexicon, however, 'consciousness' denotes a sphere of activity which is entirely independent of the world – which *confronts* the world, indeed, as selfhood to otherness. The alienation of subject and object is for them not an undesirable product of this activity of consciousness which must be corrected, but the very basis of their world view; indeed, this is confirmed in the opening remarks to their book, where 'reality' is defined in terms that, they claim, the 'man in the street' would recognize – that is to say, as 'a quality appertaining to phenomena that we recognize as having a being independent of our own volition'. Knowledge, meanwhile, is described as 'the certainty that phenomena are real and that they possess specific characteristics.'[6] The presupposition of their thesis is the *fact* of man (implicitly his male, European, 'modern' exemplars) as the summit of possible conscious experience, a being entirely responsible for building the conceptual world around him, and who is required only to acknowledge his authorship of the world in order to experience wholeness and completion. This 'fact', it doesn't need pointing out, is for Berger and Luckmann exterior to human consciousness; anxiety has no place in the Berger-Luckmann thesis, which takes for granted man's usurpation of the place of God as a progressive stage of modernity.

Berger and Luckmann are explicit in their opposition to the relation of the *ici-bas* and the *au-delà* signposted by Girard: for them the idea of another order of existence, of which this world is but an imitation, is precisely an example of reified perception; thus (they write), 'the entire order of society [is] conceived of as . . . a microcosm reflecting the macrocosm of the total universe as made by the gods. Whatever happens "here below" is but a pale reflection of what takes place "up above".'[7] Here, the theorist of reification effectively abandons the aspiration towards a truly 'dereified' society (the transcendent possibility in the name of which the Marxist critique of reification is conducted) under the auspices of a more rigorous materialism. For Berger and Luckmann, 'dereification' involves nothing so radical as a projected new world or a revolution in structures of thought, but is achieved simply by abandoning the false promises and goals of a 'Messianic' consciousness, whether these are articulated in Christian or Marxist revolutionary terms; and this abandonment, of course, is facilitated, rather than impeded, by capitalist modernity. For Berger and Luckmann the dereification of the world is equivalent to the process of secularization – 'a comparatively late development in history and in any individual biography'.[8] This dereifying process is relatively untroubled and unproblematic; Berger writes elsewhere of how the increased contact between different cultures in late capitalism is similarly dereifying, as it leads to a crisis in 'knowlege' and a further weakening in 'the reified fixedness of the old world'.[9] It seems irrefutable that a theory of reification which ignores its status as, primarily, anxiety, is destined to reproduce the alienation of subject and object at every point in its analysis.

Marriage is both the archetypal self–other relationship and, for several theorists of reification (including Berger and Luckmann), the epitome of a reified institution, in which the other (the wife, presumably) becomes the source of a detraction from the (inevitably male) self. In this example, assert Berger and Luckmann, an ongoing human production is reified 'as an imitation of divine acts of creativity, as a universal mandate of natural laws, as the necessary consequence of biological or psychological forces, or, for that matter, as a functional imperative of the social system'.[10] The third term constitutes in each case the projection of human phenomena into a non-human or superhuman dispensation – whether in the less specific form of a natural (or simply 'objective') order of things, or the more specific invocation of the divine cosmos. Thus the 'shudder of metaphysical dread' felt by an illiterate peasant couple being married is, for Berger and Luckmann, a 'reifying' rather than a dereifying experience, a falsification of the objective world in which the attitudes of the subjects themselves are immaterial, rather than a subjective–objective liberation from institutional tyranny.

Adorno, writing almost contemporaneously, provides a brilliant corrective to this view, although he is concerned here not with the religious but the artistic aura: 'If through the demythologization of the world consciousness freed itself from the ancient shudder, that shudder is permanently reproduced in the historical antagonism of subject and object.'[11] The 'shudder of metaphysical dread', in other words, may be replaced, qua metaphysical shudder, only by a relation that is infinitely more 'reifying' and degrading than the belief in God – a belief which, not merely imaginatively, establishes God as overseer of the marriage and thus as the vehicle of a synthesis of the relation between subject and object, self and other. This transcendent 'synthesis' is no less real on account of the fact that it takes place at the level of consciousness; indeed, the *conscious* experience of the synthesis is a condition of any true mediation of subject and object. For Berger and Luckmann reification is a much less nuanced and less subtle process, amounting merely to the identification of the individual 'with his socially assigned typifications';[12] there is no apparent awareness of the extent to which such identification might be understood at the same time as *de*reification, nor of the impossiblity of deciding the arguments as to whether it is one or the other, nor of the fact that the 'autonomous individual' him- or herself is the most solid and intransigent of all reifications.

It is as an analogous development to Berger's and Luckmann's thesis that we may trace the generalization of an anxiety towards reification across contemporary culture – the expression of which almost always leaves intact the alienated subject of modern capitalism, who sees the solution in a kind of Fichtean solipsism. One might read in Sam Mendes's film *American Beauty* (1999) the proposal of a Proustian aestheticism as a solution to the reified existence which it detects everywhere in American life.[13] Indeed, the route to salvation of the film's protagonist Lester Burnham has the Proustian quality of springing from what one critic described as 'the least elevated of motives – dumbfounded desire for his daughter's 16-year-old schoolfriend'.[14] In the film's central scene Ricky Fitts, the boy next door, shows Lester's daughter Jane some footage he has shot on video of a plastic bag being blown by the wind. In what turns out to be the 'redemptive' lesson of the film, Ricky treats her to a discourse on aesthetic experience: he is fascinated, he tells her, by 'this entire life behind things . . . Sometimes there's so much beauty in the world I feel like I can't take it, and my heart is just going to cave in.' The scene, accompanied by a haunting, truth-signifying piano score, represents a yearning to see through the pasteboard mask of visible reality that is apparently further advanced, and more successful, than the tormented vision of Melville's Ahab; yet the reason that Ahab's attempt founders – the hubris of man's self-elevation to the place of God – has by no means been resolved in Mendes's film, but simply replaced by the solipsism of aesthetic perception. As both Proust and Adorno would recognize, *American Beauty* solves the problem of a commodified and administered existence by universalizing fetishism: the alienation of subject and object is preserved in a narcissistic shudder. Any redemption achieved by Proust's novel, by contrast, lies in its paradoxical refusal to accept that a merely aesthetic transfiguration is possible; the only solution is a solution beyond all available solutions.

Peter Weir's film *The Truman Show* (1998) and the Wachowski Brothers' *The Matrix* (1999) each produces the fiction of a totally reified individual (Truman Burbank and Thomas 'Neo' Anderson respectively) who is able ultimately to step out of his reified existence – Truman by opting to leave the set of the all-day television programme of which he has been the unwitting star and enter the real world at the end of the movie; Neo by unplugging from his virtual reality existence near the beginning of *The Matrix*, rebuilding his atrophied limbs and finally embracing his (hitherto imputed) role as The One, the saviour of mankind from its false existence within the artificial intelligence system called the Matrix.[15] There is considerable difference in emphasis between these films. *The Matrix* offers a more radical representation of false consciousness – a grotesque image of endless 'fields' of lymphatic capsules within which human beings are 'grown' rather than born, their conscious experience entirely manufactured in 'virtuality'. The film presents us with a chosen individual who, Christ-like, will redeem the world through his incarnation, death and resurrection, each of which takes place across the boundary between the real world and the Matrix. At the end of the film Neo refuses or is denied the possibility of a 'free' existence outside the virtual world, and returns to the Matrix to bring his message of redemption to all men and women – of 'a world without rules and controls, without borders or boundaries, a world where anything is possible' – a liberation which, of course, only applies and is only possible *within* the Matrix.[16]

*The Truman Show* locates its social critique in the figure of a single, utterly manipulated individual who, nevertheless, acts as a point of identification for the audience, and a focus for its anxieties. Truman is no redeemer – or rather, he is both redeemer and redeemed; his purity and innocence are responsible for the commercial success of the show in a world where such qualities have disappeared; but they are also what prompt his interrogation of a reality that is less substantial than he is. Like Neo, who at the moment of his 'transfiguration' as The One receives a 'vision' of the virtual world of the Matrix in digital code, Truman's transfiguration takes the form of a momentous insight into the falsity of the world around him, and of his omnipotence within that world. With sudden clarity, Truman realizes that he cannot be harmed as long as he remains in Seahaven – the fictional town, really a huge studio set, which constitutes his entire existence – and he tests this hypothesis by walking out in front of a bus, and by slapping a window-cleaner with his briefcase, both without repercussions. Like Voltaire's Candide, Truman is living in the best of all possible worlds – too perfect, it becomes apparent, as he begins to experience glitches in his reality: a malfunctioning 'weather-program', or the director's instructions to the actors and crew who surround Truman on set coming through on his car radio. *The Truman Show* presents us with a clearly identifiable 'They', a face behind the pasteboard, in the person of the television show's creator and 'mastermind', Christof. In a climactic sequence, Truman attempts to sail across the artificial 'sea', a bathetic restaging of Ahab's crazed pursuit of the white whale across the oceans of the globe in the *Pequod*. Lashed by a computer-controlled storm, Truman taunts his creator, Ahab-like: 'Is that the best you can do? You're gonna have to kill me!' The film ends with Truman's boat literally bumping up against the pasteboard backdrop of Seahaven's 'horizon'.

Critical reception of all three of these films has celebrated them in terms which confirm the preoccupation with reification, and their respective interest in containing the anxiety towards it. 'Watching *American Beauty*, we gradually realize we are seeing one man's journey towards redemption, towards remembering who he is.'[17] '*The Truman Show* is a moving exploration of creation-anxiety, of the fear and hope that in a post-Darwinian world the only beings with real power are distant public figures and malevolent unknown forces ringfencing our capacity for free will.'[18] 'The Wachowskis unveil a seedy utopia where mankind is preserved, protected and endlessly recycled by its own mega-computer. The alternative to this artificial stasis is, as usual, well beyond the wit of mortal proles.'[19] In the case of each film, however (with the possible exception of *The Matrix*),[20] the critique of reified existence stops short at a core of unreified, and unreifiable selfhood. Thus each film objectifies both reification and the liberation from reification in a way which reifies that freedom; each film attempts to disperse the prevalent anxiety by enjoining individualism, or scepticism towards 'reality', and thus celebration of their immunity from reification, upon its audience.

## 3

# On Reversibility

The conceptual poles of the methodological distinction I am trying to forge may be characterized using the metaphors of religion and secularism, as these have been outlined earlier. In what follows I shall explore, in order to open up, a 'religious' model of reification in contrast to the dominant 'secular' model which takes the concept at face value, seeing it not in terms of anxiety, primarily, but as a social 'phenomenon' associated with essentially malign developments in the objective world. This is the model that operates in Berger's and Luckmann's sociology; it informs indirectly the thematic concerns of numerous feature films made recently in Hollywood, which align reification with society and freedom with individuality; and it is reiterated by certain crude post-structuralisms which refuse the concept of reification altogether on the grounds of its implication in the discredited notions of the 'transcendental signified', the 'metaphysics of presence', the historical 'grand narrative', and the 'origin'. I want to contrast this secular usage with a 'religious' model articulated in Adorno's philosophy (particularly in his theory of aesthetics), in Lukács's writings on reification (in the later 'defence' of *History and Class Consciousness* even more explicitly than in *History and Class Consciousness* itself), in the anxiety-ridden *Life and its Replacement with a Dull Reflection of Itself*, in the premises of Lucien Goldmann's 'hidden god' thesis – but also, implicitly, in the fictional writings of Flannery O'Connor, in certain literary readings of René Girard and Giorgio Agamben,[1] and in the pseudonymous 'philosophical' and non-pseudonymous 'religious' writings of Søren Kierkegaard. None of these last-mentioned figures uses the concept of reification directly, but the versions of 'religious' thinking that are expressed and defended in their work are extremely resonant for the present discussion – so much so, in the case of Kierkegaard, that he may plausibly be read as the first theorist of reification, despite writing some years *avant la lettre*.

The most important corollary of the 'religious' model is its affirmation of the concept of reification *in the name* of something that is unreifiable – something, indeed, which is *only provisionally nameable* as 'the freedom from reification'. Thus, what is further affirmed is the necessarily reified status of the concept of reification itself, as well as of the religious metaphor as a solution to it. 'Religion' implies freedom from all reification – including, in the final analysis, from religion: this is the paradoxical cusp upon which all of Kierkegaard's religious writings are riven. The mind which sees 'religion' *per se* as an idealistic, nihilistic, metaphysical or teleological world view is a product of the reified consciousness which 'true' religiosity simply supersedes. Not only is the concept of reification implicitly 'religious' or 'idealistic' (all those critics of the concept on this basis were absolutely right); the concept itself, and the profound unhappiness of those theoretical and philosophical approaches which refuse it, attest to the *innate religiosity* of mankind and the world. This 'religiosity', however, is an immensely complex claim, implying as it does the essential *reversibility* of all concepts – not only abstractions such as religion, reification, idealism, Christianity, marriage, but also more 'concrete' concepts such as table (which Marx knew all about) or spoon (an example from *The Matrix*).[2] Reversibility implies a certain underlying assumption: that there is an other to language, something completely outside the text and inarticulable by it; that the text is as nothing, merely thinglike, in relation to this outside; and that to speak in the name of this inarticulable otherness is necessarily to elaborate, or simply to presuppose the contradictory aspect of everything that constitutes the here and now.

My reference in the case of 'table', of course, is the section on the fetishism of commodities in the first volume of *Capital*, where Marx turns the wooden table on its head at the point at which it becomes a commodity, thereby transcending its 'sensuous' existence – just as, earlier, he has stood the 'idealism' of Hegelian dialectic on its feet.[3] Indeed in *Capital* he goes further, all but imbuing the table with the power to dance 'of its own free will'.[4] It is from this section of *Capital* that Lukács's theory of reification takes its point of departure; yet it is important to realize that in neither of its configurations is Marx's table 'the right way up'. Indeed Marx insists that the table continues to stand with its feet on the ground even while, 'in relation to all other commodities, it stands on its head.' Commodity fetishism is not falsification as such, but a moment of *reification* – which implies not simply the 'petrifaction' or 'ossification' of the object but, simultaneously and far more radically, its thoroughgoing conceptual instability, its *reversibility*. With the insight that the logic of reification implies *its own reified status*, reification becomes a volatile concept which may denote mutability as well as fixity, openness as well as closure, remembering as well as forgetting, homogeneity as well as difference.

This reversibility is also true of Marx and Engels's critique of Hegelian idealism, even though the Moore and Aveling translation of *Capital* has Marx turning the dialectic 'right side up again'. This has been corrected in the most recent English version: 'It must be inverted [*umstülpen*], in order to discover the rational kernel within the mystical shell.[5] Such a process of 'inversion' of everything that exists is the true dialectical critique, not one of setting things aright. 'It is self-evident,' write Marx and Engels in *The German Ideology*, 'that "spectres", "bonds", "the higher being", "concept", "scruple", are merely the idealistic, spiritual expression, the conception apparently of the isolated individual, the image of very empirical fetters and limitations, within which the mode of production of life and the form of intercourse coupled with it move.'[6] What is also self-evident, however, is that such 'spectres' may at the same time, and to the identical degree, be the vehicle of a consciousness which has long consigned *the world as it is* – including all such spooks and spectres – to the sphere of thingitude. For Lukács the transformation from being to becoming, from fact to process, from objects to relations, a corollary of the emergence of a truly proletarian consciousness, is not a 'correction' of reality but its 'mediation'; not the replacement of one reality by another, but the dissolution of bourgeois reality itself into 'an unbroken process of its production and reproduction' – a dissolution which, incidentally, Lukács describes in terms of a reality higher than 'the empirical "facts"'.[7]

This 'higher reality' seems in no way incompatible with such definitions of God as Nicholas of Cusa's, as 'the coincidence of contradictories', or Pascal's, as the meeting point of infinity and nothingness, or Alfred Jarry's, as 'the tangential point between zero and infinity', or the Apostle John's in the Book of Revelation, as 'the Alpha and Omega, the first and the last, the beginning and the end'.[8] The essential reversibility of the concept of God is an implication both of his real existence outside language – that is to say, of the total inadequacy of all language in respect of his being – and of his inseparability from humanity itself; for he is both self and other, both the particular and the universal, both the here and now and the beyond, 'who is and who was and who is to come'.[9] God, in fact, is *the possibility of the dissolution of bourgeois reality itself*, meaning (among other things) the reversibility of every term and concept. It is easy to see that from this point of view God has very little to do with the 'Christian state', and rather more to do with the structure of dialectical thought, in both its 'idealist' and 'materialist', 'religious' and 'secular', 'Hegelian' and 'Marxian' traditions. The dialectic, properly considered, is irreducible to either pole in these respective oppositions.

Kierkegaard's last book *Attack Upon 'Christendom'*, made up of articles published in the journal *Fatherland* (*Fædrelandet*) and the ten issues of his self-published broadsheet the *Instant* (*Øieblikket*), is concerned with the reversible nature of Christianity itself. It is a text convulsed by the anxiety which runs through all his works to some degree, and which he never convincingly conquers, even though the entire corpus may be seen as a systematic engagement with this profoundly subjective experience. For Kierkegaard, at the end of his life, both of the following statements are true:

> We are Christians to such a degree that, if among us there lived a Freethinker who in the strongest terms declared that the whole of Christianity is a lie, *item* in the strongest terms declared that he was not a Christian – there is no help for him, he is a Christian; according to the law he may be punished, that is a different thing, but a Christian he is.[10]

> The truth is that not only are we not Christians but we are not so much as pagans, to whom the Christian doctrine could be preached without embarrassment; but by an illusion, a monstrous illusion ('Christendom', a Christian state, a Christian land, a Christian world), we are even prevented from becoming as receptive as the pagans were.[11]

These passages are from issues of the *Instant* dated a month apart, in June and July 1855 respectively (Kierkegaard died a few weeks after the final issue, in November of that year). Their apparent discrepancy involves not simply a distinction between 'Christendom' and Christianity, between the state religion of contemporary Denmark and that of the individual believer (although such distinctions are also implied in Kierkegaard's critique), but, far more drastically, the thoroughgoing incompatibility between the devotional life on earth and *everything which it presupposes* in the life beyond. These passages cannot be reconciled by a process of historicization – by pointing out that the institutional link between the Danish Lutheran Church and State is far less revocable than that of modern-day Christianity, for example; by reiterating that unless you were an unconverted Jew, Turk or Moslem, simply being born on Danish soil in the nineteenth century made you a Christian automatically.[12] On such grounds, however, Walter Lowrie argues that *Attack Upon 'Christendom'* represents a final lapse from dialectical thinking on the part of 'this very dialectical man'.[13] For Lowrie, the texts in the *Instant* are primarily satires, a fact which alone justifies their exaggerated, 'vigorously one-sided' view of the priesthood. Such an argument enables one to restrict the relevance of Kierkegaard's critique to the established Church of nineteenth-century Denmark, or to the merely 'consolatory' aspects of religion, rather than its 'perturbations'.[14]

On the contrary, it is quite clear from *Attack Upon 'Christendom'* that such orthodox, apparently doctrinal practices of Christianity as the wedding ceremony or the act of worship are as absurd and hypocritical as its formal paraphernalia: its vestments and sacraments, its liturgical garniture, its clergy stipends and, by association, its political quietism. Even to 'worship' God is, for Kierkegaard, to treat him as a fool, for one thereby transforms 'the God of Spirit into . . . ludicrous twaddle'.[15] Authentic Christianity has long vanished from Kierkegaard's Denmark, such that its very practice has become impossible, and the New Testament ceased to be a guide for Christian living.

On one hand then, the most urgent act for anyone wishing to become a Christian is to admit honestly 'that they are not *and will not be* [a] Christian' – this in itself is deeply paradoxical.[16] On the other hand, therefore, it is no longer possible to differentiate between what Christianity is and what it might be – between what we have and what we might one day have. Here Kierkegaard concedes that 'what we call a Christian is indeed to be a Christian'[17] – at which point the argument comes full circle. The interpretation of Christianity according to which 'we are all

Christians' – that is to say, the Christianity which saturates legal, moral and civic life in European society – is for Kierkegaard, it seems finally, the most usable, meaningful and authentic sense of the term.

The discrepancy in these two relations to the term 'Christianity' which runs through *Attack Upon 'Christendom'* is unresolvable or undecidable, yet this has nothing to do with a lapse in Kierkegaard's theoretical attention or his flagging intellectual energy, nor is it a symptom of merely 'historical' factors – the idiosyncrasies of the social and political structure in contemporary Denmark, or the location of his thought at a particular 'stage' of world history. This 'unresolvability' is also not a theological position in itself, a statement of resignation, of the kind that concludes with God's categorical 'incomprehensibility'.[18] Rather, *Attack Upon 'Christendom'* is testament to the survival of Kierkegaard's earliest philosophical innovation, the 'either/or', into his mature religious thought. A journal entry from 1853, written while he was preparing the assault on 'Christendom', illuminates the incorporation of this category into his understanding of Christianity: 'Any cause not served by either/or (but both-and also, etc.) is *eo ipso* not God's cause; yet it doesn't follow that every cause served by either/or is God's cause.'[19] Only either/or expresses the true reversibility of Christianity, and of every concept and thought; yet either/or is no resolution of or corrective to Christian orthodoxy – in fact, any such resolution would inevitably crystallize into a new doctrine, which would all too soon require its own 'corrective'.

Kierkegaard's reversible concept of Christianity demonstrates the absolute centrality of something like the concept of reification, as I have been elaborating it here, to his thinking. The most cogent statement of the link between reversibility and reification occurs in one of the last letters which Theodor Adorno wrote to Walter Benjamin, dated 29 February 1940, a response to Benjamin's essay 'On Some Motifs in Baudelaire' (which discusses Proust's distinction between *mémoire voluntaire* and *mémoire involuntaire*). Adorno writes:

> all reification is a forgetting: objects become purely thing-like the moment they are retained for us without the continued presence of their other aspects: when something of them has been forgotten. This raises the question as to how far this forgetting is one that is capable of shaping experience, which I would call epic forgetting, and how far it is a reflex forgetting . . . In this regard, I hardly need to add that there is absolutely no question for us of merely repeating Hegel's verdict upon reification here,[20] but rather of formulating a proper critique of reification, i.e. of unfolding the contradictory moments that are involved in such forgetting; or one could also say, of formulating a distinction between good and bad reification.[21]

Martin Jay explains this passage as a negotiation of two quite distinct uses of the term 'reification', each of which, on its own, fails to grasp its essence. Adorno's is a 'heterodox' use, a mediation between Lukács's 'Hegelian' usage and a posited 'Nietzschean' sense. According to Adorno, ending reification in the first sense simply leads to its perpetuation in the second;[22] in other words, reification qua ossification/petrifaction may only be *replaced* by reification qua mutability and instability. The characterization of reification as forgetting therefore needs to be qualified. Adorno mentions 'epic' forgetting and 'reflex' forgetting as a way of differentiating between 'good' and 'bad' reification – thus inverting Proust's distinction between *mémoire voluntaire* and *mémoire involuntaire*. For Proust, 'recollection' is a sensuous and involuntary mode of recalling the past, exemplified by his transporting experience with the piece of madeleine; voluntary memory, on the other hand, is the attempt to recapture the past 'intellectually', a labour which is doomed to fail since it 'preserves nothing of the past itself'.[23] *Mémoire voluntaire* is inevitably a mode of 'reflex' forgetting, implies Adorno, since it works with existing categories of thought; it thus falsifies the past in the very process of retrieving it – as when the 'memory' of past love affairs enables us to shape and recreate them in the present, abstracted from their true complexity.[24] In his early study of Proust, Samuel Beckett describes *mémoire voluntaire* as 'the application of a concordance to the Old Testament of the individual'.[25] *Mémoire involuntaire*, meanwhile, is for Proust a symbol of the indeterminacy of life, of the condition of antinomy that infuses worldly existence, and which perpetually frustrates any attempt at its conscious interpretation or transcendence. *Mémoire involuntaire*, then, is the facility by which the past reveals itself, irrespective of our attempts to evoke it. The experience is always embedded in the moment, furthermore, and is evanescent; with every additional mouthful of tea-soaked madeleine the effect is diminished. We might talk, therefore, about *mémoire involuntaire* as closely related to the experience of anxiety, the presupposition of which, as Kierkegaard describes it, is the freedom of individuals; which is to say, the possibility of effectively intervening in and changing their own lives; which is to say, the indeterminacy of human experience by objective causation; which is to say, the existence of God as, at the very least, the principle of contradiction of the world itself. The moments of transfiguring recollection in *À la recherche du temps perdu* often interrupt – or are themselves interrupted by – feelings of intense anxiety, the human experience which underpins the possibility of transfiguration and is inseparable from it. Proust's description of this experience is strongly reminiscent of the concept of anxiety as it is formulated by Kierkegaard and Sartre:

> Now I feel nothing; it has stopped, has perhaps sunk back into its darkness, from which who can say whether it will ever rise again? Ten times over I must essay the task, must lean down over the abyss. And each time the cowardice that deters us from every difficult task, every important enterprise, has urged me to leave the thing alone, to drink my tea and to think merely of the worries of today and my hopes for tomorrow, which can be brooded over painlessly.
>
> And suddenly the memory revealed itself . . .[26]

Likewise, the transportation effected in *À l'ombre des jeunes filles et fleurs* by the 'fusty smell' of a public lavatory, a 'delicious, soothing' pleasure, 'rich with a truth that was a lasting, unexplained and sure', comes hard on the heels of a moment of intense anxiety, arising out of Marcel's sense of his failure to communicate to Swann 'the purity of his intentions' and 'the goodness of his soul' in a sixteen-page personal letter. 'But perhaps', the narrator considers, 'it was simply that Swann knew that nobility is often no more than the inner aspect which our egotistical feelings assume when we have not yet named and classified them.'[27] Marcel's idea of his own inner 'goodness', and his desire for Swann's recognition, is simply a manifestation of his love for Swann's daughter Gilberte in an abstract, reified form; although what Swann has failed to realize, in Marcel's tortured speculations at least, is that this 'love' is as questionable as the 'goodness' of his soul, since it is in a state of immaturity – undifferentiated from himself, and thus alienated from 'the common experience of humanity'. Marcel's state of mind is one of profound uneasiness concerning the relation between the intangibility of inner qualities and their social *forms* – an anxiety arising directly, it would seem, from the *reversibility* of reification; for the undifferentiated (internal) 'love' and the abstracted (external) 'nobility' are equally falsifications. It is no wonder that Proust draws on a Kierkegaardian phraseology to describe his feelings: 'I was in despair' (*j'étais désespéré*).[28] It is at this point, precisely, that he experiences his moment of transporting recollection.

The indeterminacy of life, its unaccountability within the categories of conscious existence, is the reason why, as Adorno writes in his letter to Benjamin, 'our own best thoughts are invariably those that we cannot entirely think through.' Yet Adorno also questions Benjamin's willingness to see Proust's distinction as analogous to the Freudian categories of conscious and unconscious, a correlation which would suggest that the experiences of *mémoire voluntaire* and *mémoire involuntaire* are *qualitatively* different – along with those of forgetting and remembering, and of reification and dereification. For Adorno the concept of reification presupposes, rather, a 'dialectical theory of forgetting', meaning that these concepts need to be elaborated as truly reversible. Forgetting is as much a foundation of *mémoire involuntaire* as of its contrary, a point that must be incorporated into Benjamin's analysis, Adorno tells him, if it is to acquire 'universal social potential'.[29]

In *American Beauty*, Ricky describes his aesthetic philosophy to Lester in terms of remembering: 'Video's a poor excuse I know. But it helps me remember. I need to remember.' Ricky's aestheticism undoubtedly disrupts 'everyday consciousness', the logic of the 'ipso facto' as Homi Bhabha calls it;[30] yet Ricky's voyeuristic relation to the world – materialized through the lens of his camera – is a deeply fetishistic and thus deeply reifying activity. The video sequences of a plastic bag in the wind or a dead bird on the college lawn represent a total suspension of history and context.[31] At what point on the continuum between remembering and forgetting does the disruption of everyday consciousness become politically and psychologically damaging? Is it possible to say that disruption of the 'ipso facto' will eventually draw the individual into a domain of subjectivist isolation – or that, conversely, such disruption is a precondition and a guarantee of subjective, political liberation? Is there a point at which remembering is completely subsumed by forgetting, and another at which remembering and forgetting fall into categorical separation?

In fact the relation between remembering and forgetting, or between *mémoire voluntaire* and *mémoire involuntaire*, should be conceived neither as an opposition nor as an economy. Rather, all remembering is *necessarily* a forgetting, and vice versa – this is what Adorno means when he writes of 'the contradictory moments that are involved in such forgetting'. Memory is a reversible concept *par excellence*; its operation in *À la recherche du temps perdu* is characterized as such by Samuel Beckett in an image which anticipates Gayatri Spivak's 'homoeopathic' elaboration of the *pharmakon*: memory, he writes, is 'a clinical laboratory stocked with poison and remedy, stimulant and sedative'.[32] We need to bear in mind that even this 'reversibility' of remembering and forgetting is a symptom of reification, a necessarily flawed attempt to make sense of the world this side of Paradise. In Kierkegaard's *Either/Or*, it is among the papers of 'A', the worldly advocate of the 'aesthetic' life, that we find the assertion that memory and forgetting are identical, not in the 'ethically' motivated responses of his critic 'B', Judge Vilhelm.[33]

The relationship between attaining to Paradise and the duality of memory and forgetting is dramatized by Dante in the final cantos of the *Purgatorio*, where the poet tells of his first encounter with Beatrice prior to his passage through the heavenly spheres. His admission into the final sphere is conditional upon a double immersion, in the rivers of Lethe and Eunoë respectively; the first erases all memory of sin, while the second restores the memory of one's good deeds.[34] This representation of the contradictory aspects of redemption might be read in terms of Adorno's distinction between good and bad reification; yet we can amplify this somewhat. Drinking from the waters of Lethe, notes Mark Musa, 'takes away the *emotional* memory of sin';[35] in other words, Lethe removes the anxiety which infuses worldly life by casting *everything that exists* in the light of the imminent revolution, or revelation. This event constitutes a third term, transcending and nullifying the world, or in any case inaugurating its reversibility – the form in which, prior to its revelation, we are able to glimpse the future. For Kierkegaard's 'A', reversibility is presented as the 'skilfully achieved identity' of forgetting and memory, and 'the Archimedean point with which one lifts the whole world'.[36] This dialectical critique of the present is equivalent to the immersion of Dante's Pilgrim in the waters of Lethe, and it represents a first stage in the mediation of reality, a symbolic annihilation of existing conditions comparable to the 'ruthless criticism of everything existing' imagined in Marx's famous letter to Ruge.[37] This process may also be described precisely as the provisional mobilization of the concept of reification.

Eunoë, a secondary immersion, signals the passage into the promised land. Eunoë restores the memory of one's good deeds, or the possibility of meaning once the anxiety towards meaning has been dispelled. The waters of Eunoë are primarily redemptive; they symbolize the moment at which the moment of forgetting is itself forgotten, a gesture of faith in the possibility of a society unimaginable from the point of view of the present. Drinking from Eunoë is an act in which the concept of reification is subjected to its own critique, and thereby transcended. If *History and Class Consciousness* represents Lukács's discovery of Lethe, his later renunciation of the book – commonly reckoned to have taken place in the mid-1920s, articulated most clearly in the 1967 preface to the book, but in fact, as I have argued earlier, all but simultaneous with it – represents his libation from the waters of Eunoë. In reality, the moments of forgetting and remembering – the immersions in Lethe and Eunoë – are always simultaneous; it is significant that Canto 28 of the *Purgatorio* reveals the two rivers to have a single source. Their simultaneity is captured in the Hegelian concept of *aufheben* (Kierkegaard's Danish equivalent is *ophæve*), which expresses both negation and preservation – the identity (or reversibility) of remembering and forgetting. (One might speak alternatively of a deconstruction reconceived as redemption, a methodology in which the categories of deconstructive critique – undecidability, aporia, trace – are taken as affirmative of the utter thingliness of everything that exists in respect of what is possible. Derrida writes famously, *contra* Lacan, that 'a letter can always not arrive at its destination'. Yet this is the falsest possible formula of the range of possibilities for any given letter. It would be far truer to say, for example, that 'a letter will never not have arrived at its destination'; or even – Lacan's original statement – that 'a letter always arrives at its destination'.[38])

The two moments of Lethe and Eunoë are non-dissociable therefore; liberation from anxiety will never be total until we have built a society free of reification, and vice versa. It may be that this simultaneous freedom from anxiety and from reification will never come to pass. It may be that there will never be a revolution, that the 'proletariat' will never pass from a condition of imputedness to one of actuality. This argument is immaterial however – literally so; for the concept 'never' is one of those which pass into oblivion the moment one takes a draught from the waters of Lethe. 'Never' is a reification, a spectre; this is obvious as soon as one begins to think about time in dialectical rather than teleological or ontological terms. As a dialectic, the moment and the eternal are inseparable, just as the particular and the universal, or the individual and the race are inseparable. Throughout *The Concept of Anxiety* Kierkegaard stresses the gravity of the situation of the person who thinks in such reified categories; his example is the inquisitive individual who dares wonder what would have happened if Adam hadn't sinned – a curiosity which implies both the alienation of the questioner from the sins of the race, and a reified notion of time itself. 'He *sins* who lives only in the moment as abstracted from the eternal', writes Kierkegaard.[39] The same could be said of those reactionary thinkers who ask whether the failure of the international proletarian revolution doesn't invalidate the Marxist theory of history, or those earnest 'revolutionaries' who see the division of labour, say, or the moment of primitive accumulation as the root of our common predicament, a Fall located in the distant past – each of which is elevated upon a sinful, reified conception of time and the separation of subject and object. Certainly, 'never' is reversible into 'always', such that they are in fact identical: thus the simultaneous freedom from anxiety and from reification *may always* come to pass; there *may always* be a revolution; the proletariat *may always* be at the point of embracing its historical identity. Redemption works forwards as well as backwards, as Walter Benjamin knew well – but these categories are in any case identical.

★

# 4

# The Threatened Intimacy of Creation: Flannery O'Connor

The state of innocence, writes Kierkegaard in *The Concept of Anxiety*, is not something that existed once, only to be annulled, nor is it something that may be *recovered* through the process of redemption. Rather, innocence is created at the same moment that it is annulled; in the Fall, innocence 'comes into existence as that which it was before being annulled [*ophævet*] and which is now annulled.'[1] This essential reversibility of the concept of innocence is opposed to a dualistic idea of the Fall as an event located in the distant, irrevocable past which divides the history of the world in two. Such an understanding is 'sinful', says Kierkegaard, since it approaches the Fall in a contemplative or 'aesthetic' attitude; this perception is thus thoroughly alienated from its own implication in the sinfulness of the world.

The American Catholic novelist and short story writer Flannery O'Connor makes a similar distinction between her own understanding of 'the central Christian mystery' and the 'Manichaean' perception of the 'average Catholic reader', who tries to separate nature and grace, the here and now and the beyond, as much as possible. Her 1957 essay 'The Church and the Fiction Writer' is a defence of art as an attitude of humility 'in the face of what-is', and of the writer's role as that of teasing out the presence of grace 'as it appears in nature'. Fiction, she writes, 'should reinforce our sense of the supernatural by grounding it in concrete, observable reality.'[2] The Manichaean vision, by contrast, sees the natural and the supernatural as diametrically opposed.

A sophisticated concept of reification, associated with received notions of the relation between sin and redemption, can be shown to inform the thought of both Kierkegaard and Flannery O'Connor. Thus O'Connor identifies two literary effects of the reified perception of nature. The first, sentimentality, is the result of the idealized collapse of nature and innocence, in which the latter is 'overemphasized' to such a degree that it becomes its opposite, cut off from grace entirely. 'We lost our innocence in the Fall', contests O'Connor,

> and our return to it is through the Redemption which was brought about by Christ's death and by our slow participation in it. Sentimentality is a skipping of this process in its concrete reality and an early arrival at a mock state of innocence, which strongly suggests its opposite.[3]

The second effect of the reification of nature in literature is pornography, the result of an alienated perception of sexuality as so disconnected from 'its meaning in life' as to become 'an experience for its own sake'.[4] This idea of nature as 'obscene' is as misguided as its sentimental idealization. Works of literature which offend and scandalize, O'Connor insists, may be just as 'permeated with a Christian spirit' as those that do not.[5] The question is not whether the work itself is pornographic, but whether its readers are 'equipped' to read such books in the first place; O'Connor's argument is directed against those Catholics who demand that 'the writer limit, on the natural level, what he allows himself to see' in order to free up his imagination for the task of proving the truth of the Faith.[6] For O'Connor it is the ability to see the grace of God in immediate reality, seeping from the pasteboard mask itself, that constitutes a life filled to the brim with Christian spirit. One can see that O'Connor's artistic and critical approach is one of *mediation*, in which received notions of the natural and the supernatural are inverted and recast in the light that emanates from the will of God.

On the face of it, her novel *The Violent Bear It Away* represents the distinction between the 'secular' and the 'religious' starkly and unambiguously. The novel tells the story of Francis Marion Tarwater, a boy brought up in solitude deep in the American South by his great-uncle Mason Tarwater, a self-styled religious prophet. The thematic opposition which structures the novel, and in which the boy Tarwater is caught for most of it, is between old Tarwater's extreme, eccentric Christianity and the atheistic rationalism of his nephew, a schoolteacher named Rayber and the brother of the boy's dead mother, from whom the old man 'rescued' Tarwater as a baby, baptizing him and carrying him off to his backwoods property in Powderhead, a clearing in Tennessee, to bring up 'according to the truth'.[7]

At one level *The Violent Bear It Away* presents the Tarwaters' unorthodox Christianity as a solution to the problem of reification, thereby reversing the prevalent 'materialist' view of religion as the epitome of reified consciousness. O'Connor's view of the schoolteacher, which builds in intensity over the course of her novel, is that it is his secularism, rather than the apparently deranged religion of the Tarwaters, which constitutes reified consciousness – a view deeply bound up with her stated conviction that Rayber in *The Violent Bear It Away* is at least motivated by the Devil, if not quite identifiable with him.[8] As the great-uncle says to Tarwater early on in the novel: 'I saved you to be free, your own self! . . . and not a piece of information inside his head! If you were living with him, you'd be information right now, you'd be inside his head, and what's furthermore, . . . you'd be going to school.' A page or so later the narrator ventriloquizes Tarwater's own thoughts: 'If the school teacher had got hold of him, right now he would have been in school, one among many, indistinguishable from the herd, and in the schoolteacher's head, he would be laid out in parts and numbers.'[9]

This view of education as falsification is a well rehearsed position within Marxist analyses of ideology, particularly in the Althusserian tradition. Étienne Balibar makes the connection explicitly between education as a process of ideological 'interpellation' and violence: 'Any rudimentary process of education is a way of integrating the individual into the structure of hegemony . . . It not only "normalizes" its subjects, but also constructs their individuality by making them the bearers of society's values and ideals.'[10] Balibar is wrong, however, when he compares the ideological function of the educational state apparatus to 'religious conversion', if only because the governing assumptions of these two experiences are quite different. Whereas secular education is founded upon the false premise of a rationally comprehensible and perfectible world, and thus on the possibility of the removal of violence from it, religion is predicated upon the *heteronomy* of the truth of the world from the various categories which the world puts forward to make sense of it – that is to say, on the irreducibility of the violence necessary to create the world anew, or (again), the discrepancy between the devotional life and everything that it presupposes in the life beyond. 'Education' commits the individual to a set of worldly categories which, in claiming to 'enlighten' or liberate from 'illusion', fetter him or her to the world as it actually is. Religious conversion, on the contrary, is an experience analogous to the necessary violence of removing violence from the world – what Balibar describes (using the dialectical term *Gewalt*) as a violence which includes 'permanently intertwined with it . . . a glimpse of another world, another reality'[11] – much more so than to the worldly perpetration of ideological violence on the subjectivities of individuals.

O'Connor's awareness of the intimate but complex relation between violence and redemption is apparent from the title of her novel, taken from a passage in Matthew's gospel which (in the Douay-Rheims version) appears as the novel's epigraph: 'From the days of John the Baptist until now, the Kingdom of Heaven suffereth violence, and the violent bear it away.'[12] The passage is fascinating in itself, given that it is concerned with the arrival of the 'kingdom of heaven' in the person of Jesus, the moment when the law and the prophets are fulfilled, and with the violence which defines and characterizes that arrival. John the Baptist is a transitional figure who, although the greatest of men born up until that moment, is himself excluded from the kingdom; thus Jesus says in the preceding verse: 'Truly, I say to you, among those born of women there has risen no one greater than John the Baptist; yet he who is least in the kingdom of heaven is greater than he.'[13] John is the herald of the new order, but his vision and quality of understanding is entirely of the old.

This revolutionary situation is steeped in violence – like the colonial society analysed in Frantz Fanon's *The Wretched of the Earth*, and the age of 'absolute sinfulness' diagnosed in Lukács's *Theory of the Novel*. It is also a society in the grip of intense religious fervour and anxiety, in which the abstinence of John the Baptist and the appetites of Jesus Christ are equally causes of the people's suspicion.[14] All conventional values are in turmoil, or in the process of being reinvented. No passage illustrates this more than the Sermon on the Mount, several chapters earlier in Matthew's gospel, where the kingdom of heaven is introduced as a dispensation which inverts all norms and received wisdoms, from the opening 'beatitudes' – according to which the hungry shall be satisfied, the reviled rewarded, and the meek inherit the earth – up until the moment when Jesus enjoins his followers to 'Love your enemies and pray for those who persecute you'.[15] This is a transvaluation of values which is emulated rather than subverted by the spirit of reversibility of Kierkegaard's *Attack Upon 'Christendom'*.

For Flannery O'Connor, violence itself has a 'homoeopathic' or 'reversible' quality – a characteristic, as we have seen, of all theoretical analyses which subscribe explicitly or implicitly to the concept of reification. Violence, she said in 1963, is 'the extreme situation that best reveals what we are essentially, . . . a force which can be used for good or evil, and among other things taken by it is the kingdom of heaven.'[16] For O'Connor, violence is a quality specific to a revolutionary or emancipatory condition; her rhetoric recalls Fanon's paeans to the truth-telling, even 'cleansing' qualities of violence in *The Wretched of the Earth*. 'The man in the violent situation,' says O'Connor, 'reveals those qualities least dispensable in his personality, those qualities which are all he will have to take into eternity with him'.[17] She is referring to her story 'A Good Man is Hard to Find', about a criminal psychopath calling himself The Misfit, who slaughters a grandmother and her family in cold blood; but the remarks illuminate what is so fascinating about her novel *The Violent Bear It Away* for thinking about the relationship between religion and reification. For O'Connor, violence is associated with the anxiety of a world in suspension – a world, that is to say, in wait for the Messiah who will clarify everything. The world depicted in *The Violent Bear It Away* is that transitional world which *is* life on earth, shrunken to a few square miles in the American South over a few hot, timeless weeks in 1952.

The schoolteacher Rayber is perhaps the most troubled character in O'Connor's novel. Having, like Tarwater, been 'rescued' from his parents and baptized by the old man at a young age, and been 'rescued' from Powderhead in turn by his father, a life insurance salesman, the adult Rayber is set upon exorcizing the demon of 'superstition' that old Tarwater introduced into him. For much of the novel, which opens with the death of the great-uncle, the struggle between Rayber and Tarwater seems to signify a tension between secularism and religion. Each of these characters, however, is an entanglement of anxiety; neither regards his designated identity with anything like the old man's level of conviction.

Rayber aestheticizes old Tarwater, an attitude which characterizes the magazine article he writes about him. 'Uncle, you're a type that's almost extinct!' he tells him;[18] yet Rayber is beset by moments of deep uncertainty towards his own rationalism. For Kierkegaard, anxiety is a sign of perfection in human beings; neither beasts nor angels experience anxiety, and both are therefore 'less perfect than man'.[19] Once the metaphysical faculty has been introduced it is there for good – this is also the logic of Kierkegaard's insistence that 'we are all Christians'. Rayber tells his uncle: 'You infected me with your idiot hopes, your foolish violence. I'm not always myself, I'm not al . . .' and he breaks off, belatedly recovering his dignity.[20] As the old man reflects in relation to Rayber: 'Good blood flows in his veins . . . And good blood knows the Lord and there ain't a thing he can do about having it. There ain't a way in the world he can get rid of it.'[21] There is certainly something fervent about Rayber's resolution to 'save' Tarwater from his great-uncle's legacy; when he turns his glistening eyes upon the boy in the heat of his proselytizing rationalism he takes on the aspect of a 'fanatical country preacher'.[22] Rayber's atheism has the quality of something determined upon, rather than a system of belief he is at all at ease with.

Tarwater's consciousness, meanwhile, is compelled by an 'either/or' that is Kierkegaardian in its severity. Is he really a prophet, as his great-uncle told him, and as the 'silence' which surrounds him seems to insist? Alternatively, was his great-uncle deluded, as Rayber believes, and as the diabolical voice in Tarwater's head assures him? Which, of his uncle or his great-uncle, inhabits the real world? Which is his saviour? This process of interrogation reaches its most intense and its most concrete stage with the question which weighs upon Tarwater towards the end of the book: should he baptize Rayber's 'idiot child' Bishop – the mission old Tarwater enjoined upon him – or drown him?

In *Either/Or* Kierkegaard formulates the difference between the ethical and the aesthetic life not as a choice between good and evil, but as the distinction between choosing and the failure to choose: 'someone who lives aesthetically does not choose, and someone who, once the ethical has become apparent to him, chooses the aesthetic, does not live in the aesthetic sphere for he sins and comes under the category of the ethical, even if his life must be described as *un*ethical.'[23] Tarwater's dilemma is whether to abandon his 'vocation' and enter the world, or abandon the world and take up his mission, condemning himself thereby to the 'silence' of the elect. Merely deciding, however, irrespective of his choice, will take him to a spiritual stage beyond that of Rayber, whose defining characteristic is an inability either to act or to choose. As Tarwater tells the reception woman at the lodge by the little lake, the setting for the novel's climactic episode:

'You got to show you're not going to do one thing by doing another. You got to make an end of it. One way or another.'[24] If Tarwater drowns the boy, he will certainly be unable to baptize him; if he baptizes him, the inner voice tells him, he'll be baptizing people for the rest of his life. The real choice in life is between choosing and not choosing; Rayber's weakness is not his having chosen wrongly, but his failure to choose at all – or, more accurately, his desire to return to the stage prior to his 'conversion' by old Tarwater, a stage in which the 'choice' between good and evil appears merely irrelevant, a superstitious anachronism.

The opposite of belief, as I have said earlier, is not atheism but agnosticism. It is this that Rayber is guilty of, despite his espousal of atheistic principles; for these are revealed to be spurious simply by his anxiety-ridden and – from the 'ethical' point of view – *sinful* yearning for the state of what Kierkegaard calls 'spiritlessness'.[25] 'To wish that sin had not entered the world is to take humanity back to something less perfect', says Kierkegaard's ethical representative ('B' – Judge Vilhelm) in *Either/Or*.[26] This makes sense in the light of *The Violent Bear It Away*, in which good and evil are shown to be dialectically interpenetrated; one cannot yearn for a world without sin without yearning for a world without the good either. Rayber is shown already to be 'in' the good by his wish to get out of it. Even sin is higher than innocence, which is only inaugurated alongside it. This interpretation is bolstered by an observation which O'Connor made after the novel's publication; among writers of fiction, O'Connor is almost uniquely forthcoming about the theology which underpins her work: 'Most of us have learned to be dispassionate about evil, to look it in the face and find, as often as not, our own grinning reflections with which we do not argue, but good is another matter. Few have stared at that long enough to accept the fact that its face too is grotesque, that in us the good is something under construction.'[27]

In 'A Good Man is Hard to Find' The Misfit explains himself to the grandmother, moments before he shoots her throught the chest, as follows:

> If [Jesus] did what He said, then it's nothing for you to do but thow [sic] away everything and follow Him, and if He didn't, then it's nothing for you to do but enjoy the few minutes you got left the best way you can – by killing somebody or burning down his house or doing some other meanness to him . . . I wisht I had of been there . . . It ain't right I wasn't there because if I had of been there I would of known. Listen lady, . . . If I had of been there I would of known and I wouldn't be like I am now.[28]

In a situation of metaphysical doubt, the violence of The Misfit establishes a degree of certainty, in the immediate physical world at least. For the Tarwaters likewise it is the ability to act, as against Rayber's impotence and indecision, that confirms their real freedom. The line between the ugly, violent actions of The Misfit and the supposedly divine inspiration of the Tarwaters is extremely thin; perhaps it doesn't exist at all. In fact their proximity is evidence of the essential *reversibility* of good and evil, of the sacred and the profane, and of their allied hostility to the deadening, reifying influence of the Raybers of the world. O'Connor once commented that the character of The Misfit was meant, in some other story perhaps, to become a prophet;[29] certainly The Misfit and the Tarwaters are equally removed from Rayber's ineffectual rationalism.

The passage in Matthew's gospel which gives the novel its name is a statement of the irreducibility of the moment of violence in any passage to a world that exists in the realm of possibility, which as yet is only dreamed of. O'Connor's stories and characters too are the product of a theological imagination in which every possible means of escaping from or changing the world is necessarily implicated in the debased values of that world. Tarwater's baptism of Bishop, completed in the same moment that he drowns him, is the gateway to his own transfiguration; only by this synthesis of opposites can he both express and realize – bring to realization – his sense of the thingly character of all worldly notions, including the ceremony of baptism and the prohibition against murder. The episode recalls the simultaneous sacrifice and murder of Isaac demanded of his father Abraham – another incomprehensible and unjustifiable infanticide – except that no angel of the Lord appears at the final moment to stay the hand of Tarwater. In a world of absolute sinfulness, the anathema and the anointed are identical in their capacity to point the way towards a life of grace.

Reversibility, as a quality of the world and all its notions, must define the thoroughly worldly concept of reification as well. In separate passages in *The Violent Bear It Away*, Rayber and Tarwater are shown attempting consciously to delimit their apprehension of reality. The impulse in each case is the reverse of Captain Ahab's obsession with the façade of the white whale and what lies behind it, or Marcel Proust's persistent attendance on the enlightenment promised by the hawthorns at Combray or the steeples at Martinville.[30] What seems to torment Tarwater and Rayber is not the elusiveness of revelation, but the prospect of it:

> [Tarwater] tried when possible to . . . keep his vision located on an even level, to see no more than what was in front of his face and to let his eyes stop at the surface of that. It was as if he were afraid that if he let his eye rest for an instant longer than was needed to place something – a spade, a hoe, the mule's hind quarters before his plow, the red furrow under him – that the thing would suddenly stand before him, strange and terrifying, demanding that he name it and name it justly and be judged for the name he gave it. He did all he could to avoid this threatened intimacy of creation.[31]

> [Rayber's] normal way of looking on Bishop was as an *x* signifying the general hideousness of fate . . . the little boy was part of a simple equation that required no further solution, except at the moments when with little or no warning he would feel himself overwhelmed by the horrifying love. Anything he looked at too long could bring it on. Bishop did not have to be around. It could be a stick or a stone, the line of a shadow, the absurd old man's walk of a starling crossing the sidewalk. If, without thinking, he lent himself to it, he would feel suddenly a morbid surge

> of the love that terrified him – powerful enough to throw him to the ground in an act of idiot praise. It was completely irrational and abnormal.[32]

The 'threatened intimacy of creation' is O'Connor's phrase for what Marx, in the first chapter of *Capital*, calls fetishism – the moment when things appear to dance of their own free will, when they assume a familiarity with men and women which is alienating and falsifying. Tarwater, it seems, attempts to preserve the use value of objects as their sole determining quality against the exchange value that threatens to take them over, thereby, in a sense, setting them free of their context. Rayber, meanwhile, deflects his 'irrational' love for Bishop in an effort to rationalize the existence of his child in purely aetiological, that is to say scientific terms. The love that would overwhelm him comes from outside the economy of cause and effect; thus it is of the same order as anxiety: 'It was love without reason, love for something futureless, love that appeared to exist only to be itself, imperious and all demanding, the love that would cause him to make a fool of himself in an instant.'[33] What is most striking about these passages is the almost irresistible force with which reality in its transcendent, 'terrifying' aspect presses itself upon its perceivers; it is all one can do to prevent the spectre from usurping habitual consciousness, which for Rayber and Tarwater is a rationalist and utilitarian rather than spiritual order of awareness. In *The Violent Bear It Away*, the latter rather than the former (which would turn everything into 'information') is closest to truth.

Thus O'Connor's conception of the relation between the immediate world and its 'phantasmagorical' transformation is an inversion of both the Marxist theory of false consciousness and Marx's account of the fetishism of commodities in *Capital*. The feeling described so vividly by O'Connor is no mystical falsification of the world but a manifestation of the grace of God, which not only pushes through the pasteboard mask of visible objects but emanates from the mask itself, revealing simultaneously its falsity and its truth. The 'strange and terrifying' spectre, in fact, constitutes the *disruption* of everyday consciousness, the truthful *mediation* of reality rather than the opposite, and the means by which the world is both annulled and completely transformed.

Can we be sure that Karl Marx and Flannery O'Connor are talking about the same process? How can fetishism be ascribed both to a quasi-religious consciousness, as the classical Marxist account would have it, and to a thoroughly secular materialism, as it is required to in this reading of *The Violent Bear It Away*? Old Tarwater, after all, might more conventionally be read as an exemplary case of reified consciousness, in which religion – a reality *produced* by man – has been allowed to cavort freely and grotesquely as if it were 'a natural phenomenon' alien to mankind.[34] Religious belief – a paradigm of false consciousness, which flourishes in geographically or culturally provincial settings such as rural Tennessee – has been transmitted with varying degrees of success to the characters of Tarwater and Rayber, with devastating and destructive results. Any Marxist must surely read O'Connor's novel, insofar as it is concerned with ideology and subjective liberation, as mystifying and reifying in the extreme. And if not, is this not due to the incoherence and near uselessness of the term 'reification', which neither Marx nor O'Connor uses, and which is forced by this juxtaposition to span so wide a range of significations that its meaning is effectively lost? Why should two fictional passages dealing with the subjective perception of the natural world bear any comparison to a theoretical analysis of the relations of men and women to the products of their labour under capitalism?

If we look again at the two passages from *The Violent Bear It Away*, however, it is clear that neither is about the *phenomenon* or the *event* of the transformation of reality, in the direction either of reification or dereification. Rather, each is concerned with the prospect of that transformation, the *anticipation* of it, the *anxiety* towards it. Tarwater's and Rayber's perceptions should not be regarded as displays of subjective resistance towards the 'true consciousness' represented by 'the horrifying love', the imminence and inevitability of which is apparent everywhere. For the truth, when it comes, confounds all expectations, rendering even its anxious anticipation a violation of it; this, indeed, is what marks it out as truth. Neither Rayber nor indeed Tarwater, until the last few pages of the book at least, has access to truth, except negatively, in the form of this insistent anxiety towards the thingness of the world as it is.

The novel concludes with Tarwater's real transfiguration at Powderhead, when he receives a vision of a multitude being fed loaves and fishes from a single basket at dusk. His transformation at this point is a qualitative one, the repercussions of which extend retroactively through the book as a whole. Most significantly, Tarwater's experience transcends and annihilates all the earlier signifiers of religiosity we have encountered in the text: the girl preacher watched by Rayber through a window of the pentecostal tabernacle; Bishop's affliction taken as a sign of his holiness; the old man's obsession with baptism – each of which is revealed by the text to be a product of ignorance, exploitation, superstition, even madness. The logic of this multiple abrogation even includes the language of prophecy, hellfire and 'the freedom of the Lord Jesus Christ' used by the Tarwaters – this despite the fact that such language seems closest to the inclinations of the novelist herself.[35] Tarwater's singular vision is marked by a sudden realization of the falseness of the world, a falseness which covers every worldly conception of what lies beyond:

> He felt his hunger no longer as a pain but as a tide. He felt it rising in himself through time and darkness, rising through the centuries, and he knew that it rose in a line of men whose lives were chosen to sustain it, who would wander in the world, strangers from that violent country where the silence is never broken except to shout the truth.[36]

'That violent country' refers, of course, to the kingdom of heaven, yet it is a country of silence – meaning that its content, its substance, is necessarily removed from this world, and incomprehensible to it. The description of Tarwater's vision is conspicuously lacking in specifically religious imagery; even the multiplied loaves and fishes, we read, would be insufficient to satisfy his hunger; and when he hears the command 'GO WARN THE CHILDREN OF GOD OF THE TERRIBLE SPEED OF MERCY', the words are 'as silent as seeds opening one at a time in his blood.' Something more than the truth of Christianity or the authenticity of Tarwater's prophetic calling is being signalled in these concluding pages. O'Connor's grotesque rendition of the Tarwaters – the characters with whom, in the closed world of the text, her sympathies most clearly lie – is a statement of the violent, violative nature even of the most 'otherworldly' and thus most meaningful attempts to present what is unpresentable.

Tarwater's transfiguration, accompanied by an awareness 'of the object of his hunger' and that 'nothing on earth would fill him', is comparable to Neo's vision of the 'reality' of the Matrix in digital code and Truman's sudden sense of the falseness of Seahaven and his own invincibility there. At the moment of transfiguration all anxiety disappears, an event that is so strongly tied to the transformative sense of the falseness of the world as to be indistinguishable from it. This applies also to the transfigurations in *The Matrix* and *The Truman Show*, where the sudden omnipotence of Neo and Truman signals the realization not only that another world is possible, but that it is *inevitable*. This conviction produces an immediate liberation from the burning anxiety which defines their lives up until that moment; each life is confronted with an outside which gives it meaning in the here and now. For Tarwater and Neo at least, liberation is not deferred until the next world; the outside does not remain outside but rather, simply by its acknowledgement and acceptance, is made a constituent element of this one, which is changed radically as a result.

Stanley Spencer is another visionary in whose works a sense of the falseness of the world is vividly present; his religious paintings in particular presuppose the reality of another world existing alongside everyday life and acting as a perpetual corrective of it.

Spencer's biblical scenes, for example, take place in recognizable twentieth-century provincial settings – a juxtaposition of the universal and the particular made more striking by the extreme specificity of Spencer's locations. The omnipresence of Christ in Spencer's world has a powerful transformative and redemptive effect; the prevailing mood of the awakening characters in *The Resurrection, Cookham*, for example, is one of serenity and ease, the total absence of anxiety. Spencer described the effect as follows:

> No one is in any hurry in this painting. Here and there things slowly move off but in the main they resurrect to such a state of joy that they are content and happy to remain where they have resurrected. In this life we experience a kind of resurrection when we arrive at a state of awareness, a state of being in love, and at such times we like to do again what we have done many times in the past, because now we do it anew in Heaven.[37]

In Spencer's vision, as in Tarwater's, a reified notion of time is replaced with a dialectical conception of the moment as interpenetrated with the universal, of the individual as interpenetrated with the race, of the life hereafter as interpenetrated with life on earth, and of the moment of redemption as interpenetrated with the continuity of sin. What Spencer and O'Connor have most in common is not their 'religious' concerns as such – plenty of artists and writers have those – but a sense of the reification of the world, of the reversibility of good and evil, of redemption as attained by the affirmation of an outside which is free of thing-itude, and of religion as the most accessible and intelligible vehicle for such an affirmation. As an artist Spencer is far less aware than O'Connor of the repulsive, even monstrous appearance of a life lived 'beyond anxiety'. He seems to have lived and worked in ignorance and disregard of the violent character and the destructive results of his own otherworldliness. While O'Connor's readers are spared the likely repercussions of Tarwater's mission in the 'dark city' towards which he sets off from Powderhead at the close of the book, we are in no doubt as to the generally calamitous effects of the old man's faith in terms of the social values of the modern world – values which O'Connor by no means unfairly stacks her book against. A common interpretation of O'Connor, pointed up by David Eggenschwiler, is that she, 'like Milton, was of the devil's party without realizing it'.[38] This statement is no more true of O'Connor than it is of Milton. Her vision is one which ultimately transcends and annuls the Manichaean conception of the relation of good and evil. O'Connor faces up to the other-worldly, radical, deeply discomfiting nature of truth, and the falsification which attends any simple affirmation of terms which the world already accepts.

# 5

# The Coincidence of Contraries

The religious world, emphasizes Marx, is only a reflection [*Widerschein*] of the real world. And these religious reflections can vanish 'only when the practical relations of everyday life between man and man, and man and nature, generally present themselves to him in a transparent and rational form'.[1] Religion is a symptom of a reified society, which is to say that it is an expression of the anxiety towards reification. It arises out of the disjunction between thought and actuality; it is a means by which that disjunction can be bridged, the anxiety assuaged. Religion will vanish only when a solution to reification is available in a non-religious form, when the gap between subject and object is 'genuinely' rather than 'artificially' closed, when the truth of liberation which inheres in religion is no longer understood as *its* truth, a quality of the religious world, but as *the* truth, when anxiety comes into focus *as* anxiety. At this point religion will fade from view, will in fact already have become obsolete; this is an inversion of the pre-modern situation when religion provided the governing conceptual framework of the universe, and was thus invisible *as such*.

An elaboration of reification as an essentially reversible structure – a concept that implies its own repudiation, that is inseparable from the anxiety towards it – is one way of making such a solution available. There is no rightness or wrongness to such a strategy; for to maintain that the solution to reification will be *substantially* different, depending on whether it takes a religious or a non-religious form, perpetuates not only a fetishistic attachment to the categories of worldly knowledge which the concept of reification puts into suspension, but a reified notion of truth as separate from history – from the events which take place and from the structures of thought which produce and are produced by them. The obsolescence of religion is not a political project – as a symptom, religion is as potentially liberating as it is potentially oppressive – but a cultural-historical process. The obsolescence of religion is a product of its reversibility, of the dawning awareness that true religion implies its own repudiation, its overcoming.

Thus, the question of an eventual 'non-religious' solution to the problem of reification may just as well be approached from the other side, from the side of religion itself; indeed, such an approach makes sense, given that religion is still largely familiar and accessible to us as a paradigm of thought. The question is not one of spirituality versus materialism, God versus man, Christianity versus atheism, however, but of infinitude versus finitude, possibility versus necessity, freedom versus coercion. 'Whoever does not wish to sink in the wretchedness of the finite' writes Kierkegaard in *The Concept of Anxiety*, 'is constrained in the most profound sense to struggle with the infinite.'[2] If Kierkegaard's term for the stage on which this struggle with the infinite takes place is the 'religious', his understanding of this term is such as to imply its identity with its opposite. The relation between religion and non-religion I am trying to imagine is one in which each is always at the point of collapsing into the other; religion, like the concept of reification itself, is comprehensible only as a system of thought on the brink of its own obsolescence. Kierkegaard insists that the struggle with the infinite represents 'education by possibility', as opposed to the 'education by finitude' which Rayber makes available to Tarwater – an education bound by the categories of worldly thought. Although the later Kierkegaard reproaches the institutions of Christianity for getting pulled down by finitude, religious principles are in general particularly receptive to elaboration in the direction of 'possibility', a process which might begin by stressing the ways in which religious categories comprehend and embrace their own opposites. Three examples from Christianity illustrate such a process of elaboration: the concept of marriage, the ceremony of the Eucharist, and the tradition of martyrdom.

The second volume of Kierkegaard's *Either/Or* begins with two long letters from B, the fictional Judge Vilhelm and the advocate of an 'ethical' life view, to A, the fictional aesthete of Volume One of the book. The first letter attempts to justify marriage aesthetically, but from an ethical point of view, while the second defines the relationship of the ethical and the aesthetic as one of equilibrium, or – to reiterate a term which I have been using here – *reversibility*. Throughout Volume One, A has written of marriage as a potential inhibition of his freedom, an incarnation of finitude, convention and boredom, and an offence against aesthetics, which values youth, nature and beauty over independence, coquetry and 'piquancy' – the qualities one is likely to find in any wife.[3] In the essay 'Crop Rotation' and the pseudonymous 'Seducer's Diary' – a novel found among A's papers and penned, suspects Kierkegaard's fictitious editor Victor Eremita, by A himself under the pseudonym 'Johannes' – marriage is discredited as ordinary and predictable by comparison with the poetic adventure that is first love. While marriage keeps to 'the middle of the king's highway', love prefers to beat its own track, favouring an intimate 'penetration' into Grib's Forest over any respectable promenading.[4] In 'Crop Rotation', A contrasts the subjective integrity of the single life to the progressive loss of freedom in domestic life:

> One must always be careful not to enter into any life-relation in which one can become several . . . When you are several you have lost your freedom and cannot order travelling boots when you will, cannot roam aimlessly about. If you have a wife it is difficult; if you have a wife and may have children, it is troublesome; if you have a wife and do have children, it is impossible.[5]

Vilhelm's argument with A, sustained through some two hundred pages, is that marriage is not only ethically superior to the immediate, supposedly more intense and evanescent pleasures of first love, but *therefore* aesthetically superior too. Marriage transcends the worldly distinction between ethics and aesthetics, revealing life to be most beautiful precisely when it is most ethical. His contention is not that A has erred in choosing the aesthetic, but that the aesthetic is the consequence of a failure to choose. The aesthete accedes in the values of the world by relinquishing all possibility of intervening meaningfully in it. Everything is conceived under the category of chance; thus the aesthetic life lacks the freedom which is commonly attributed to it. Only the ethical is authentically both ethical and aesthetic; only the ethical – or better, the religious – transcends the difference between ethical and aesthetic. Only the religious is both spiritual *and* material, worldly *and* otherworldly, timeless *and* rooted in the historical moment. In one of the most economical and suggestive remarks in *Either/Or*, B writes to A that the life of the married man 'is truly poetical, he solves the great riddle: to live in eternity yet so to hear the parlour clock strike that its striking does not shorten but prolongs his eternity . . .'[6] Marriage is a dialectic, a process of the unfolding of love (and truth), rather than the signal of its attainment. This theory of marriage is firmly contrary to the prevailing view (put forward in the works of romantic novelists, for example) of marriage as the *end* of first love – as the summation of the process. 'After the many twists of fate they have overcome,' says Vilhelm, 'the lovers finally fall into each other's arms, the curtain falls, the book ends, but the reader is none the wiser . . . What is false in [such works] is that the struggle, this dialectic, is entirely external, and that love comes out of the struggle as abstract as it entered into it.'[7] The fact that first love is easier to 'represent' than marriage – and aesthetically compelling depictions of marriage are as rare among today's cultural forms as they were in the romantic literature of nineteenth-century Denmark – testifies to its worldliness, and to the superficiality of the aesthetic life-view itself. 'All that I am talking about here can be represented aesthetically' insists Vilhelm; 'not, however, through poetic reproduction but by one's living it, realizing it in actual life.'[8]

This apologia for marriage is actually a critique of marriage as such, as a thing. Marriage is defensible only to the extent that it is nothing in itself; it *is* only as a *relation* – of the singular and the universal, of the world and what is not the world, of the moment and the eternal. Marriage *is* only insofar as it is not *marriage*, not a thing, but a necessarily worldly mode of reaching towards what is beyond the world; a combination of finitude and infinitude, of the everyday and the divine; a vehicle of their interpenetration, a means of comprehending the infinitude which dwells in all finitude, the universal which suffuses singularity. Marriage retains immense critical potential by remaining in a world which it simultaneously transcends. 'Married love has its conflict in time, its victory in time, its blessing in time,' says the Judge, spelling out this paradoxical relation to the historical moment.[9] First love, by contrast, is 'an instant lying outside time, a mysterious something about which one can make up any lie'. First love is *in essence* an abstraction, entirely separate from history and from humanity. Vilhelm couldn't be more explicit as to its thingly quality:

> The first love remains an unreal *An-sich* which never acquires inner substance because it moves merely in an outer medium; in the ethical and religious intention, marital love has the possibility of inner history and distinguishes itself from first love as the historical from the non-historical.[10]

In simply opposing himself, his insights and his values to the way of the world, A puts himself in the place of God. He illustrates the equivalence of cynicism and romanticism, both of which cherish the dream of a 'place in the sun' which is untouchable by history or society – a dream which is thoroughly bourgeois in its dimensions. A's unworldliness is of a type that falsifies everything around it – even himself, to the extent that he ever appears in the world. 'I would not even take a drive in the woods with you,' B tells him, 'because your participation is always a falsehood, for if you really take pleasure, one can always be certain it is not in something we others are taking pleasure in . . ., but in something you have *in mente* . . .'[11] The married man, by contrast, is able to take pleasure in the world, to be both inside and outside it. He knows another scale of values which enables him all the more to enjoy what the world has to offer. He is both more fully in the world than the aesthete, and more completely removed from it, but this is not a relation of 'undecidability'; for in the realm of possibility these things are identical.

This ability of religion to combine opposing terms is exemplified, secondly, in the Catholic Eucharist, which expresses neither an ambiguity between the material and the spiritual, nor an economy between them, but their identity. Flannery O'Connor expresses her grasp of the dialectical subtleties of the ritual in a letter written in 1959: 'The Mass is a memorial, but it is a memorial in which Christ is "really, truly, and substantially" present under the forms of bread and wine.'[12] The sacraments are not *symbols* of the body and blood of Christ, which exist in some other conceptual or physical realm; rather, the bread and the wine are, precisely, his body and his blood – *and vice versa*. O'Connor is quoting from the Council of Trent ruling of 1545–63 on the doctrine of transubstantiation – yet her understanding of the ceremony seems hardly orthodox. The relation between the sacraments and the substantiality of Christ, in its most progressive and dialectical form, is a reversible one. Neither term is privileged; transubstantiation takes place on *both sides*. A better term for what happens in the Eucharist is therefore *intersubstantiation*. Christ's body and blood are everywhere around us – the implication of which is that there is no ontological difference between what O'Connor calls 'the ultimate reality' and 'the present reality'. The Incarnation is both, she says in another of her letters; not one more than the other, but one *insofar* as it is the other. For O'Connor, in fact, there is only one reality.[13] This is the opposite of mystical; it is what is referred to as the 'intimacy of creation' in *The Violent Bear It Away*, where the true *reversibility* of reality – the sacredness of the mundane, the mundanity of the sacred – presses in on the consciousnesses of Tarwater and Rayber as the imminence of the world's transfiguration.

This thoroughly paradoxical structure of the Eucharist is illustrated in an early seventeenth-century engraving by Hieronymus Wierix, in which Christ is depicted inside an enormous wine press, with God the Father behind him turning the screw which bears down upon the cross of the crucifixion on his back, forcing his blood through the press and into the Communion goblets of the pilgrims below.[14] The mystic wine press, a popular image in late Medieval Europe, *equates* Christ's blood with the wine of the sacraments, such that a timeless, merely 'metaphorical' interpretation of the conjunction is interrupted. Neither a purely symbolic nor a purely physical reading of the eucharistic transformation may easily be derived from the picture, for Christ is himself present, alongside his 'metaphorical' substitute. The truth of the Holy Communion is the *preserved contradiction* between the spiritual and the material world, not – as in the Protestant tradition – its translation or resolution in the form of 'symbolism'. The Eucharist ascribes an otherness precisely to the world as it is. If there is any symbolism at all in the sacraments, it operates metonymically rather than metaphorically; the bread and wine stand for the whole of creation rather than for anything outside it (such as the Creator). One should therefore resist the temptation to *interpret* the Eucharist, to translate it into psychoanalytic or philosophical terms, for example. Instead, by allowing it to be, the mystery of creation, or the hiddenness of God, is preserved.

Hieronymus Wierix, *Christ in the Wine Press* (c. 1600).

Dogma, writes Flannery O'Connor pertinently, 'is the guardian of mystery.'[15]

Michele Nicoletti has written, thirdly, of the tradition of the Christian martyr as the model for a politics inspired by Kierkegaard's thought. 'Only martyrs are able to rule the world at the crucial moment', writes Kierkegaard in a preface intended for *The Book on Adler*,[16] a statement which Nicoletti mines as the key to a 'Kierkegaardian' politics on the basis that the martyr, by definition, mediates the opposition of finitude and infinitude. The martyr 'is prepared to die, rather than to betray not only the truth but also finitude. The martyr dies in the world because she wants to "bear witness" to the truth in the world. The martyr maintains not only the importance of the truth but also the relevance of the world as the only place where a person has to live and can realize the truth.'[17] Thus the martyr understands the internal structure of reality as characterized by antagonism (or reversibility). She is uniquely qualified to undertake its 'real government', since the world offers her nothing substantial that she doesn't already possess, and nothing she remotely desires. The Christian is fulfilled according to another order of gratification; the Christian 'has already more than conquered,' writes Kierkegaard, 'despite all the world's confusion and rebellion'.[18] For the Christian, therefore, the task of ruling is no personal indulgence, since there is nothing she can gain from it; it is rather a responsibility and a suffering. Ever since the appearance of the fourth estate, says Kierkegaard – that is to say, ever since the decline of the rule of the tyrants, ever since the advent of democracy – it has not been possible to govern secularly. 'As soon as the fourth estate is established, governing can be done only divinely, religiously.'[19]

Despite the pains which he takes elsewhere to differentiate religion from the worldly concerns of politics, here the relation between politics and religion is confirmed as analogous to the relation between finitude and infinitude – as similarly defined by reversibility. Kierkegaard's characterization of politics as a 'vortex', a foundationless movement which replaces the underlying stability of religion with the illusion of 'a fixed point ahead',[20] is a rejection of established religion as much as of established politics, both of which are set upon a course of secular reinvention in nineteenth-century Europe. Kierkegaard's religiosity, by implication, affirms a truly revolutionary *politics* for which everything proposed by the world is annulled from the outset. This is a politics which has always already triumphed, for which every failure or moment of suffering is merely incidental to the victory achieved in eternity.

As a model for politics in the twenty-first century, Kierkegaard's knight of faith may seem essentially otherworldly, even apolitical. In the preface to *The Book on Adler*, written in that revolutionary year 1848 (although never published in his lifetime), Kierkegaard satirizes the attempt to achieve equality on earth, the secular extreme of which, he writes, is represented in 'communism'. Just as false, however, but on precisely the same grounds, is its apparent opposite, 'pietism', a version of 'religiosity' which is equally worldly, insofar as it is attached to the reified forms of that religion, including a concept of eternity which is entirely separate from the present moment – a 'fixed point ahead', in effect.[21] Kierkegaard's critique is directed towards all manifestations of politics and religion which remain devoted to the forms of the world as it is, which are thus condemned to be forever engaged in an interminable adjustment of priorities, and to be constantly subject to – and powerless in the face of – accusations of corruption:

> To worldly passion it can deceptively look as if it were possible to bring about equality between persons in worldliness if only one remains indefatigable in calculating and computing. In any case the finite dialectic will be able to make an unbelievably great number of combinations. The constant refrain will become: treachery, treachery. No, when it is done in another way, when one subtracts a little *here*, adds a little *there*, and then divides equally the more that is there, without forgetting the difference there, collated with the difference here, and there and here and here and yonder and up and down – then it must necessarily be

> possible to find the equality, the divisor, the monetary standard for human-likeness in worldliness, that is, in difference, the equality for the *worldly* human-likeness, that is, for the – different – equality . . . Worldliness is an enormous variegated composite of more and less, a little more and a little less, much, some, a little, etc., that is, worldliness is difference.[22]

Worldliness, for Kierkegaard, is predicated on differentiation, and thus on an administrative agenda of anatomizing and reconciling difference. Such a process must lead to a gradual exacerbation of the levels of anxiety experienced by humankind, as differences inevitably multiply, becoming ever less manageable. Kierkegaard goes on to describe a positive correlation between bureaucratization and anxiety: 'In the midst of all this, this series of paragraphs or this series of administration changes, the human race will become more and more confused, just as a drunken man, the more violently he storms around, gets more intoxicated, even though he does not get more to drink.'[23] Kierkegaard's confessed 'incomprehension' of politics is a rejection of the parsimonious agenda which emanates from a secular understanding of the world. His category of the 'religious' – a category which has only an incidental relation to the worldly forms of religious thought – represents for Nicoletti 'the destruction of the absolutist pretensions of politics'.[24] The religious proposes the 'purification' of politics by revealing the internal incoherence of the secular model, and of bourgeois reality. The religious is an event which, by presenting a new, wholly unimaginable world, makes possible the recovery of politics and of the existing world itself.

Martyrdom, in this context, is a figure for the willingness to affirm a truth that is greater than oneself, a truth far greater, certainly, than the worldly representation of that truth. The last thing the martyr does is affirm the authority of the Christian Church, just as the last thing the married man or woman celebrates is the institution of marriage as such. No martyr lays down her life for the Church; indeed, martyrs are often killed or betrayed precisely by the 'worldly' representatives of their faith, whose tenets they have outraged – as was the case, say, with Jesus of Nazarath, Joan of Arc, Thomas Cranmer, Malcolm X, Leon Trotsky. Martyrdom is thus both the fulfilment of religion and its annihilation.

From the side of 'religion', then, marriage, the Eucharist and martyrdom may each be elaborated as a way of preserving the contradiction between the physical and the spiritual, finitude and infinitude, the literal and the symbolic, the world and what is not the world, in a form which is immediately accessible to comprehending consciousness. These concepts express the reversibility of Christianity itself. Kierkegaard's view of marriage, O'Connor's view of the Eucharist, Nicoletti's view of martyrdom, all accept the necessary 'otherworldliness' of a solution to reification, while simultaneously importing this otherworldliness into the world itself. Each affirms the 'beyond' in a form which immediately cancels itself out – or rather, which remains both incidental to and inseparable from its truth content; this is the meaning of the term *intersubstantiation*, introduced here to denote an event in which both 'world' and 'beyond' are transfigured. Each seizes on a category of religious thought as a bearer of truth, amplifying it to the point at which its 'worldly' religiosity is transcended, revealed as a mere distraction.

From the side of the nonreligious, however, a similar reversibility may be attributed to the commodity, the essence of which is both thingitude and dethingitude, object and spectre, mysticism and materiality. The situation of the worker confronted by the object of his labour, described by Marx in his analysis of the commodity form, is a dialectical inversion of the individual confronted by his or her own possibility, as described by Kierkegaard in *The Concept of Anxiety*. Marx's 'materialism', in other words, is as much a struggle with the infinite as Kierkegaard's 'religiosity'. Gillian Rose writes of Marx's theory of commodity fetishism as 'the presentation of a contradiction between substance and subject', or between 'actuality and its misrepresentation'. The substantive term of this formulation is not 'actuality' or 'misrepresentation', but 'contradiction'.[25] This is confirmed by reading the section on the fetishism of commodities in the first chapter of *Capital*, by the end of which the character of the commodity is no less 'enigmatic' than at the beginning. The same contradiction between subject and object underlies Tarwater's and Rayber's anxiety when faced with the 'threatened intimacy of creation', or the 'horrifying love' which seeps into Rayber's world in the presence of his son Bishop. Tarwater's trepidation at Powderhead is anticipated by Kierkegaard, writing in his journal in 1839: 'The whole of existence makes me anxious, from the smallest fly to the mysteries of the Incarnation. It's all inexplicable, myself most of all. For me all existence is contaminated, myself most of all.'[26] In the gap between creation and its 'contamination' (or reification), or between the subjectivity of the worker and his objectification (or reification), is consciousness, anxiety – and it is to anxiety, therefore, that we must look for a solution to the disjunction.

# 6

# Kierkegaard as a Theorist of Reification

Judge Vilhelm's letters to the unnamed aesthete in Kierkegaard's *Either/Or* are important for my argument, because the temperament he is taking issue with may be characterized, among other things, as an anxiety towards reification. A's unhappiness is explicable as a fear of the dissipation of the 'singularity' of love into the universal. 'You want to rejoice in what is peculiar to your love,' writes Vilhelm;

> you want to let all the passion of love blaze up in you, and you do

> not want to be disturbed by the thought that Peter and Paul do the same . . . but your reasoning conceals a reflection that has disturbed the first love. Love is, as noted above, a unity of the universal and the singular, but the sense in which you want to enjoy the singular shows a reflection that has put the singular outside the universal.[1]

A's approach to love, which sees the singular as incompatible with the universal, reveals very clearly the general structure of the relation between reification and the anxiety towards it. This anxiety is rooted in a finite world which extends no further than the boundaries of the immediate present. Its sense of self is fragile, its values entirely dependent on those of other men and women. The world of the aesthete is a Manichaean universe, a closed *economy* where the limits of the 'self' are defined solely by differentiation from the 'other', where subjectivity is absolute and objectivity profane, and where finitude and infinitude are polar, irreconcilable opposites. In such a world, love between two people can offer no transcendence, except of a purely subjective and fleeting kind.

At the end of the 'Seducer's Diary', immediately prior to his long awaited tryst with Cordelia, Johannes is in a frenzy of anticipation, which he expresses in solipsistic terms highly reminiscent of Fichte's yearning for transcendence: 'Everything is image; I myself am a myth about myself, for is it not rather as a myth that I hasten to this meeting? Who I am has nothing to do with it. Everything finite and temporal is forgotten, only the eternal remains, the power of love, its longing, its bliss.'[2] In his last letter to Cordelia he wrote: 'When we keep together we are strong, stronger than the world, stronger than the gods themselves.' After their appointment, however, Johannes returns deflated and depressed; in giving herself to him, he writes in the final diary entry, the girl has lost everything, all her innocence and fragrance, and he declares dejectedly: 'I want never to see her again'. The strength of first love is indomitable and yet, simultaneously, utterly fragile. The aesthetic elevation of first love over marriage is hubristic and solipsistic; the bullheaded challenge it raises to the world is only sustainable, to use B's phrase, '*in mente*'. The sublimity of first love is not transferable outside the self; its happiness is doomed, its 'uniqueness' a mere spectre in the mind of the lover. In seeking to elevate itself above a contemptible world, first love constructs a dualism, according to which its triumph is achievable only with the defeat of the world, and vice versa. 'Freed' from the demands and the contingencies of finitude, its claim to infinitude simply evaporates.

This profound anxiety is destined to be unsatisfied for as long as it remains within the stupidity of a 'secular' world view which thinks to account for everything that exists with a binary model of self and other. Johannes's rejection of the pieties of married life leaves intact the pieties of the aesthetic. This temperament is unable to abstract from the actuality in front of it. The aesthete, embedded in and tormented by actuality, fails to connect with any perspective which looks upon possibility as higher than actuality, and from which everything that exists is false by definition. Everything which the secular, dualistic consciousness perceives (including and above all itself) is a reification. Johannes's rejection of 'religion' is a rejection of nothing at all, of a ghost, a mere spectre, and nothing is changed by it. His critique of religion qua religion fails to dent the totality of relations in the slightest; the aesthetic consciousness colludes in the inclinations of the world to be allowed to be just what it appears to be. Johannes's aestheticism leaves reality intact; his rejection of marriage qua marriage has no critical consequences for the metaphysical edifice on which marriage is built. In each case Johannes merely replaces one illusion, God/marriage, with another, Man/the pleasures of seduction. It is not surprising that at the end of the 'Seducer's Diary' we find Johannes's anxiety not only intact, but more acute than ever.

By contrast, marriage comprehends and incorporates its own opposite, achieving a real transcendence of all existing conditions which casts everything that exists, including itself, into a symbolic abyss. The wedding ceremony, says Vilhelm, offers 'the universal and the singular together', by presenting love in the context of the union of the first human couple. Every marriage, like every human life, is 'an individual and a symbol at the same time'.[3] The universal in marriage is no meaningless abstraction, therefore, but a material presence in the consciousness of every married person. In his letters to A, Vilhelm constructs a critique of reification which is at the same time a critique of the *concept* of reification. Marriage frees its participants from reification by freeing them from the *anxiety* towards reification – from the anxiety that the demands of the other, or the authority of the institution, detract from the integrity of the self. The belief in a God who oversees the marriage lifts both wife and husband out of the finitude which seems to threaten and corrode everyday life; this is also what makes everyday life anything but mundane. Married love 'is the divine through being the everyday'. Far from detracting from the self, marriage augments and completes it.[4] Husband and wife attain a sense of purpose and meaning which is both completely individual and completely collective – they are bound together in their indissoluble uniqueness. In this way, marriage is the opposite of restricting or enslaving. 'If she now thanks God for the loved one,' writes Vilhelm of the believing wife,

> her soul is safe against suffering; being able to thank God means she can put the loved one at just enough distance for her to be able to draw breath. And that occurs not as a result of an anxious doubt. She knows no such thing. It happens immediately.[5]

In Kierkegaard's ethical thought it is precisely the *difference* between subject and object, rather than either pole in itself – one could say alternatively the difference between husband and wife, a difference which God both bridges and maintains – which takes on the status of the universal.[6]

All anxiety is anxiety about reification, because all anxiety *suffers* from reification, from the (atheistic) perception that 'this' is all there is – or conversely, the (deistic) belief in an unapproachable 'beyond' that is categorically removed from human possibility. Anxiety, in Kierkegaard's usage – fear which lacks an object – is the temperament which is dominant in modern society; it is the feeling expressed in the following soliloquy, from Jean-Luc Godard's 1966 film *2 ou 3 choses que je sais d'elle*:

> I know sometimes what it is I desire. At other times, I don't know. For example, I know there's something missing in my life, but I don't really know what. Or else I feel scared though there's nothing particular to be frightened about. . . . Something can make me cry, . . . but the reason for those tears is not directly connected with the actual tears that trickle down my cheeks. . . . Everything I do can be described but not necessarily the reasons for which I do it.[7]

It would be easy to situate the appearance of anxiety in modernity in the gap opened up by the 'death of God'. Such a procedure would find anxiety to be merely the residue of an outdated delusion, one which must soon follow the delusion itself into obsolescence. The truth, however, is not that God is dead, but that he is hidden, and that the process of his disappearance takes place not primarily on the physical plane but on the conceptual one. The reality of God is non-dissociable from the spiritual life of real men and women; yet the existing ideational forms of God – including, in large part, the very concept of God – are no longer adequate to his actuality. God represents a possibility of transcending the self which coexists with and is inseparable from the self. God signifies the otherness of the self, a disjunction within the self, the dissolution of the self; God is the possibility of arriving at a state of intimacy with creation which is accessible from every point within it. This series of paradoxes is what is signalled by the Hegelian concept of 'spirit' (*Geist* – or in Danish, *Aand*) – a vehicle of truth according to which spirituality is embedded in materiality, seeps from it, but cannot be abstracted from it. Spirit is the medium of human history; it expresses the identity of the individual with the race, and of the instant with eternity, and of transcendence with materiality. God, the prevailing signifier of spiritual truth, is produced by human beings; he is therefore as real as human beings themselves, and the hinge between our universality and particularity.

In a society in which the dominant spiritual temperament is anxiety, that anxiety is the prevailing form of the manifestation of God. We are confronted not merely by a hidden God, but a God who has departed from the existing conceptual apparatus of his presentation – which means that the object of our desires and our fears is no longer even *conceptually* available to us. Anxiety arises when there is a disjunction between the actuality of truth and the forms in which it resides – when those forms appear inadequate or too rigid. Hence the object of anxiety is always a nothing – a gap, a space, an absence. Anxiety is so prevalent in late capitalist society that it has become a defining quality of that society. Not only is reification inseparable from the anxiety towards it; anxiety is always anxiety about reification. The effect of anxiety is reification (and vice versa) because anxiety *presupposes* reification – a disparity between soul and form which is dissolved by the awareness of their dialectical reversibility, the identity which inheres in their very disparity. Johannes reifies Cordelia and himself in his certainty that love for the other results in the partial loss of the self, that the only love that escapes falsification is momentary, a love which experiences and discards its object in a instant; this philosophy is a grotesque falsification of the object, as well as of the subject. Ahab's pursuit of the white whale, like Johannes's ventures in seduction, projects a false antagonism between subject and object; his anxiety towards the pasteboard reality which presses in on him is the very process which reduces reality to the quality of pasteboard. Anxiety is the consciousness of reification; reification is the anxiety towards reification. Neither can exist without the other.

*

# 7

# Total Reification (III): Reading Hardt and Negri

The prevalence of anxiety is also expressed in the concepts of 'omni-crisis', 'permanent exception' and 'endemic corruption' with which Michael Hardt and Antonio Negri characterize the contemporary situation.[1] For Hardt and Negri, the use of the term 'corruption' has no moral overtones but is an implication of the disappearance of the 'ontological' basis of human existence, and thus of any stability or knowability from the objects of human fear and desire. The disappearance of ontology denotes an absence of anything outside discourse and, concomitantly, a rejection of the idea that power is located somewhere beyond its representation, or outside the bounds of its dominion.

Hardt and Negri's 'endemic corruption' is thus a characteristic post-structuralist statement. Certainly their analysis builds on the work of Deleuze, Foucault and Derrida; the deontologization of power presupposes, for example, the deconstruction of the inside/outside opposition found in the work of all three thinkers.[2] Where Hardt and Negri's book *Empire* differs from the classic texts of post-structuralism is in its relatively straightforward translation of this idea to the discipline of political science, and in its willingness to undertake the ontological 'violence' of elaborating this state of affairs in terms of a linear historical narrative. 'Deontologization', in other words, is a real political development – but it is one which inaugurates a new global situation of the impossibility of real political developments.

This situation, paradoxically, is one of liberation as much as the reverse. Hardt and Negri develop the concept of 'Empire' to describe a world order in which sovereignty no longer resides in the nation state but in what they call the 'multitude', an updated form of Lukács's hypothesis of the 'revolutionary proletariat'; indeed, the concept of 'imputedness' is explicitly present in Hardt and Negri's use of the term 'virtuality'. The evolution of the multitude takes place in a world whose values are not determined by any 'transcendent power or measure' but by 'humanity's own continuous innovation and creation' – that is to say, in the realm of the virtual.[3] The multitude itself is virtual; if it is the new locus of resistance, its sole province is 'the nexus between virtuality and possibility' – a statement that recalls Lukács's definition of the proletariat as simply that vehicle in which 'the dialectical contradictions of the development as a whole become conscious'.[4] The multitude exists only insofar as the passage from virtuality to possibility takes place. The multitude is an imputed concept by definition; with the absence of ontology, all its activities are necessarily experimental. Thus, the precise form the insurgence of the multitude will take, and the impact it will have, (always) remain to be seen.

Empire is a power structure which has no outside, no other – or rather, the other of Empire exists within it, operating simultaneously against it and beyond it, 'at the same level of totality'.[5] Empire is a historical successor to the age of imperialism; the concept of Empire represents the *realization* of the aims of imperialism as concurrent with their *failure*. Empire is the historical conjuncture at which the identity of these supposed opposites becomes apparent, along with the antagonistic structure of reality itself. Empire is an eminently reversible concept; it denotes both the fixation of 'the existing state of affairs for eternity'[6] and the inherent volatility of that state of affairs – deontologization as a new ontology; universal corruption as a new innocence. *Empire* might be read as the radicalization of the theory of 'reflexive modernization' (described in Part Two): its completion by a theory of 'genuine reversibility' in which the scale of the crisis is not limited by a belief in the final triumph of capitalism, or by a positivistic faith in the immunity of concepts.

A 'deontological' world is one in which possibility is everywhere; in which nothing – or (which amounts to the same thing) everything – is reified; and in which revolutionary activity is as far from political anachronism as it ever was. The idea of a 'totally administered' society, one which is difficult to refute in the face of a globalizing world economy, simply cannot have the catastrophic implications evoked by the Frankfurt School thinkers – even though for Hardt and Negri the 'negativity' of those thinkers, the 'refusal to participate' expressed in their work, emerges from an experience of 'damaged life' which anticipates the 'life in the desert' of today's multitudes, and provides ways of reflecting on the possibilities for liberation specifically generated by a world in which crisis is the prevailing human and social condition.[7]

The concept of Empire intersects with the concept of anxiety, defined by Kierkegaard as 'freedom's possibility' – a state of mind which 'consumes all finite ends and discovers all their deceptiveness'.[8] Anxiety is determined by the absence of ontology; its very existence testifies to the impossibility that the world is limited ontologically. Kierkegaard's concept of anxiety, writes William F. Fischer, is 'an experiential state, constituted by the individual's awareness of his own possibilities, by his realization that he has no objective justification for choosing them, and by his limited capacity to foresee all the consequences of a possible choice.'[9] Anxiety lives and struggles in a world from which all certainty has been eroded. For Kierkegaard, the appearance of anxiety in the individual is a stage in the progression towards a freedom free of the bonds constituted by a naive opposition between freedom and unfreedom. Anxiety, indeed, is 'entangled freedom', meaning that freedom is 'not free in itself but entangled, not by necessity, but in itself'.[10] Anxiety frees one from reification, from the falsity of believing that a world without sin ever existed – of believing, by extension, that a freedom which is completely free of unfreedom might be possible. The crucial distinction for Kierkegaard is between two ways of living: that of 'actuality', which accepts the things of this world as they appear, which believes in the substantiality of existing terms and concepts, and is thus resigned to the 'finitude' of the world itself, and that of possibility, which refuses them – which values things which don't exist higher than those which do, and is able to imagine the world in reverse. The distinction is analogous to the one I have been making in this book between 'secular' and 'religious' models of thought.

The 'education by possibility' that Kierkegaard prescribes for his readers is an education in the concept of reification, which is also an education according to one's own infinitude: 'Only he who passes through the anxiety of the possible is educated to have no anxiety, not because he can escape the terrible things of life but because these always become weak by comparison with those of possibility'.[11] In a vivid image he describes what this 'education' is like, the degree to which it involves rejecting the consolations which the world proffers to men and women, and the risks of this process should the meaning of anxiety be misunderstood – namely, suicide; yet its end is a liberation from anxiety, in the form of its conceptualization as something which 'possibility' requires that one remain *with*, a conceptualization which is no longer deceived by 'its countless falsifications':

> He who sank in possibility – his eye became dizzy, his eye became confused, so he could not grasp the measuring stick that Tom, Dick, and Harry hold out as a saving straw to one sinking; his ear was closed so he could not hear what the market price of men was in his own day, did not hear that he was just as good as the majority. He sank absolutely, but then in turn he emerged from the depth of the abyss lighter than all the troublesome and terrible things in life.[12]

Kierkegaard's concept of anxiety looks like an individualistic category. The simplest way of achieving this education, says Kierkegaard, is to place the 'pupil of possibility' in the middle of the Jutland heath where, cut off from human society and events, 'he will experience everything more perfectly, more accurately, more thoroughly than the man who received the applause on the stage of world history . . .'[13] Transcending anxiety is an experience, it seems, of cementing the individual into his or her individuality, thus to achieve a temporary but decisive identity of self and other with which to return to the world. The falseness of the world is associated with the values of society, such that it is only in separation from the world that one is able to comprehend its nullification. Yet the truth that may be grasped in separation from society is not an individualistic truth. Fichte's solipsism arises out of the need to preserve the unity of the self *against* society; for Kierkegaard, by contrast, the truth of solitude is predicated upon the *dissolution* of the self, upon the reversibility of self and other which becomes apparent in isolation.

In Godard's 1962 film *Vivre sa vie*, the French philosopher of language Brice Parain is engaged by the protagonist Nana in a discussion about the relation between speaking and not speaking – about the desire to live without speaking, and the impossibility of doing so. In order to speak well, he tells her, we have to pass through a stage in which a recognition of the violence of language actually prohibits its use: 'I believe one learns to talk well only when one has renounced life for a time . . . Speaking is almost a resurrection in relation to life. Speech is another life from when one does not speak. So, to live in speech one must pass through the death of life without speech . . . There is a kind of ascetic rule that stops one from talking well until one sees life with detachment.'[14] This dialogue comes towards the end of a story in which Nana has been treated by the men she meets in progressively more objectified terms. The film begins with her descent into prostitution, and ends with her being traded by her pimp and finally shot dead during the exchange. The encounter with Parain is a moment of redemption in an otherwise bleak film, its sole episode of genuine human interaction. It expresses not only the possibility of living amidst horror, but the need to pass by the horror in a spirit of refusal in order eventually to transcend it.

For Kierkegaard, the education in possibility represents just such a passage through – rather than a descent into – asceticism.

The anxiety towards reification is a profoundly subjective and lonely, indeed reifying experience; the *concept* of reification, as Lukács discovered very quickly, is itself reifying. The education in possibility is an education in the simultaneity of the anxiety towards reification with its opposite, liberation from it. In reality, death and resurrection occur simultaneously. As Parain says to Nana, 'we swing between the two because it's the movement of life. From everyday life one rises to a life we call superior: the thinking life. But this life presupposes that one has killed the everyday, too elementary life.'

Liberation from reification is a process that requires both the anxiety towards it, which kills the everyday, and the acknowledgement of its obsolescence, which resurrects it. The task for the pupil of possibility is to develop a relation to the world in which the renunciation of life and its resurrection by speech can take place *simultaneously*. Such a relation has far less to do with irony than with earnestness. The only 'irony' that is worth anything at all, observes Kierkegaard, is in a profound sense deadly earnest; it knows what to be earnest about, and is thus able to speak lightly of the things of this world, secure in the knowledge that the 'thingliness' of the world is not the whole of it.[15] For Parain in *Vivre sa vie*, not only do words betray us; *we* also betray *them* – meaning that words are only as false, as thing-like, as corrosive of reality as our anxiety towards them allows them to be.[16]

The relevance of Hardt and Negri's *Empire* is in providing a political-theoretical model for a society which operates according to a principle of the reversibility of all concepts and values. Empire is a theoretical structure in which oppression and liberation, like the rivers of Lethe and Eunoë in Dante's *Purgatorio*, have the same source. In Empire, victory and defeat are simultaneous. Deterritorialization, a process in which the sites of production become unyoked from specific localities under capitalism, is also a process of territorialization, as the bargaining position of labour is progressively weakened and the systems of control centralized and extended.[17] For Hardt and Negri capitalism is reifying and dereifying in the same measure; the spiritual becomes progressively less dissociable from the material as resources tend more and more to the production of values rather than of goods. With the emergence of Empire, and the gradual replacement of ontology by the spectre of possibility, anxiety becomes a generalized state of consciousness, and the principal expression of a society's spiritual truth.

The authors of *Empire* decline to spell out the implications of their analysis in the direction of a new 'political programme', for reasons that are intrinsic to the analysis itself. The significance of the book is primarily diagnostic; for my purposes its importance lies in the development of a terminology to anatomize a situation of 'total reification' which is simultaneously one of dereification, and its boldness in translating the theme of 'reversibility' (as I have formulated it here) to the political sphere. The concept of Empire describes very well the prevailing human condition at the beginning of the twenty-first century – and perhaps at other periods too: 'we are situated precisely at that hinge of infinite finitude that links together the virtual and the possible,' write Hardt and Negri towards the close of the book.[18] The concept of Empire is an example of those dialectical approaches to the idea of totalization described at the end of Part One. For both Lukács and Fanon, an acknowledgement of the extremity – the *totality* – of the situation is a condition for changing that situation; totalization is a quality of any situation which requires urgent change, and in which change is imminent. Empire, like the 'age of absolute sinfulness', or the thoroughly deformed reality of colonial society, is a 'transitional diagnosis of a transitional epoch'. As such, it must be articulated in totalizing terms; indeed, the possibility of a totalizing articulation is a precondition of any transitional moment.

We are not speaking here of rhetorical exaggeration, or a metaphorical characterization of society designed to excite resistance against it, but of a dialectical analysis in which both extremes – totality and transience – are simultaneously and necessarily true. In the tradition of thinkers, including Fanon and Lukács, who have looked creatively and dispassionately at their society, Hardt and Negri hazard the attempt at a conceptualization which holds for every particular of that society; in so doing, they make irrevocable and irreversible the process of its transformation. Anxiety is the constitutive consciousness of all such situations; anxiety is the spirit of possibility which seeps from the analysis of every totality. The concept of Empire, like the concept of reification itself, imbues existing reality with an otherness which, at the level of consciousness and beyond, ensures its imminent and radical transformation.

# 8

# Conclusion: Towards Intimacy

We are living in a world which perpetually threatens us with its intimacy. Tables and chairs have long been dancing of their own accord, but the conversations they seem determined to hold with us are increasing in volume, to the point at which we may feel we can no longer hear ourselves think. Attempts to keep these spectral discourses at bay range from the crude to the sophisticated. Naomi Klein begins her book *No Logo* with a curious echo of Tarwater's desire, in *The Violent Bear It Away*, to subdue the world around him: 'If I squint, tilt my head, and shut my left eye,' she writes, 'all I can see out the window is 1932, straight down to the lake.'[1] In the same book she quotes Tocqueville's fears about the 'fantastic' quality of democratic art, and the 'strange creations' awakened by poets with democratic brains; she declares that we are 'surrounded now by the realization of Tocqueville's predictions: gleaming, bulbous golden arches; impossibly smooth backlit billboards; squishy cartoon characters roaming fantastically fake theme parks.'[2]

*No Logo* is punctuated by expressions of concern over the

The *Guardian* (*G2* supplement) front cover, 9 July 2001.

power of the brand and the logo to define our reality for us, and our susceptibility to what she calls 'the seductions of fake'. Its account has been hugely influential – or perhaps the book is merely symptomatic of wider anxieties – and 'branding' has become an 'issue' to be discussed and debated, a subsection in bookshops, a cultural brand in itself. 'What do brands really mean to us?' asks a newspaper supplement, illustrating the question with a cartoon depicting a scene of urban consumerism in which every product speaks volumes: a T-shirt announces 'I Understand Irony', while another identifies a 'Media type'; carrier bags give away a 'Discerning Customer' and the recent purchase of 'Something French'; and the mere name of a bar assures patrons that it is a 'Safe Pub For Girls'.[3]

Naomi Klein's answer is unambiguous: 'Branding, in its truest and most advanced incarnations, is about corporate transcendence.'[4] What distinguishes the brand from the 'product', she continues, is its 'spiritual' component – meaning, of course, the propensity to evolve out of its brain (wooden or otherwise) 'grotesque ideas'. With great tenacity, Klein sets about demolishing the pasteboard world constructed by American corporatism. Her success is more palpable than the aestheticism of *American Beauty*, and less ambiguous than the attempts of Melville's Captain Ahab to 'strike through the mask' – but then so is her antagonist. For the truth beneath the 'inviting plasticity'[5] increasingly defining America's collective consciousness is revealed by Klein to be a complex of global factors, which include the restrictive practices of Western corporations, the manoeuvring between governments and business, and a movable infrastructure of 'sweatshops' located throughout Asia and Latin America. Her journey in search of what lies behind 'the slick veneer'[6] – closely following, incidentally, the trail of the *Pequod* – is the journey taken by capital itself as it chases the lowest labour costs in the world. Klein maps the route through the South China Sea and the Pacific Ocean, from Taiwan, Korea and Japan to Indonesia, China, Thailand and the Philippines: 'The migration patterns have been clearly documented with Reebok's manufacturers. In 1985, Reebok produced almost all its sneakers in South Korea and Taiwan and none in Indonesia and China. By 1995, nearly all those factories had flown out of Korea and Taiwan and 60 percent of Reebok's contracts had landed in Indonesia and China.'[7]

It becomes possible, on the basis of this movement of capital, for companies to establish the identities of brands in increasingly elevated terms. 'Out-sourcing', the prevailing mode of production of contemporary capitalism, constructs a *cordon sanitaire* between marketing and manufacture, or between the 'spiritual' and the 'material' worlds, such that Western corporations are no longer responsible for producing the goods they sell. The business of the company becomes that of pure *fetishism* or *reification*: the systematic production of abstraction, and thus the further mystification of society itself. Nike is a 'sports and fitness' company, aiming to 'enhance people's lives', rather than a shoe manufacturer; Polaroid is a 'social lubricant', not a camera; IBM sells 'business solutions' rather than computers, and so on.[8] We live and move in a world saturated by ethereal values; all visible objects abound in 'metaphysical subtleties and theological niceties';[9] we are forever being addressed in riddles. Contemporary capitalism, notes Klein, is more 'spiritual' than ever before, although the term is used here in a quite un-Hegelian sense: 'After establishing the "soul" of their corporations, the superbrand companies have gone on to rid themselves of their cumbersome bodies, and there is nothing that seems more cumbersome, more loathsomely corporeal, than the factories that produce their products.'[10]

*No Logo* tends towards political economy rather than cultural criticism; thus Klein explicitly eschews 'content critiques' of advertisements in place of empirically-charged attacks on 'the corporations that paid for them'.[11] Nevertheless, the book should be read as an expression of a broader cultural anxiety, as much as an analysis of a particular global-economic set of relations; for the process of commodity fetishism that concerns Klein is not a new one – and yet, in a sense, it is produced anew in her anatomization of it. The analysis has a 'homologous' relation to its object of study. *No Logo* produces the very reification it recoils from, in its delineation of a two-tier model of global capitalism: a manifest world of spectacular artifice, branding and cod 'spirituality', in which the Nike 'swoosh' is ubiquitous, and a hidden, undifferentiated world of toil, production, exploitation, and no logos. This binary model is reminiscent of *The Matrix*, in which a vivid, seductive, virtual existence is counterposed to a monotonous and repulsive reality. Klein's description of a 'free-trade zone' in Cavite, outside Manila in the Philippines, has all the grotesque immediacy of the world of revolutionary uniforms, industrial hardware and liquid nutrition into which Neo is inducted by Morpheus:

> Manufacturing is concentrated and isolated inside the zone as if it were toxic waste . . . Windowless workshops made of cheap plastic and aluminum siding are crammed in next to each other, only feet apart. Racks of time cards bake in the sun, making sure the maximum amount of work is extracted from each worker, the maximum number of working hours extracted from each day. The streets in the zone are eerily empty, and open doors – the ventilation system for most factories – reveal lines of young women hunched in silence over clamouring machines.[12]

The two-tier model is present even in the epigraph to Klein's book, a quotation from the Indonesian writer Y. B. Mangunwijaya: 'You might not see things yet on the surface, but underground, it's already on fire'. The message is clear: life in a consumer society is a collective hallucination. Cavite is the 'other' of advanced capitalism, its hidden truth – the disclosure of which throws into relief its familiar, merely 'phenomenal' aspect. Klein's radical hippy parents, it seems, were right all along: war toys, moulded plastic and fast food are the negation of 'verdant farmland and majestic mountains'.[13] In *No Logo* we see the anxiety of contemporary capitalism expressed in yet another binary, explicitly secular form: the desire for an other that will right the plastic, thingly condition of a fallen self.

This conceptual structure is reiterated by *No Logo*, even while the existence of the book is a material refutation of it. Klein's book, after all, emerges wholesale from the upper level of that structure – not an anomaly within it, but an exemplary, perfectly judged 'product' of it. The book was created and marketed with the manifold resources of a global publishing operation. *No Logo* is implicated in the process of the 'impoverishment' of the world, even as it describes and indicts the relations of production and exploitation which make that process inevitable. *No Logo* is an expression of the *reversibility* of that 'impoverishment', therefore, since it is materially underpinned by it, and cannot be separated from it. Consequently, the substantiality of its adversary – 'multinational capital', or 'global corporatism' – dissolves the moment it is named as such – the moment, that is to say, at which it is urged to 'step forth' in a transcendent form – whereupon it finds itself confronted with and admonished by its own inverted actuality.

*No Logo* is an extraordinarily compelling narrative of the anxiety which characterizes, perhaps even defines, the consciousness of advanced capitalist society. In a discussion of capitalism's propensity to appropriate signifiers of political radicalism, Klein mentions 'Situationism', the revolutionary–theoretical movement which anticipated and, in part, provoked the events of May 1968 in Paris. The most coherent and well-known expression of what is more formally referred to as the 'Situationist International' is Guy Debord's 1967 manifesto *The Society of the Spectacle*. 'Never Work', 'It Is Forbidden to Forbid', 'Take Your Desires for Reality', genuinely subversive messages in the 1960s, Klein points out, now sound like slogans for a Sprite or a Nike campaign.[14] Yet *The Society of the Spectacle* is the text which it is most appropriate to read alongside Klein herself. 'The spectacle is the self-portrait of power in the age of power's totalitarian rule over the conditions of existence', writes Debord, describing a relation in which both *No Logo* and *The Society of the Spectacle*, as products of that society, are implicated. In *No Logo* we see the world of multinational capitalism *speaking to itself*, as any 'political-economic' rather than 'content' analysis of the book could not fail to conclude.

None of this is intended as criticism of Klein's book, which has catalysed what is arguably the largest, certainly the most visible radical political movement in the Western world in recent years. In any case, such reflexive knowledge is an intrinsic element of *No Logo*'s overall critique. Certainly Klein is aware of the degree to which the book is implicated in the relations of commodity fetishism she describes; the fact is wittily acknowledged by a photograph of an infant wearing a 'No Logo' hooded top in the front of the book. Yet her conception of the struggle against capitalism also seems formed by a recognition of its reversibility, and of the impossibility of a critical perspective which is untouched by its object: 'anticorporate campaigns draw energy from the power and mass appeal of marketing, at the same time as they hurl that energy right back at the brands that have so successfully colonized our everyday lives.'[15] According to Klein, we have the brands themselves to thank for giving us a 'crash course' in global mobilization.[16] In these respects, the approach of *No Logo* may be counterposed to the painstaking attempt of *Life and its Replacement with a Dull Reflection of Itself* to create a theoretical space free of implication in the progressive 'impoverishment' of the world. Klein has absorbed the contradictory nature of capitalism far more thoroughly than the found text analysed earlier, such that what the Pleasure Tendency theses describe, in a somewhat apocalyptic tone, as the 'decentralization' of power is an assumption tacitly present at every point in her book.[17]

My account of *No Logo* is offered not to support a position of commodity or reality 'pietism', to use Gayatri Spivak's provocative phrase, but as further illustration of three of the central assertions of the present work: (i) the inseparability of the subjective and the objective aspects of reification, meaning that the anxiety towards reification is an element intrinsic to the concept itself; (ii) the centrality of this anxiety to the constitution of the modern capitalist subject; and (iii) the reversibility of all terms and concepts as an implication of any thorough elaboration of the concept of reification. *No Logo* is caught in a tension between its author's revulsion from her childhood 'seduction by fake' and her recognition of the real liberation from the world of immediacy that may be achieved by, say, a Nike 'swoosh' tattoo on one's ankle, or a child's Barbie doll fetish. Such gestures are more akin to religious devotion than anything else in our society; they are an expression of the tension which is constitutive of modern capitalist subjectivity itself. In a reified and reifying society, the sphere of consumption can, indeed must, perform a liberating, 'spiritual' function.

The disappearance of religion, to restate a theme of this book, is only possible with the disappearance of reification. The key to removing both events from the merely speculative dimension is *the recognition of their reversibility*. The disappearance of religion is identical to the realization of its truth, to the manifestation of its objects of devotion, to the erasure of the semiotic disjunction between faith and *parousia*, an event which religion itself could not survive. Likewise, the disappearance of reification would be identical to its totalization. Reversibility is not only an implication of the concept of reification as I have been elaborating it here, but a feature which pertains to the concept itself. And the Nike swoosh – like the cross of Christ, the banns of marriage and the Mau Mau panga – is a reversible signifier *par excellence*.

As a philosophical statement of reversibility, Kierkegaard's dialectic of non-religious religiosity has the merit, for the purposes of this investigation, of imaginative clarity founded in the appropriation of an already existing theoretical formation: Christianity. It is this clarity that drew both the young Lukács and the young Adorno to his writings. Kierkegaard is arguably the first theorist of reification; he is as far from orthodox Christianity as he is from Fichtean subjectivism, the two charges most frequently levelled at his work. Truth for Kierkegaard, writes Adorno in 1939, 'is no "result", no objectivity independent of the process of subjective appropriation, but really consists in the process of subjective appropriation itself.'[18] On the other hand, this is no more than to say that truth 'exists in the living process of Faith, theologically speaking, in the imitation of Christ'. Here, despite the negative judgement which he finally delivers upon Kierkegaard's work, Adorno seems alert to the reversibility which is always latent in his thought, and which is embodied in a stand-off between the tedious 'verbosity' of his religious writings and the paradoxical rationality of the philosophical works. Kierkegaard wants to 'rejuvenate' Christianity into 'what it was supposed to be during St. Paul's times', writes Adorno: 'a scandal to the Jews and a folly to the Greeks. The scandal is Kierkegaard's Christian paradox. The folly to the Greeks, however, is the laborious simplicity which Kierkegaard stubbornly upholds throughout the religious sermons.'[19]

*The Concept of Anxiety* is the text in which Kierkegaard comes closest to bridging this impasse. It is also the first of his pseudonymous works not to have been published alongside an 'upbuilding discourse' under his own name – suggesting, as Gordon D. Marino observes, that the book has a directness of expression which the other pseudonymous works lack.[20] The consequences of this 'directness of expression' are far from straightforward, however; for the project of mediating the opposition between religion and philosophy demands that each is perpetually and simultaneously inverted into the other; discourse is pushed to its limits in *The Concept of Anxiety*, so as to point towards the truth which it is itself unable to grasp. The book undertakes both 'the transplantation of theology into the philosophical realm', as Adorno writes of Kierkegaard's work in general, and the reverse. Kierkegaard's thought strives towards the 'abdication' of philosophy, which may approach the Absolute only by such an act of self-sacrifice.[21] Any successful elucidation of Kierkegaard's Christianity or of his philosophy must proceed by way of the category of reification, which, unnamed, occurs everywhere in his works, and nowhere more so than in *The Concept of Anxiety*.

In his earlier *Kierkegaard: Construction of the Aesthetic*, published in 1933, Adorno dismisses Kierkegaard's existentialist

Christianity as a 'consolatory' discourse, the product of a 'shallow idealism' which 'comfortably divides up its objects into internal and external, spirit and nature, freedom and necessity'.[22] Yet Adorno here underestimates the extent to which for Kierkegaard these concepts are always reversible, always identifiable with their opposite. Kierkegaard's opposition to the 'privations' of an 'incipient high-capitalism' takes place not 'in the name of a lost immediacy', as Adorno states,[23] but in the name of the world of spirit, an 'eternal divine order' of justice and fairness[24] – a projected future which is indescribable except in the reified, 'idealistic' terms of an impoverished present. Adorno, this is to say, misses or ignores the extent to which a strong concept of reification, comparable in subtlety and stringency to Adorno's own use of the term, permeates and qualifies every word of Kierkegaard's philosophical interrogation and defence of Christianity.

In *The Concept of Anxiety* Kierkegaard coins the term 'spiritlessness' (*Aandløsheden*) to designate a state of consciousness which fails to realize that it is embedded in sinfulness, in thingitude – which fails, in effect, to recognize its own unhappiness, or to acknowledge the anxiety pressing in upon it. Spiritlessness is 'the consequence of that sin which is absence of the consciousness of sin'.[25] Spiritlessness is reified consciousness, 'the stagnation of spirit' and 'the caricature of ideality',[26] which are the same thing. At a certain stage in history, spiritlessness may even possess the whole content of spirit, says Kierkegaard, 'but mark well, not as spirit but as the haunting of ghosts, as gibberish, as a slogan, etc. It may possess the truth,' he continues, 'but mark well, not as truth but as rumour and old wives' tales.'[27] In some cases, he says,

> spiritlessness can say exactly the same thing that the richest spirit has said, but it does not say it by virtue of spirit. Man qualified as spiritless has become a talking machine, and there is nothing to prevent him from repeating by rote a philosophical rigmarole, a confession of faith, or a political recitative.[28]

Identical statements or formulations may, in only minutely differing circumstances, be truth-telling or falsifying. Spiritlessness is a form of consciousness which is condemned to falsity, because it apprehends its truths in terms which imply their ontological limitation by the *forms* of their apprehension. Spiritlessness is secure in the knowledge that it possesses the truth; such certainty renders it further removed from truth than ever. Spiritlessness is anxiety in the form of absence of anxiety. It is a secular consciousness which deals with its anxiety – the disturbing intuition of something other in the core of the same – by ruthlessly expunging all traces of it. Spiritlessness is the conviction that nothing exists beyond the immediate world, a conviction which may as frequently appear in the form of 'religious' belief as a 'secular' world view, for Kierkegaard's phrase 'the caricature of ideality' refers to a complacent faith in the *existing conceptual forms* of the Absolute. Religious belief still exists overwhelmingly in forms which are as far removed as possible from the structure of 'religiosity' as I have been attempting to redefine it in this book.[29]

Adorno writes that for Kierkegaard religion 'brings rescue from the extremity of reification'.[30] This is only superficially true; for religion, as well as embodying 'the logic of an inverted world in popular form', is also, as Marx and Engels write in the *Communist Manifesto*, one of many abstractions of bourgeois prejudice, 'behind which lurk in ambush just as many bourgeois interests'.[31] The last thing the present work seeks is a *reconciliation* of Marxism with Christianity, that concessionary political formation which Marx and Engels dismiss with the term 'feudal socialism' – 'half lamentation, half lampoon; half echo of the past, half menace of the future'.[32] Only in Kierkegaard's peculiar sense of Christianity as reversibility, as dialectical thought, as the critique of everything that exists, is 'religiosity' a means of genuine liberation from reification. Such liberation does not entail a *dissolution* of the anxiety towards reification, but the mobilization of its energies towards a mode of engagement in which the conceptual forms of the present are regarded in the light of an unimaginable and yet imminent future. In the name of that future is produced the *identity* of Marxism and religious thought, a complex which may be represented as the simultaneous rejection and redemption of each: the triumph of materialism as the apogee of idealism.

The usual assumption of revolutionary thinking is that critique loses its properly political dimension when it becomes a critique of reality *per se*; that political thought is thereby transformed into armchair metaphysics; that its objectives simply recede into what Hegel called a 'bad' or 'spurious' infinite – meaning, as he writes in the *Science of Logic*, a concept of infinity which is 'qualitatively distinct' from the finite.[33] The moment theory turns into philosophy is the moment when radical thought enters into a relation with the world which is destined never to be satisfied, when the dimension of possibility is shunted into impossibility, when infinity – that which by definition does not exist – is produced as an abstraction entirely and forever removed from the here and now.

This assumption should be countered with a reminder that the critique of reality *per se*, the 'total' critique, necessarily encompasses this prevailing, 'spurious' concept of infinity as well as the 'finitude' it is so futilely opposed to. The 'total' critique speaks in the name of a true infinity which is more, not less comprehensive than Hegel's 'spurious' infinity, given that finitude itself comes under its scope. The true infinite, therefore, implies the *reversibility* of infinite and finite. Infinity, as Nicholas of Cusa realized,[34] is a signifier of reversibility; and the same must be true of its opposite, 'total' reification, which includes the concept of reification within its critique. The rationale which insists upon the *totality* of reification is the same as that which makes inevitable Lukács's disavowal of the concept almost as soon as he formulates it.

Politically revolutionary critique must be articulated in totalizing terms. This is not simply a theoretical axiom; for, as any thorough survey of the consciousness of advanced capitalist society must reveal, reification is fast approaching the stage of totality;

probably it arrived there long ago. This is not to say that the possibility for radical intervention in the world no longer exists, but rather that such intervention is imminent and inevitable – that it *cannot but* take place. Moreover, in a situation of total reification, effective critique will inevitably appear in a violent form, one which may be abhorrent to all liberal sentiments – indeed, it may well have no obvious relation to the respectable forms of 'anti-capitalist' protest that have prevailed hitherto. New forms of revolutionary critique may – indeed must – emerge from a consciousness that is as 'reified' as the reality it is attempting to displace.

The figure of 'total reification' is, despite its apparent idealism, an appropriate one for a world in which a new generation of spectres is proliferating before our eyes. 'Advanced capitalism' is a totally reified society which mystifies everything, including all manifestations of otherness, which it *produces* in forms which appear completely alien to itself. The accuracy of this diagnosis is confirmed when acts of extreme violence, especially violence on a grand scale, effect a temporary displacement of this reification – operate as a 'cleansing force', to use Fanon's phrase, upon a reality which is as petrified in Manichaean falsity as, say, colonial Algeria. Recognizing the totality of this situation is necessary for any real change. Not only is the pasteboard façade an illusion, but the grotesque reality beneath as well; not only the reified manifestation, but the critique of reification which exposes it. Reification is both total and illusory – a total illusion. Reification so completely conditions the present reality of human consciousness that the critique of reification is thoroughly implicated in it. Herbert Marcuse expresses this in a concise, enigmatic formulation at the end of *One-Dimensional Man*: 'if the abstract character of the refusal is the result of total reification, then the concrete ground for refusal must still exist, for reification is an illusion.'[35] The grounds for an 'absolute refusal' of the violence of reification exist irrespective of the violence of that refusal; for the 'absolute refusal' promises to upset the very order according to which truth and illusion, reality and ideology, object and subject, inhabit two distinct arenas. The totality of reification, in other words, implies its own reversal – which is to say, dereification. The reversibility of the concept of reification is the key to its rehabilitation, and to the dereification of the world.

The solution to the experience of reification which I have tried to put forward in this book may appear somewhat removed from the traditional notion of 'praxis', the term commonly used to denote 'the unity of theory and practice', but which Marx defined more concisely as 'practical, human-sensuous activity'.[36] 'Reversibility' in this work designates a structure of critical intellection, the dialectical mediation of reality – predicated upon the actuality and ubiquity of the phenomenon of reification, its simultaneity with the anxiety towards it, and the inseparability of that anxiety from the experience of human consciousness. Reversibility is, among other things, an attempt to forestall the very much more bloody and physically exacting 'total critique' which is otherwise, and perhaps in any case, on its way. Yet the apparently abstract nature of this proposal is not simply a flight from politics into idealism, but a response to the real idealization of politics itself, a process of the gradual correspondence of subjective experience and objective reality. The event of 'total reification' signals the collapse of the absolute *alienation* of subject and object into their absolute *identification*. We are living under what Slavoj Žižek has called 'the reign of "real abstraction"',[37] a period dominated by processes and forces so far beyond the practical or intellectual reach of men and women that universalizing those forces, or simply identifying with them, is unavoidable. Theodor Adorno diagnoses an era of 'absolutized praxis', within which thought is no longer possible, only 'reaction' – a degraded rationality based on the false premises of the existing world.[38] 'Real abstraction' and 'absolutized praxis' are of course identical. Each describes a situation in which the prevailing form of ideology is an emphasis upon 'real people with their real worries', a distraction, which only serves to obscure the fact that, in Adorno's phrase, the doors are barricaded. In a society of 'real abstraction', the only action which has any impact is that which 'overdoes and aggravates itself for the sake of its own publicity'.[39] Acts of spectacular destruction on the physical plane, and the thoroughgoing mediation of every conceptual form on the theoretical one, are the only means of displacing a world which has solidified in opposition to all that is right and true. In an age of 'real abstraction', however, 'practical, human-sensuous activity' is located wholly on the side of the latter; for the former moves within what Adorno calls 'pseudo-reality', a product of the false society. Extreme violence *expends* itself upon the material world, leaving the abstract reality intact. Its success, albeit limited, in throwing into temporary relief the contradictions of that reality is a symptom of an age in which drastic action in the service of political reality is all but unheard of. Adorno is undaunted in his insistence on the need for critical thinking in such a period: 'It is up to thought not to accept the situation as final. The situation can be changed, if at all, by undiminished insight.'[40] With determination and momentum, this transformation may even be effected on a revolutionary scale.

The resources I have found to think the reversibility of all terms and concepts include writers who have long been recognized for their dialectical subtlety: Hegel, Adorno, Lukács, Proust, John Donne and Søren Kierkegaard – as well as others not conventionally thought of as theoreticians at all: Flannery O'Connor, Dante and Herman Melville. Yet the implications of the thesis advanced here are that such resources might potentially be found in any text at all, from the most spiritually vapid or politically obnoxious, to those which regard the world from a position of religious sanctimony, or which present to us the basilisk gaze of technocratic mediocrity. Every text is subject to conditions of worldly thingitude which must be mediated to reveal its truth content, and that of the world itself.

I have tried to avoid lengthy statements of methodology in this book; yet it may be appropriate to point up the extent to which the perspective adopted here attempts to invert the usual procedure of critical-theoretical thought. Rather than discard the concept of reification on the grounds of its covert religiosity,

I have sought to discard the prohibition on 'religiosity' within critical thinking – or rather, to *mediate* the opposition between secularism and religion – thereby to rehabilitate the concept of reification. This strategy may be described as a 'redemptive' one; redemption, I would claim, and not 'construction' or 'reconstruction', is the true alternative to deconstruction, and its logical consequence. It is an approach which might be pursued with regard to deconstruction itself; this is not something I have been able to undertake here, although the idea of reversibility clearly points the way towards a redemptive reorientation of the Derridean notion of undecidability.

Perhaps, following the example of Lukács's theory of reification, or that of Kierkegaard's distinction between the aesthetic and the ethical stages, the best that can be hoped for with this work is that its conceptual model become obsolete as quickly as possible; that the reversibility of all terms and concepts be superseded by a theoretical willingness to take up residence within them, in serene acknowledgement of their ontological inadequacy; that the simultaneity of reification with its opposite be succeeded by a thoroughgoing liberation from the category; that anxiety no longer be a condition of human consciousness but a fetter to be cast aside; that the 'virtual multitude' give way to a theory of political change predicated on the recovered model of proletarian revolution. Least significant among the effects of this longed-for abrogation, however, would be the corroboration of everything put forward in these pages. Among the more significant would be the arrival of humanity at a state of intimacy with the created and the uncreated world.

# Notes

## Preface

1 Georg Lukács, *The Theory of the Novel: A historico-philosophical essay on the forms of great epic literature*, trans. Anna Bostock, Cambridge, MA: MIT Press 1971, p. 29.

2 Don DeLillo, *Underworld*, London: Picador 1998, p. 103.

3 Glenn Brown, quoted Julian Stallabrass, *High Art Lite: British Art in the 1990s*, London: Verso 1999, p. 101.

4 Michael Wood, 'Foreword: Happy Days', in Peter Biskind, *Seeing is Believing: How Hollywood Taught us to Stop Worrying and Love the Fifties*, London: Bloomsbury 2001, p. ix.

5 Andrew O'Hagan, 'Everything Must Go!', *London Review of Books*, Vol. 23, No. 4 (13 December 2001), p. 3.

6 Leszek Kolakowski, *Main Currents of Marxism* Vol. 3: *The Breakdown*, trans. P. S. Falla, Oxford: Oxford University Press 1978, pp. 334–5.

7 Lukács, *The Theory of the Novel*, p. 34.

8 Theodor Adorno, *Minima Moralia: Reflections from Damaged Life*, trans. E. F. N. Jephcott, London: Verso 1978, §49, pp. 78–9

9 See Mazisi Kunene, 'Introduction' to Aimé Césaire, *Return to my Native Land*, trans. John Berger and Anna Bostock, Harmondsworth: Penguin 1969, p. 32.

10 Aimé Césaire, *Notebook of a Return to My Native Land*, trans. Mireille Rosello with Annie Pritchard, London: Bloodaxe 1995, p. 125.

11 Frantz Fanon, *Studies in a Dying Colonialism*, trans. Haakon Chevalier, London: Earthscan 1989, p. 47. David Macey discusses the ambiguities of the term 'negritude' in *Frantz Fanon: A Life*, London: Granta 2000, pp. 177–87.

12 Theodor Adorno, 'Messages in a Bottle' (excised fragments from *Minima Moralia*), *New Left Review* I/200 (July/August 1993), §VIII, p. 10.

13 Ibid., pp. 10–11.

## PART ONE: FALL

1 Georg Lukács, *Record of a Life: An Autobiographical Sketch*, trans. Rodney Livingstone, London: Verso 1983, p. 181.

### 1 Obsolescence of a Concept

2 See Karl Marx, *Economic and Philosophical Manuscripts,* in *Early Writings*, trans. Rodney Livingstone and Gregor Benton, Harmondsworth: Penguin 1975, esp. pp. 322 ff.

3 Karl Marx, *Capital: A Critique of Political Economy*, Volume 1, trans. Ben Fowkes, Harmondsworth: Penguin 1990, p. 165.

4 Georg Lukács, 'Reification and the Consciousness of the Proletariat', in *History and Class Consciousness: Studies in Marxist Dialectics*, trans. Rodney Livingstone, London: Merlin 1971, p. 83; John Rees, 'Introduction' to Georg Lukács, *A Defence of* History and Class Consciousness: *Tailism and the Dialectic*, London: Verso 2000, p. 13.

5 See Gillian Rose, *The Melancholy Science: An Introduction to the Thought of Theodor W. Adorno*, London and Basingstoke: Macmillan 1978, p. 30.

6 Herbert Marcuse, *Reason and Revolution: Hegel and the Rise of Social Theory* (2nd edn), London: Routledge and Kegan Paul 1955, pp. 112–13 ff.

7 Peter Berger and Stanley Pullberg, 'Reification and the Sociological Critique of Consciousness', *New Left Review* I/35 (January–February 1966), p. 62.

8 Lucien Goldmann, *Lukács and Heidegger: Towards a New Philosophy*, trans. William Q. Boelhower, London: Routledge and Kegan Paul 1977.

9 See for example Ben Brewster's 'Comment' on Peter Berger and Stanley Pullberg's article, *New Left Review* I/35 (January–February 1966), p. 73.

10 Georg Lukács, 'Reification and the Consciousness of the Proletariat', pp. 149 ff. and 177 ff.

11 Lucien Goldmann, 'La Réification', *Recherches Dialectiques* (3rd edn), Paris: Gallimard 1959, p. 64n.; as quoted and translated by Mitchell Cohen in *The Wager of Lucien Goldmann: Tragedy, Dialectics, and a Hidden God*, Princeton, NJ: Princeton University Press 1994, p. 179.

12 See Goldmann, 'La Réification', p. 66.

13 Martin Jay, *Adorno*, Cambridge, MA: Harvard University Presss 1984, p. 68.

14 Goldmann, *Lukács and Heidegger*, p. 34.

15 Ibid., p. 135.

16 Theodor Adorno, *Minima Moralia: Reflections from Damaged Life*, trans. E. F. N. Jephcott, London: Verso 1978, §147, p. 229.

17 Joseph Gabel's *La fausse conscience* appeared in France in 1962, and in an English translation (as *False Consciousness: An Essay on Reification*) in 1975. More recent texts include Burke C. Thomason, *Making Sense of Reification: Albert Schutz and Constructionist Theory* (Macmillan 1982), and Hugh Grady, *Shakespeare's Universal Wolf: Studies in Early Modern Reification* (Clarendon 1996); yet each of these is concerned less with the concept itself as with its application in the context of certain highly specific scholarly analyses. Edward Said's *Culture and Imperialism* (London: Chatto & Windus 1993), Fredric Jameson's *The Political Unconscious* (London: Methuen 1981) and Gillian Rose's *The Melancholy Science* (London: Macmillan 1978) all include highly useful and relevant discussions of reification, but each expresses certain reservations about the concept, and none offers an overall theory *of* it. Indeed, it is arguable whether even Lukács, in his classic essay on the subject, really offers a theoretical exegesis of the term. In a 1967 afterthought to *History and Class Consciousness*, published as a preface to the 1971 English translation, Lukács criticized the book, and implicitly the account of reification that was central to it, for 'subjectivism' and 'messianic utopianism' (p. xviii). This self-critique should certainly not be taken at face value; yet Rose has commented that in Lukács 'reification', along with 'mediation', operates as a 'shorthand' for the Marxist critique of capitalism, rather than as a sustained critical theory (see Gillian Rose, *Hegel Contra Sociology*, London: Athlone 1981, p. 29).

Jameson writes similarly that in Lukács's later aesthetic writings in particular, the term is used as 'simple shorthand for value judgement and for the repudiation by association of the various modern styles' (*The Political Unconscious*, pp. 226–7).

18 Lukács, 'Reification and the Consciousness of the Proletariat', p. 149. See Marx and Engels, *The Holy Family, or Critique of Critical Critique*, trans. R. Dixon, Moscow: Foreign Languages Publishing House 1956, p. 51.

19 The importance of this future-historical perspective – what Jean-François Lyotard has in a different context referred to as the mode of the 'future-anterior' – is demonstrated in another passage which Lukács elsewhere quotes from *The Holy Family*: 'It is not a question of what this or that proletarian, or even the whole proletariat, at the moment, *regards* as its aim. It is a question of *what the proletariat is*, and what, in accordance with this *being*, it will historically be compelled to do.' See Georg Lukács, *A Defence of* History and Class Consciousness: *Tailism and the Dialectic*, trans. Esther Leslie, London: Verso 2000, p. 66.

20 Louis Althusser, 'Ideology and Ideological State Apparatuses (Notes Towards an Investigation)', *Lenin and Philosophy and Other Essays*, London: New Left Books 1971.

21 Adorno, *Minima Moralia*, p. 15.

22 Lucien Goldmann, *The Hidden God: A Study of Tragic Vision in the Pensées of Pascal and the Tragedies of Racine*, trans. Philip Thody, London: Routledge & Kegan Paul 1964, p. 105.

## 2 Marxist Anxieties

1 Rose, *The Melancholy Science*, p. 49

2 See Burke C. Thomason, *Making Sense of Reification*, esp. chapter 5: 'Reification as a Constructionist Concept', pp. 114 ff. Other non-Marxist, similarly expansive accounts of the term are found in Peter L. Berger and Thomas Luckmann, *The Social Construction of Reality: A Treatise in the Sociological Critique of Consciousness*, New York: Doubleday 1967, and Berger and Pullberg, 'Reification and the Sociological Critique of Consciousness'.

3 This is strictly true only if one restricts one's attention to Derrida's written (and therefore more circumspect) enunciations. In conversation with Richard Kearney in 1981, when challenged as to whether the political position of deconstruction might be described as one of

'responsible anarchy', Derrida gave a qualified assent, but went on to speak of the danger that such terms as 'responsible' and 'anarchy' may become 'reified and unthinking dogmas'. See Richard Kearney, *Dialogues with Contemporary Continental Thinkers: The Phenomenological Heritage*, Manchester: Manchester University Press 1984, p. 121.

4 See Gayatri Chakravorty Spivak, 'Translator's Preface', in Jacques Derrida, *Of Grammatology*, trans. Gayatri Chakravorty Spivak, Baltimore and London: Johns Hopkins University Press 1976, pp. xii–xiii; Homi K. Bhabha, *The Location of Culture*, London: Routledge 1994.

5 Gayatri Chakravorty Spivak, *A Critique of Postcolonial Reason: Towards a History of the Vanishing Present*, Cambridge, MA, and London: Harvard University Press 1999, p. 76n.

6 Karl Marx and Frederick Engels, *Manifesto of the Communist Party*, trans. Samuel Moore, Peking: Foreign Languages Press 1975, pp. 36–7.

7 Ellen Meiksins Wood, 'The Communist Manifesto 150 Years Later', in Karl Marx and Friedrich Engels, *The Communist Manifesto*, New York: Monthly Review Press 1998, p. 93.

8 Marx and Engels, *Manifesto of the Communist Party*, pp. 38, 36.

9 Spivak, *A Critique of Postcolonial Reason*, p. 69n.

10 Neil Lazarus, 'Hating Tradition Properly', *New Formations* 38 (Summer 1999), pp. 13–14; see Samir Amin, *Eurocentrism*, trans. Russell Moore, London: Zed 1989, p. 72.

11 Spivak, *A Critique of Postcolonial Reason*, p. 83.

12 See Jacques Derrida, 'Plato's Pharmacy', *Dissemination*, trans. Barbara Johnson, London: Athlone 1981, esp. p. 98.

13 Spivak, *A Critique of Postcolonial Reason*, p. 84.

14 Lukács, 'Reification and the Consciousness of the Proletariat', p. 199.

15 Gayatri Chakravorty Spivak, 'Speculation on reading Marx: after reading Derrida', in Derek Attridge, Geoff Bennington and Robert Young, eds., *Post-structuralism and the Question of History*, Cambridge: Cambridge University Press 1987, p. 30. However, this perspective is belied in the more recent *A Critique of Postcolonial Reason*, throughout which, she states, she has 'quietly changed "sublation" [*Aufhebung*] to "*différance*" as the name of the relationship between capitalism and socialism' – this, she says, as a direct response to 'globalization'. See *A Critique of Postcolonial Reason*, p. 70.

## 3 Reification and Colonialism

1 See Karl Marx, *Capital: A Critique of Political Economy*, Volume 1, trans. Ben Fowkes, Harmondsworth: Penguin 1990, p. 931n.

2 See for example Gayatri Chakravorty Spivak, 'Scattered Speculations on the Question of Value', *In Other Worlds: Essays in Cultural Politics*, New York and London: Methuen 1987, pp. 160–61.

3 Some explanation may be needed for readers outside the UK, where the Lawrence case became a *cause célèbre*. On 22 April 1993 Stephen Lawrence, an eighteen-year-old sixth-form student, was stabbed to death in a racist attack at a bus stop in Eltham, south London. Three of the five suspects initially arrested for the murder were subsequently acquitted in a private prosecution, brought by the Lawrence family after the Crown Prosecution Service failed to prosecute the five on the grounds of 'insufficient evidence'. The other two suspects were discharged at the private prosecution, also for lack of evidence. The names of all five suspects were widely publicized. 'The five boys in the Stephen Lawrence case didn't have an O-level between them,' said Stuart Hall pertinently, several years later. 'The only time [people like them] can feel English is when they can kick shit out of the Dutch or the Belgians. If you're serious about a multicultural society, you would address the sense of alienation of white working-class people, who have to be won to a new conception of themselves where Britain's not lording it from a gunboat.' Maya Jaggi, 'Prophet at the margins', *Guardian* (Saturday Review), 8 July 2000, p. 9.

4 The point is that reification provides a principle, a technology by which to identify these apparently opposing currents; in so doing it transforms particular events into an abstract illustration of a universal process.

5 Joseph Conrad, *Heart of Darkness*, Harmondsworth: Penguin 1983, pp. 31-2.

6 F.R. Leavis, *The Great Tradition: George Eliot, Henry James, Joseph Conrad*, Harmondsworth: Penguin 1962, p. 196.

7 Edward W. Said, 'Conrad: The Presentation of Narrative', in *The World, the Text, and the Critic*, London: Vintage 1991, p. 90.

8 Ibid., p. 95.

9 Conrad, *Heart of Darkness*, pp. 69, 83.

10 Ibid., p. 67.

11 Ibid., p. 40.

12 Ibid., p. 57.

13 Edward W. Said, *The World, the Text, and the Critic*, pp. 108-9, 95-6.

14 Fredric Jameson, 'Romance and Reification: Plot Construction and Ideological Closure in Joseph Conrad', in *The Political Unconscious: Narrative as a Socially Symbolic Act*, Ithaca, New York: Cornell University Press 1981, pp. 236–7.

15 Jameson, 'Romance and Reification', p. 237.

16 Perry Anderson, *The Origins of Postmodernity*, London: Verso 1998, p. 76.

17 Sean Homer, 'Marxism, *Fredric Jameson: Marxism, Hermeneutics, Postmodernism*, Cambridge: Polity 1998, p. 169.

18 Fredric Jameson, *The Geopolitical Aesthetic: Cinema and Space in the World System*, London: British Film Institute 1992, p. 212.

19 Anderson, *The Origins of Postmodernity*, p. 76.

20 See Chinua Achebe, 'An Image of Africa: Racism in Conrad's *Heart of Darkness*', in *Hopes and Impediments: Selected Essays 1965–87*, London: Heinemann 1988. Said accords the defence of Conrad on the grounds of his cultural and historical limitation more legitimacy than Achebe does: 'As a creature of his time,' writes Said, 'Conrad could not grant the natives their freedom, despite his severe crtique of the imperialism that enslaved them.' See *Culture and Imperialism*, p. 34.

21 Ernest Mandel, *Late Capitalism*, trans. Joris De Bres, London: Verso 1978, pp. 505–6.

## 4 From Adorno to Jameson

1 Jameson, *The Political Unconscious*, p. 226; my emphasis.

2 Theodor Adorno, *Minima Moralia: Reflections from Damaged Life*, trans. E. F. N. Jephcott, London: Verso 1978, §32, pp. 52-3. In his essay 'Hating Tradition Properly' (*New Formations* No. 38 [Summer 1999]), Neil Lazarus subjects this passage to an intense reading in an attempt to liberate Adorno from his marginalization at the hands of postcolonial critics. See also Neil Lazarus, *Nationalism and Cultural Practice in the Postcolonial World*, Cambridge: Cambridge University Press 1999.

3 See Conrad, *Heart of Darkness*, p. 75: 'I don't think a single one of them had a clear idea of time, as we at the end of countless ages have. They still belonged to the beginnings of time – had no inherited experience to teach them, as it were.' See Gayatri Spivak's critique of Hegel's

Eurocentric, 'orientalist' version of the 'timelessness' of India, in her *A Critique of Postcolonial Reason*, pp. 41 ff.

4 Theodor W. Adorno, 'Resignation', in *Critical Models: Interventions and Catchwords*, trans. Henry W. Pickford, New York: Columbia University Press 1998, p. 289. Adorno's essay, a response to attacks on the Frankfurt School intellectuals for their 'absenteeism' during the May 1968 demonstrations, inverts the equation of theory with contemplation and of action with praxis.

5 Ibid., p. 291.

6 Perry Anderson, *The Origins of Postmodernity*, pp. 75-6.

7 See, for example, Simon Jarvis, *Adorno: A Critical Introduction*, Cambridge: Polity 1998, p. 76. It is difficult to defend Adorno from the charge of defeatism in the face of such extreme statements as the following, in *Dialectic of Enlightenment* (trans. John Cumming, London: Verso 1979, p. 167): 'The most intimate reactions of human beings have been so thoroughly reified [*verdinglicht*] that the idea of anything specific to themselves now persists only as an utterly abstract notion: personality scarcely signifies anthing more than shining white teeth and freedom from body odour and emotions.' Nonetheless, the complexity of the concept of reification as developed in later writings – most notably *Aesthetic Theory* – indicates that it is through the dialectical elaboration of the concept, rather than the search for ever more rarefied strategies of evasion of it, that liberation from reification is possible.

8 See 'The Dialectic of Utopia and Ideology', Jameson's conclusion to *The Political Unconscious*.

9 Fredric Jameson, *Postmodernism, or The Cultural Logic of Late Capitalism*, London: Verso, 1991, p. 383; 'On Jargon', *The Jameson Reader*, ed. Michael Hardt and Kathi Weeks, Oxford: Blackwell 2000, p. 118.

10 Ernest Mandel, *Late Capitalism*, p. 506. See Theodor W. Adorno, *Critical Models: Interventions and Catchwords*, p. 269. The reference to Jürgen von Kempski is to the latter's conclusion, in a 1949 article, that the superiority of state weapons technology in advanced industrial societies performs an equivalent function in preventing 'revolutions' to the bureauracratic command structures which foiled the German coup of 20 July 1944; see the translator's note to the passage on p. 382 of *Critical Models*.

11 Most notably in 'Free Time', in Theodor W. Adorno, *Critical*

*Models: Interventions and Catchwords*; but see also *Minima Moralia*, §84, pp. 130–31.

12 Georg Lukács, *A Defence of History and Class Consciousness: Tailism and the Dialectic*, London: Verso 2000.

## 5 Messianism, Historical Materialism, Post-structuralism

1 *The Political Unconscious* p. 285. *'Une Promesse de bonheur'* is the phrase coined by Stendhal in *De l'Amour* to describe the experience of beauty, and made famous by Nietzsche's quotation in the *Genealogy of Morals*. See Stendhal, *Love*, trans. Gilbert and Suzanne Sale, London: Merlin 1957, ch. XVII, p. 46; Friedrich Nietzsche, *On the Genealogy of Morality*, trans. Carol Diethe, Cambridge: Cambridge University Press 1994, p. 78 (3rd essay, section 6).

2 Jameson, *The Political Unconscious*, pp. 286–7.

3 'On Jargon', *The Jameson Reader*, p. 118.

4 Jameson, *The Political Unconscious* p. 293

5 Max Raphael, *The Demands of Art*, trans. Norbert Guterman, London: Routledge & Kegan Paul 1968, p. 201.

6 Jameson, *The Political Unconscious*, p. 288.

7 Sean Homer, *Fredric Jameson: Marxism, Hermeneutics, Postmodernism*, Cambridge: Polity 1998, p. 158.

8 *The Political Unconscious* p. 287.

9 Ibid., p. 283.

10 Ibid., p. 283.

11 Edward Said, 'Traveling Theory', in *The World, the Text, and the Critic*, London: Vintage 1991, pp. 236-7.

12 Jameson, *The Political Unconscious*, p. 283.

13 Lucien Goldmann, *The Hidden God: A Study of Tragic Vision in the Pensées of Pascal and the Tragedies of Racine*, trans. Philip Thody, London: Routledge & Kegan Paul 1964, p. 90.

14 Jameson, *The Political Unconscious*, p. 63.

15 Jameson, *The Political Unconscious*, p. 102; *The Jameson Reader* p. 136.

16 Mary Evans, *Lucien Goldmann: An Introduction*, Brighton, Sussex: Harvester 1981, p. 60.

17 Ibid., p. 64.

18 Goldmann, *The Hidden God*, p. 301.

19 Jameson, *The Political Unconscious*, pp. 284–5.

20 Goldmann, *The Hidden God*, p. 300.

21 'Always historicize!' are the well-known opening words to Jameson's *The Political Unconscious*.

22 Jameson, *The Political Unconscious*, p. 285.

23 Goldmann, *The Hidden God*, p. 15.

24 Ibid., p. 25.

25 Ibid., p. 17.

26 Lucien Goldmann, *Towards a Sociology of the Novel*, trans. Alan Sheridan, London: Tavistock 1975, pp. 10–11.

27 See Theodor W. Adorno, *Hegel: Three Studies*, trans. Shierry Weber Nicholsen, Cambridge, MA,. and London: MIT 1993, p. 64.

28 Goldmann, *The Hidden God*, p. 376.

29 Jameson, *The Political Unconscious*, pp. 20, 19; see Anderson, *The Origins of Postmodernity*, pp. 53–4.

30 Spivak, *A Critique of Postcolonial Reason*, p. 208 (Spivak's emphasis). See Jameson, *The Political Unconcsious*, p. 20; Sartre, *Existentialism and Humanism*, trans. Philip Mairet, London: Methuen 1948, pp. 46–7. This should be compared to another of Sartre's 'notorious' statements – discussed by Jameson in *Postmodernism, or The Cultural Logic of Late Capitalism* – that one would not be able to read a *nouveau roman* in an 'undeveloped' country. The true target of the remark is not, of course, the Third World but the *nouveau roman* – specifically Alain Robbe-Grillet. See '"A Long, Bitter, Sweet Madness": An Interview with Jean-Paul Sartre, *Encounter*, Vol. XXII, No. 6 (June 1964), p. 62; Fredric Jameson, *Postmodernism, or The Cultural Logic of Late Capitalism*, p. 145. See also Maurice Cranston, 'Sartre's Commitment', *Encounter*, Vol. XXIII, No. 2 (August 1964), pp. 43–5.

31 Goldmann, *The Hidden God*, p. 12.

32 Roland Barthes, 'The Death of the Author', in *Image – Music – Text*, trans. Stephen Heath, New York: Farrar, Straus and Giroux 1977, pp. 147, 146.

33 Augustine, *The City of God against the Pagans*, trans. R. W. Dyson, Cambridge: Cambridge University Press 1998, p. 3; see Jameson, *The Political Unconscious*, p. 18.

34 Geoffrey Bennington, 'Not Yet', *Legislations: The Politics of Deconstruction*, London: Verso 1994, pp. 82, 80.

35 Jean-Paul Sartre, *Existentialism and Humanism*, p. 47.

36 Adorno, *Hegel: Three Studies*, p. 67.

37 Georg Lukács, *A Defence of* History and Class Consciousness: *Tailism and the Dialectic*, trans. Esther Leslie, London: Verso 2000, p. 112.

38 Goldmann, *The Hidden God*, p. 303.

39 Ibid., p. 305.

40 Ibid., p. 4.

41 Ibid., p. 19.

42 See Michel Foucault, 'Nietzsche, Genealogy, History', trans. Donald F. Bouchard and Sherry Simon, in *The Foucault Reader*, ed. Paul Rabinow, Harmondsworth: Penguin 1986, p. 85.

43 Ibid., p. 80.

44 Ibid., p. 81 (my emphasis).

45 Ibid., p. 94.

46 Ibid., pp. 88-9; Foucault is quoting from Nietzsche's *Daybreak* (trans. R.J. Hollingdale, Cambridge: Cambridge University Press 1982, §130, pp. 131–2).

47 Michel Foucault, 'Nietzsche, Genealogy, History', p. 89. See Jürgen Habermas's critique of Foucault on similar grounds in *The Philosophical Discourse of Modernity*, where he writes of the 'involuntary presentism of a historiography that remains hermeneutically stuck in its starting situation', and of the genealogical understanding of history as 'meaningless kaleidoscopic changes of shape in discourse totalities that have nothing in common apart from the single characteristic of being protuberances of power in general': Habermas, *The Philosophical Discourse of Modernity: Twelve Lectures*, trans. Frederick Lawrence, Cambridge: Polity 1987, pp. 276–7.

48 Goldmann, *The Hidden God*, p. 18.

49 Ibid., pp. 19–20.

50 Ibid., pp. 7–8.

51 Ibid., p. 29.

52 Jacques Derrida, 'Force and Signification', in *Writing and Difference*, trans. Alan Bass, London: Routledge & Kegan Paul 1978, p. 4.

53 Spivak, *A Critique of Postcolonial Reason*, pp. 207, 208.

54 Derrida, 'Force and Signification', p. 3.

55 Jacques Derrida, *Of Grammatology*, trans. Gayatri Chakravorty Spivak, Baltimore and London: Johns Hopkins University Press 1976, p. 67.

56 Geoffrey Bennington and Jacques Derrida, *Jacques Derrida*, trans.

Geoffrey Bennington, Chicago and London: University of Chicago Press 1993, p. 72.

57 The strategy of *sous rature* is of course a gesture towards such a discourse.

58 Romans 7: 1 (New International Version).

59 Lucien Goldmann, *The Human Sciences & Philosophy*, trans. Hayden V. White and Robert Anchor, London: Jonathan Cape 1969, p. 14.

## 6 The Translation of God into Man

1 Edward W. Said, *The World, the Text, and the Critic*, London: Vintage 1991, p. 290.

2 Ibid., p. 291.

3 Ibid., p. 290. This critique is discussed in more detail in section 10, below, pp. 69–70.

4 Flannery O'Connor, 'The Artificial Nigger', in *A Good Man is Hard to Find & Other Stories*, London: The Women's Press 1980, p. 129; my emphases.

5 Goldmann, *The Hidden God*, p. 307.

6 'Commitment', trans. Francis McDonagh, in Ernst Bloch et al., *Aesthetics and Politics*, London: Verso 1980, p. 194.

7 Georg Simmel, 'Christianity and Art', in *Essays on Religion*, trans. Horst Jürgen Helle in collaboration with Ludwig Nieder, New Haven and London: Yale University Press 1997, p. 72.

8 'The Dual Nature', in Gabriele Finaldi et al., *The Image of Christ: The Catalogue of the Exhibition SEEING SALVATION*, London: National Gallery 2000, p. 45; 'despised and rejected of men' is a quotation from Isaiah 53: 3.

9 Edward W. Said, *The World, the Text, and the Critic*, p. 291.

10 Goldmann, *The Hidden God*, pp. 60-61. Goldmann adds a footnote to the effect that since writing those lines in 1952, both Sartre and Merleau-Ponty have changed their positions, albeit 'in opposite directions' – Sartre, presumably, towards a more explicit commitment to revolutionary politics, Merleau-Ponty towards 'neutrality' and resignation.

7 Marxism and the Hidden God

1 Jameson, *The Political Unconscious*, p 51.

2 'A materialist theory of immortality' is one of the claims of Ben Watson's book *Art, Class & Cleavage* (London: Quartet 1998). The linguistic theory of V. N. Voloshinov, as put forward in *Marxism and the Philosophy of Language* (trans. Ladislav Matejka and I. R. Titunik, New York and London: Seminar Press 1973) is Watson's principal resource for this idea. Watson unfortunately imperils the integrity of his dialectical methodology in the very moments at which he declares his allegiance to it most strenuously – as when he writes of Voloshinov having salvaged 'the promise of immortality from Christian lies', and of Voloshinov's 'rational and secular understanding of Biblical promises of eternal life' (pp. 335–6). Nevertheless, Voloshinov's theory of the 'multiaccentuality' of the ideological sign, its 'inner dialectic quality' (that is to say, its reversibility), represents one route to the replacement of secular individualism with a dialectical thought predicated upon human 'immortality'. Another is found in Alain Badiou's insistence on Man's 'singularity': his ability *in extremis*, sustained by that which is 'incalculable' and 'un-possessed', to exceed the ontological category of 'living being'; see Badiou's *Ethics: An Essay on the Understanding of Evil*, trans. Peter Hallward, London: Verso 2001, esp. pp. 10–16.

3 Fredric Jameson, *Marxism and Form: Twentieth-Century Dialectical Theories of Literature*, Princeton, NJ: Princeton University Press 1971, p. 416.

4 Lukács, *History and Class Consciousness*, p. 85.

5 Goldmann, *The Hidden God*, p. 308.

6 Ibid., pp. 306, 307.

7 Isaiah 45: 15: *Vere tu es deus absconditus: deus Israel saluato.*

8 Goldmann, *The Hidden God* p. 391.

9 John Cairncross, 'Jean Racine', in Jean Racine, *Iphigenia, Phaedra, Athaliah*, trans. John Cairncross, Harmondsworth: Penguin 1970, p. 24.

10 Goldmann, *The Hidden God* p. 105.

11 Ibid., p. 180.

12 Ibid., p. 379.

13 Marshall Berman, 'Georg Lukács's Cosmic *Chutzpah*', in *Adventures in Marxism*, London: Verso 1999, p. 192.

14 Leszek Kolakowski, *Main Currents of Marxism Vol. 3: The Breakdown*, trans. P. S. Falla, Oxford: Oxford University Press 1978, p. 332.

15 Goldmann, The Hidden God, p. 284

16 Slavoj Žižek, 'Postface', in Georg Lukács, *A Defence of* History and Class Consciousness: *Tailism and the Dialectic*, London: Verso 2000, p. 164.

17 Ibid., p. 163.

18 Jameson, *The Political Unconscious*, p. 35.

19 Ibid., p. 102.

20 Sean Homer, *Fredric Jameson*, p. 158.

21 Making no reference to Goldmann's *The Hidden God*, Malcolm Bull has generalized the process of the disappearance of God as one of of 'coming into hiding', by which he means the gradual appearance of truth as a fact of disunity, disequilibrium and hiddenness, the setting in of a permanent mismatch between reality and forms of representation. Malcolm Bull, *Seeing Things Hidden: Apocalypse, Vision and Totality*, London: Verso 1999.

22 Jameson, *The Political Unconscious*, pp. 53–4.

23 Ibid., p. 43.

24 Walter Benjamin, 'Theses on the Philosophy of History', *Illuminations*, trans. Harry Kohn, New York: Schocken 1968, pp. 254–5.

25 Malcolm Bull, *Seeing Things Hidden*, p. 156.

26 Walter Benjamin, *The Arcades Project*, trans. Howard Eiland and Kevin McLaughlin, Cambridgc, MA: Harvard University Press 1999, pp. 462, 463 (my emphasis).

27 Blaise Pascal, *Pensées and Other Writings*, trans. Honor Levi, Oxford: Oxford University Press 1995, p. 172; see Goldmann, *The Hidden God*, p. 307.

## 8 Post-structuralism and the Absent God

1 Jacques Derrida, *Positions*, trans. Alan Bass, London: Athlone 1987, p. 51.

2 Gilles Deleuze and Félix Guattari, *Anti-Oedipus: Capitalism and Schizophrenia*, trans. Robert Hurley, Mark Seem, and Helen R. Lane, London: Athlone 1984, p. 107. An interesting exception to this tendency within post-structuralism (to stretch the category a little) is the case of Jacques Lacan, in whom the trope of the 'hidden God' survives in the form of the Real, or 'lack' – a very different concept from *différance*, and one in which Derrida detects a hidden metaphysical 'transcendentalism'. Lacan writes of the 'poverty' of modern

terminology, as compared to 'those that structured in their very confusion the ancient quarrels centred around Nature and Grace'; and he includes several citations from Pascal. See Jacques Lacan, 'Function and Field of Speech and Language', in *Écrits: A Selection*, trans. Alan Sheridan, London: Routledge 1989, especially p. 54, and note 24 on p. 108; Jacques Derrida, 'Le facteur de la verité', in *The Post Card: From Socrates to Freud and Beyond*, trans. Alan Bass, London: University of Chicago Press 1987.

3 Deleuze and Guattari, *Anti-Oedipus*, p. 108.

4 Ibid., p. 13; see also pp. 71–2. *Omnitudo realitatis* is Kant's term for the idea of totality; see Immanuel Kant, *Critique of Pure Reason* (Book II Chapter III Section 2: 'The Transcendental Ideal'), trans. J. M. D. Meiklejohn, ed. Vasilis Politis, London: J. M. Dent 1993, pp. 398–9.

5 Emmanuel Levinas, 'The Trace of the Other', trans. Alphonso Lingis, in Mark C. Taylor, *Deconstruction in Context: Literature and Philosophy*, Chicago and London: University of Chicago Press 1986, p. 355; 'God and Philosophy', trans. Alphonso Lingis and Richard Cohen, in Emmanuel Levinas, *Basic Philosophical Writings*, ed. Adriaan T. Peperzak, Simon Critchley, and Robert Bernasconi, Bloomington and Indianapolis: Indiana University Press 1996, p. 141.

6 Richard Kearney, *Dialogues with Contemporary Continental Thinkers: The Phenomenological Heritage*, Manchester: Manchester University Press 1984, p. 59.

7 Ibid., p. 68.

8 See Levinas, *Basic Philosophical Writings*, p. 141. *Il y a* is glossed by Phillip Blond as 'the sheer brute category of existence itself'; and by Levinas himself as 'the phenomenon of the absolutely impersonal', and 'the simple fact of being, without there being any objects'; see Phillip Blond, 'Emmanuel Levinas: God and Phenomenology', in *Post-Secular Philosophy: Between Philosophy and Theology*, London and New York: Routledge 1998, p. 210; Emmanuel Levinas, *Alterity and Transcendence*, trans. Michael B. Smith, London: Athlone 1999, p. 98.

9 Levinas, *Basic Philosophical Writings*, p. 141.

10 Emmanuel Levinas, *Proper Names*, trans. Michael B. Smith, London: Athlone 1996, p. 77; see Derrida's discussion of this passage in *The Gift of Death*, trans. David Wills, Chicago and London: University of Chicago Press 1995, p. 78n.

11 See Søren Kierkegaard, *Fear and Trembling*, trans. Howard V. Hong, Princeton: Princeton University Press 1983, p. 82.

12 Kearney, *Dialogues with Contemporary Continental Thinkers*, p. 67.

13 Søren Kierkegaard, *Either/Or: A Fragment of Life*, trans. Alastair Hannay, Harmondsworth: Penguin 1992, p. 432.

9 What is Imputed Class Consciousness?

1 Quoted by György Márkus, 'Life and Soul: the Young Lukács and the Problem of Culture', in Agnes Heller, *Lukács Revalued*, Oxford: Basil Blackwell 1983, p. 1.

2 George Steiner, 'Georg Lukács and his Devil's Pact', *Language and Silence: Essays 1958–1966*, London: Faber and Faber 1985, pp. 367, 359.

3 Jameson, *Late Marxism*, p. 25.

4 Slavoj Žižek, *The Fragile Absolute, or, Why is the Christian legacy worth fighting for?*, London: Verso 2000, p. 2.

5 Richard Crossman (ed.), *The God That Failed: Six Studies in Communism*, London: Hamish Hamilton 1950, pp. 11-12.

6 Žižek, *The Fragile Absolute*, p. 2.

7 Jacques Derrida, *Specters of Marx: The State of the Debt, the Work of Mourning, and the New International*, trans. Peggy Kamuf, New York and London: Routledge 1994, p. 88.

8 For a critical assessment of deconstruction as primarily an expression of such anxieties, see my 'Vulgar Marxism: The Spectre Haunting *Specters of Marx*', in *Parallax* 20, Vol. 7, No. 3 (July–September 2001).

9 Jacques Derrida, *Specters of Marx*, pp. 159–61.

10 Ibid., p. 89.

11 Ibid., p. 87.

12 Jacques Derrida, *The Gift of Death*, trans. David Wills, London and Chicago: University of Chicago Press 1995, p. 108.

13 Ibid., p. 115.

14 Georg Lukács, 'Class Consciousness', in *History and Class Consciousness: Studies in Marxist Dialectics*, trans. Rodney Livingstone, London: Merlin 1971, p. 51.

15 Antonio Gramsci, *Selections from the Prison Notebooks*, trans. Quintin Hoare and Geoffrey Nowell Smith, London: Lawrence & Wishart 1971, p. 126.

16 Ibid., pp. 126–7.

17 Lukács, 'Class Consciousness', pp. 51, 74; Lucien Goldmann,

*The Human Sciences and Philosophy*, trans. Hayden V. White and Robert Anchor, London: Jonathan Cape 1969, pp. 51, 112 ff.

18 Georg Lukács, *A Defence of* History and Class Consciousness: *Tailism and the Dialectic*, trans. Esther Leslie, London: Verso 2000, p. 92.

19 Lukács, 'Class Consciousness', pp. 79–80.

20 See Slavoj Žižek, 'Postface: Georg Lukács as the Philosopher of Leninism', in Lukács, *A Defence of* History and Class Consciousness, pp. 153–4.

21 Lukács, 'Class Consciousness', p. 75.

22 Lukács, 'Reification and the Consciousness of the Proletariat', p. 110.

23 Žižek, *The Fragile Absolute*, p. 14.

24 Karl Marx and Frederick Engels, *Manifesto of the Communist Party*, trans. Samuel Moore, Peking: Foreign Languages Press 1975, pp. 35–6.

25 Žižek, *The Fragile Absolute*, p. 15. Debord intends something similar when he writes in *The Society of the Spectacle* that the spectacle is 'the material reconstruction of the religious illusion . . . It is thus the most earthbound aspects of life that have become the most impenetrable and rarefied.' Guy Debord, *The Society of the Spectacle*, trans. Donald Nicholson-Smith, New York: Zone 1995, p. 18.

26 Marshall Berman is perhaps the most prominent Marxist seducee of this myth; see his *All That Is Solid Melts Into Air*, London: Verso 1983.

## 10 Reification and Decolonization

1 Gayatri Chakravorty Spivak, *A Critique of Postcolonial Reason: Towards a History of the Vanishing Present*, Cambridge, MA and London: Harvard University Press 1999, p. 76n.

2 Michael Hardt and Antonio Negri, *Empire*, Cambridge, MA and London: Harvard University Press 2000, p. 127.

3 Edward W. Said, 'Traveling Theory', in *The World, The Text, and the Critic*, p. 239.

4 Edward W. Said, *Culture and Imperialism*, London: Vintage 1994, p. 326

5 Frantz Fanon, *The Wretched of the Earth*, trans. Constance Farrington, Harmondsworth: Penguin 1967, p. 27.

6 Ibid., pp. 29–30.

7 Ibid., p. 31.

8 Lukács, 'Reification and the Consciousness of the Proletariat', p. 172.

9 Fanon, *The Wretched of the Earth*, pp. 40, 36.

10 Ibid., p. 49.

11 Ibid., p. 74.

12 Theodor W. Adorno, *Critical Models: Interventions and Catchwords*, trans. Henry W. Pickford, New York: Columbia University Press 1998, pp. 168–9.

13 Fredric Jameson, 'Third-world Literature in the Era of Multinational Capitalism', *The Jameson Reader*, p. 336.

14 Joseph Conrad, *Heart of Darkness*, Harmondsworth: Penguin 1983, pp. 113–14.

15 See Gillian Rose, *The Melancholy Science: An Introduction to the Thought of Theodor W. Adorno*, London and Basingstoke: Macmillan 1978, p. 43; Neil Lazarus, 'Hating Tradition Properly', p. 15.

16 See Theodor W. Adorno, *Critical Models*, pp. 269, 291–2. This repudiation appears at its most unrelenting and pessimistic in a nevertheless extremely suggestive passage in *Minima Moralia*, p. 231: 'Quick reactions, unballasted by a mediating constitution, do not restore spontaneity, but establish the person as a measuring instrument deployed and calibrated by a central authority. The more immediate its response, the more deeply in reality mediation has advanced: in the prompt, unresistant reflexes the subject is entirely extinguished.'

17 Fredric Jameson, 'Third-world Literature', *The Jameson Reader*, p. 336.

18 In fairness to Jameson, his essay on Third-world literature concludes on a mildly self-satirical note, with a reference to the ending of Faulkner's *Absalom, Absalom!* consisting of Quentin's overstated denial: 'I don't hate the Third World! I don't! I don't! I don't!'

19 Gayatri Chakravorty Spivak, *A Critique of Postcolonial Reason*, p. 74.

20 Ibid., p. 68n.

21 Ibid., p. 75n. Spivak omits the final clause of the sentence: '. . . just as all the particular useful forms of commodities are generally effaced in money.' The effect of this elision is to obscure the fact that the residue of 'rationality' that exists in the commodity has nothing to do with its use value but simply with its status as a 'product' of the cap-

italist mode of production. See Karl Marx, *Capital: A Critique of Political Economy*, Vol. 2, trans. David Fernbach, Harmondsworth: Penguin 1978, p. 131.

22 Spivak, *A Critique of Postcolonial Reason*, pp. 68-9n.

23 Adorno, *Minima Moralia*, pp. 46–7.

24 Žižek, *The Fragile Absolute*, p. 5. For an account of racism as an exemplary form of reified consciousness see Joseph Gabel, *False Consciousness: An Essay on Reification*, trans. Margaret A. Thompson, Oxford; Basil Blackwell 1975, discussed at greater length in Part Two.

25 Žižek, *The Fragile Absolute*, p. 13.

26 Hardt and Negri, *Empire*, p. 190.

27 See Žižek, 'Postface: Georg Lukács as the Philosopher of Leninism', pp. 153, 175.

28 V.S. Naipaul, *A House for Mr Biswas*, Harmondsworth: Penguin 1992, p. 212.

29 Theodor W. Adorno, *Aesthetic Theory*, trans. Robert Hullot-Kentor, p. 81; translation modified. In *Minima Moralia* Adorno ascribes the same liberating quality to the child's capacity for play. In opposition to Friedrich Hebbel, who ascribes the loss of 'life's magic in later years' to our realization of the truth behind the phenomenon – that such things as singing and pipe-playing marionettes need the materiality of a 'revolving cylinder' (or a means of subsistence) to set them in motion – for Adorno children's games signify rather the *disavowal* of 'the contradiction between phenomenon and fungibility', and thus an unconscious rehearsal of the unalienated life. The same liberation is also manifested in children's blissful contemplation of animals: 'I am a rhinoceros, signifies the shape of the rhinoceros'. See *Minima Moralia*, §146, pp. 227–8 ('Toy Shop').

30 *Troilus and Cressida* I. 1; I. 2; IV. 5. For a detailed discussion of the theme of reification in *Troilus and Cressida* see Hugh Grady, '"Mad Idolatry": Commodification and Reification in *Troilus and Cressida*', in *Shakespeare's Universal Wolf: Studies in Early Modern Reification*, Oxford: Clarendon Press 1996.

31 Spivak, *A Critique of Postcolonial Reason*, p. 76.

32 Karl Marx, *Capital: A Critique of Political Economy* Vol. 1, trans. Ben Fowkes, Harmondsworth: Penguin 1976, pp. 194n, 638n.

33 Theodor W. Adorno, 'Aldous Huxley and Utopia', in *Prisms*, trans. Samuel and Shierry Weber, Cambridge, Massachusetts: MIT Press 1981, p. 106.

34 Fanon, *The Wretched of the Earth*, p. 253; Adorno, 'On Subject and Object', *Critical Models*, p. 247.

35 Theodor W. Adorno, *Negative Dialectics*, trans. E.B. Ashton, London: Routledge 1990, p. 191 (translation modified). See Theodor W. Adorno, *Negative Dialektik*, Frankfurt am Main: Suhrkamp 1966, p. 190.

36 Karen Lisa G. Salamon, 'No borders in business: The management discourse of organisational holism', in Timothy Bewes and Jeremy Gilbert (eds), *Cultural Capitalism: Politics after New Labour*, London: Lawrence and Wishart 2000, pp. 137–8. Salamon is quoting Steen Hildebrandt, a professor of management studies in Denmark.

37 Ibid., pp. 149–50.

38 Spivak, *A Critique of Postcolonial Reason*, p. 68n.

39 Theodor W. Adorno, 'Aldous Huxley and Utopia', p. 106.

## 11 Total Reification (I): Reading Fanon

1 Homi Bhabha, 'Foreword', in Frantz Fanon, *Black Skin, White Masks*, trans. Charles Lam Markmann, London: Pluto 1986, pp. vii, ix. David Macey observes that the Manichaeistic 'misreading' of Fanon has not been helped by the poor quality of the English translations – the most significant error being that of the title of the fifth chapter of *Black Skin White Masks*, where 'L'Expérience vécue de l'homme noir' is rendered as 'The Fact of Blackness' rather than, say, 'The Lived Experience of the Black Man'. As Macey observes, for Fanon there is no 'fact of blackness'. See David Macey, *Frantz Fanon: A Life*, London: Granta 2000, p. 26.

2 Homi Bhabha, 'Foreword', p. viii. Typical of the attitude Bhabha has in mind is that of Jack Woddis, whose *New Theories of Revolution* notes that the title of Fanon's *Les Damnés de la terre* was taken from Eugene Pottier's original words for *L'Internationale*, the anthem of the international working class. Woddis comments, with an emphasis that is quite contrary to Bhabha's, that '[Fanon's] innermost being yearned for an end to the old world of capitalism and the creation of a cleaner, nobler world in which men could live as brothers, even though his vision of that world was blurred and confused.' Jack Woddis, *New Theories of Revolution: A commentary on the views of Frantz Fanon, Régis Debray and Herbert Marcuse*, London: Lawrence and Wishart 1972, p. 175. David Macey meanwhile identifies the probable source for the title

of Fanon's book as Jacques Roumain's poem 'Sales nègres' ('Dirty Niggers'), written in 1938 or 1939: Macey, *Frantz Fanon*, pp. 177–9.

3 Macey, *Frantz Fanon*, pp. 21–2; see Fanon, *The Wretched of the Earth*, p. 119.

4 Fanon, *Black Skin White Masks*, p. 18.

5 Fanon, *The Wretched of the Earth*, p. 117.

6 Madhu Dubey, 'The "True Lie" of the Nation: Fanon and Feminism', *Differences* Vol. 10, No. 2 (Summer 1998), p. 21.

7 Frantz Fanon, *Studies in a Dying Colonialism*, trans. Haakon Chevalier, London: Earthscan 1989, p. 128.

8 Ibid., p. 128. For Adorno also, 'free and honest exchange' is the lie of the commodity world, a circumstance in which 'the lie that denounces it', which refuses to accept its domination – for example, by proposing a different order of values – becomes a corrective. See *Minima Moralia*, §22, p. 44.

9 Fanon, *Studies in a Dying Colonialism*, pp. 85–7.

10 Fanon, *The Wretched of the Earth*, trans. Constance Farrington, Harmondsworth: Penguin 1967, p. 21. David Macey reveals that an edition of *Les Damnés de la terre* was in fact published by François Maspero in 1968 without Sartre's preface at the insistence of Fanon's widow, Josie Fanon, although a folded poster including the preface was inserted into the volume as a supplement. See Macey, *Frantz Fanon*, pp. 467–8.

11 See Fanon, *The Wretched of the Earth*, p. 237.

12 Fanon, *Black Skin White Masks*, pp. xv, 16.

13 Fanon, *Black Skin White Masks*, pp. 231, 228.

14 Fanon, Black Skin White Masks, p. 30.

15 Madhu Dubey, 'The "True Lie" of the Nation', p. 21.

16 Homi K. Bhabha, *The Location of Culture*, London: Routledge 1994, p. 51.

## 12 Total Reification (II): Reading Lukács

1 See Marshall Berman, *Adventures in Marxism*, London: Verso 1999, p. 201.

2 Ibid., p. 15.

3 Ibid., p. 193; see also Berman's *All That Is Solid Melts Into Air*, London: Verso 1983.

4 Agnes Heller, 'Lukács's Later Philosophy', in Agnes Heller (ed.), *Lukács Revalued*, Oxford: Basil Blackwell 1983, p. 178.

5 István Eörsi, 'The Unpleasant Lukács', *New German Critique* 42 (Fall 1987), p. 10.

6 Georg Lukács, *Record of a Life: An Autobiographical Sketch*, trans. Rodney Livingstone, London: Verso 1983, p. 65.

7 Georg Lukács, 'Bolshevism as an Ethical Problem', in Arpad Kadarkay (ed.), *The Lukács Reader*, Oxford: Blackwell 1995, p. 220.

8 Georg Lukács, 'Tactics and Ethics', in *Political Writings 1919–1929: The Question of Parliamentarianism and Other Essays*, trans. Michael McColgan, London: NLB 1972, p. 11. Lukács later described the essay 'Tactics and Ethics' as 'an inner balancing of accounts which made it possible for me to join the Communist Party.' See Lukács, *Record of a Life*, p. 54.

9 Georg Lukács, *The Theory of the Novel*, trans. Anna Bostock, London: Merlin 1971, pp. 152, 18. The quotation from Fichte may be found in 'The Characteristics of the Present Age', in *The Popular Works of Johann Gottlieb Fichte*, trans. William Smith (4th edn), Volume II, London: Trübner & Co. 1889, pp. 17–18.

10 István Eörsi, 'The Unpleasant Lukács', p. 10.

11 Georg Lukács, *Record of a Life*, p. 48.

12 See Žižek, 'Postface', pp. 162–4.

13 See Theodor W. Adorno, *Hegel: Three Studies*, trans. Shierry Weber Nicholsen, Cambridge, Mass. and London: MIT 1993, p. 69.

## PART TWO: INVERSION

1 Jean-Luc Godard, *Two or Three Things I Know About Her*, trans. Marianne Alexander, in *Three Film Scripts: A Woman is a Woman, A Married Woman, Two or Three Things I Know About Her*, London: Lorrimer 1975, p. 139.

### 1 The Reflexive Character of Reification

2 Georg Lukács, 'Reification and the Consciousness of the Proletariat', in *History and Class Consciousness: Studies in Marxist Dialectics*, trans. Rodney Livingstone, London: Merlin 1971, p. 95.

3 Ibid., p. 197.

4 Georg Simmel, 'The Metropolis and Mental Life', trans. Edward

A. Shils, in David Levine, (ed.), *On Individuality and Social Forms*, Chicago and London: University of Chicago Press 1971, p. 339.

5 David Frisby, *Sociological Impressionism: A Reassessment of Georg Simmel's Social Theory*, London: Heinemann 1981; Georg Lukács, 'Georg Simmel', trans. Margaret Cerullo, *Theory, Culture & Society* Vol. 8, No. 3 (August 1991), p. 146.

6 Gillian Rose, *The Melancholy Science: An Introduction to the Thought of Theodor W. Adorno*, London and Basingstoke: Macmillan 1978, p. 35.

7 Georg Simmel, *The Philosophy of Money* (Second Edition), trans. Tom Bottomore and David Frisby, London: Routledge 1990, p. 449.

8 Georg Lukács, 'Reification and the Consciousness of the Proletariat', p. 157.

9 Ibid., p. 172.

10 *Life and its Replacement with a Dull Reflection of Itself: Preliminary Theses of The Pleasure Tendency*, Leeds: The Pleasure Tendency 1984, pp. 20–1; see the discussion in Part Three, section 1, below.

11 Theodor Adorno, *Negative Dialectics*, trans. E. B. Ashton, London: Routledge & Kegan Paul 1973, p. 192.

12 Ibid., p. 190.

13 Gillian Rose, *The Melancholy Science*, p. 43.

14 Theodor Adorno, *Negative Dialectics*, p. 190.

15 Ibid.

16 Ibid., p. 191.

17 Simon Jarvis, *Adorno: A Critical Introduction*, Cambridge: Polity 1998, p. 191.

18 Nathanael West, *Miss Lonelyhearts*, Harmondsworth: Penguin 1991, p. 46.

## 2 Total Illusion: the Triumph of Capital:

1 Georg Lukács, 'Reification and the Consciousness of the Proletariat', p. 208.

2 See Nicolai I. Bukharin, *Economics of the Transformation Period* (with Lenin's critical remarks), New York: Bergman 1971, p. 52.

3 G. W. F. Hegel, *Phenomenology of Spirit*, trans. A. V. Miller, Oxford: Oxford University Press 1977, §80, p. 51.

4 Ibid., §545, p. 332.

5 Georg Lukács, 'Reification and the Consciousness of the Proletariat', p. 115.

6 Georg Simmel, 'The Conflict in Modern Culture', in *On Individuality and Social Forms: Selected Writings*, ed. Donald N. Levine, Chicago and London: University of Chicago Press 1971, p. 375.

7 Ibid., p. 393.

8 Georg Simmel, *The Philosophy of Money*, trans. Tom Bottomore and David Frisby, London: Routledge 1990, p. 469.

9 Georg Lukács, 'Reification and the Consciousness of the Proletariat', p. 121.

10 Simon Jarvis, *Adorno: A Critical Introduction*, p. 55.

11 Jean Baudrillard, 'The Masses: The Implosion of the Social in the Media', trans. Marie Maclean, in *Selected Writings*, ed. Mark Poster, Cambridge: Polity 1988, pp. 218–19.

12 Jean Baudrillard, *In the Shadow of the Silent Majorities or, The End of the Social and Other Essays*, trans. Paul Foss, John Johnston and Paul Patton, New York: Semiotext(e) 1983, p. 23. I discuss the concept of cynicism at length in my *Cynicism and Postmodernity*, London: Verso 1997.

13 Baudrillard, *In the Shadow of the Silent Majorities*, p. 13.

14 As quoted by Simon Jarvis (in his translation), *Adorno: A Critical Introduction*, p. 58; see Theodor W. Adorno, 'Reflexionen zur Klassentheorie', in *Gesammelte Schriften* Vol. 8: *Soziologische Schriften I*, Frankfurt am Main: Suhrkamp 1972, pp. 380, 377.

15 Theodor W. Adorno, 'Cultural Criticism and Society', in *Prisms*, trans. Samuel and Shierry Weber, Cambridge, MA: MIT Press 1981, p. 21.

16 Ibid., p. 29. *Theses on Feuerbach* is included in Marx *Early Writings*, Harmondsworth: Penguin 1975, pp. 421–3.

17 See Peter Sloterdijk, *Critique of Cynical Reason*, trans. Michael Eldred, London: Verso 1988, pp. 169 ff.

## 3 The 'Aesthetic Structure' of Reification

1 Virginia Woolf, 'Modern Fiction', in *The Crowded Dance of Modern Life (Selected Essays: Volume Two)*, ed. Rachel Bowlby, Harmondsworth: Penguin 1993, p. 9.

2 Immanuel Kant, *Critique of Judgement*, trans. Werner S. Pluhar, Indianapolis: Hackett 1987, p. 58.

3 *Life and its Replacement with a Dull Reflection of Itself: Preliminary Theses of The Pleasure Tendency*, Leeds: The Pleasure Tendency 1984, pp. 7, 35.

4 Søren Kierkegaard, 'The Aesthetic Validity of Marriage', in *Either/Or* Part II. This text is discussed more fully in Part Three, section 5: 'The Coincidence of Contraries'.

## 4 Post-structuralism: Anxiety Reified as *Différance*

1 Jacques Derrida, *Margins of Philosophy*, trans. Alan Bass, Brighton: Harvester 1982, p. 3.

2 Jacques Derrida, *Specters of Marx: The State of the Debt, the Work of Mourning, and the New International*, trans. Peggy Kamuf, New York and London: Routledge 1994, pp. 147–176.

3 I have quoted the Moore and Aveling translation here on account of its particularly graphic description: Karl Marx, *Capital* Vol. 1*: A Critique of Capitalist Production*, trans. Samuel Moore and Edward Aveling, London: Lawrence & Wishart 1974, p. 76; see also Karl Marx, *Capital: A Critique of Political Economy* Vol. 1, trans. Ben Fowkes, Harmondsworth: Penguin 1976, p. 163.

4 Karl Marx, *Capital*: *A Critique of Political Economy* Vol. 1, trans. Ben Fowkes, Harmondsworth: Penguin 1976, p. 169; quoted in Derrida, *Specters of Marx*, p. 164.

5 Jacques Derrida, *Specters of Marx*, p. 161.

6 Plato, *Phaedrus and Letters VII and VIII*, trans. Walter Hamilton, Harmondsworth: Penguin 1973, p. 97.

7 Jacques Derrida, 'Plato's Pharmacy', in *Dissemination*, trans. Barbara Johnson, London: Athlone 1981, p. 143.

8 Jacques Derrida, *Specters of Marx*, p. 159.

9 Friedrich Nietzsche, *Beyond Good and Evil: Prelude to a Philosophy of the Future*, trans. R.J. Hollingdale, Harmondsworth: Penguin 1990, p. 221.

10 Ulrich Beck, 'The Reinvention of Politics: Towards a Theory of Reflexive Modernization', in Ulrich Beck, Anthony Giddens and Scott Lash, *Reflexive Modernization: Politics, Tradition and Aesthetics in the Modern Social Order*, Cambridge: Polity 1994, p. 2.

11 Ulrich Beck, *The Reinvention of Politics: Rethinking Modernity in the Global Social Order*, trans. Mark Ritter, Cambridge: Polity 1997, p. 62.

12 Slavoj Žižek, '"You May!"', *London Review of Books*, Vol. 21 No. 6 (18 March 1999).

13 Georg Lukács, 'Reification and the Consciousness of the Proletariat', p. 194.

14 Ibid., p. 135.

15 Ulrich Beck, *The Reinvention of Politics*, p. 17.

16 Ulrich Beck, *Risk Society: Towards a New Modernity*, trans. Mark Ritter, London: Sage 1992, p. 11.

## 5 Reflexive Modernization: Anxiety Reified as Risk

1 Ulrich Beck, *The Reinvention of Politics*, p. 13.

2 Georg Lukács, 'Reification and the Consciousness of the Proletariat', p. 194.

3 Ulrich Beck, *Risk Society: Towards a New Modernity*, p. 183.

4 Karl Mannheim, *Ideology and Utopia: An Introduction to the Sociology of Knowledge*, trans. Louis Wirth and Edward Shils, London: Routledge 1991, p. 68

5 Georg Lukács, 'Reification and the Consciousness of the Proletariat', p. 187.

6 Scott Lash, 'Reflexive Modernization: The Aesthetic Dimension', in *Theory, Culture & Society*, Vol. 10, No. 1 (1993), pp. 2, 21.

7 Slavoj Žižek, *The Ticklish Subject: The Absent Centre of Political Ontology*, London: Verso 1999, p. 337.

8 Theodor W. Adorno, *Aesthetic Theory*, trans. Robert Hullot-Kentor, Minneapolis: University of Minnesota Press 1997, p. 45.

9 Scott Lash, 'Reflexive Modernization: The Aesthetic Dimension', p. 15.

10 Ibid., p. 14.

11 Ibid., p. 9.

12 Jacques Derrida, *Of Grammatology*, p. 158.

13 See Beck, *The Reinvention of Politics*, p. 161, where he asks rhetorically, 'What is so terrible in Foucault's insight that the institutions of liberation are in fact elaborate systems of subordination? Certainly our disappointed ideals rebel. An entire experimental order of Enlightenment proves to be the opposite of Enlightenment. But is this not an expression of the desire to unmask, the quintessential pleasure of Enlightenment, which does not even shy away from its own arrogance and its initial hopes, joyously toppling the monuments of its own tyranny?' The complacency of this inversion of Foucault lies almost entirely in its assumption that control and oppression have come to an end. For Beck, the processes of Enlightenment itself are characterized by 'joy', not struggle against oppression. And Foucault's theories are no

longer about the continuing, mutating strategies of power, but about the collapse of discourse at the end of history.

14 Scott Lash, 'Reflexive Modernization: The Aesthetic Dimension', p. 20.

15 See Michel Foucault, *Madness and Civilization: A History of Insanity in the Age of Reason*, trans. Richard Howard, New York: Pantheon 1965; *The Order of Things: An Archaeology of the Human Sciences*, New York: Vintage 1994; *The Archaeology of Knowledge*, trans. A. M. Sheridan Smith, New York: Pantheon 1972, p. 120. The adjective 'arid', as used of *The Archaeology of Knowledge*, comes from J. G. Merquior's unsympathetic and imperceptive introduction to Foucault (J. G. Merquior, *Foucault*, London: HarperCollins 1991, p. 83).

## 6 The Aesthetics of Incomprehensibility

1 Walter Benjamin, 'Franz Kafka: On the Tenth Anniversary of His Death', in *Illuminations*, trans. Harry Zohn, New York: Schocken 1968, pp. 127–8.

2 Beck, *The Reinvention of Politics*, pp. 162-3.

3 Ibid., p. 162.

4 Max Brod, ed., *The Diaries of Franz Kafka 1910-23*, trans. Joseph Kresh and Martin Greenberg, Harmondsworth: Penguin 1964, pp. 18–19.

5 Ibid., p. 393.

6 Beck, *The Reinvention of Politics*, p. 163.

7 Lukács, 'Reification and the Consciousness of the Proletariat', p. 187.

8 Samuel Beckett, *Waiting for Godot* in *The Complete Dramatic Works*, London: Faber 1986, p. 76.

9 Momme Broderson, *Walter Benjamin: A Biography*, trans. Malcolm R. Green and Ingrida Ligers, London: Verso 1996, p. 219.

10 Walter Benjamin, 'Some Reflections on Kafka' (letter to Gerhard [Gershom] Scholem, 12 June 1938), in *Illuminations*, pp. 148–9.

11 Adorno, *Prisms*, pp. 261, 246.

12 Adorno, *Aesthetic Theory*, p. 175.

13 Benjamin, *Illuminations*, p. 144.

14 Adorno, *Aesthetic Theory*, p. 339.

15 Adorno, *Prisms*, p. 246.

16 Benjamin, *Illuminations*, p. 129.

17 Marcel Proust, *In Search of Lost Time* Volume 1: *Swann's Way*, trans. C.K. Scott Moncrieff and Terence Kilmartin, London: Vintage 1992, p. 214.

18 Simon Critchley, *Very Little . . . Almost Nothing: Death, Philosophy, Literature*, London and New York: Routledge 1997, p. 149.

## 7 Ambiguity and Utopia

1 Adorno, *Aesthetic Theory*, p. 226.

2 Ibid., pp. 335–6.

3 Adorno, *Minima Moralia*, p. 130.

4 See Adorno, *Aesthetic Theory*, p. 12.

5 Ibid., p. 347.

6 Ibid., p. 153.

7 Adorno, 'Commitment', in Ernst Bloch et al., *Aesthetics and Politics*, London: Verso 1980, p. 194.

8 Adorno, *Aesthetic Theory*, p. 4.

9 Theodor W. Adorno, 'Resignation', in *Critical Models: Interventions and Catchwords*, trans. Henry W. Pickford, New York: Columbia University Press 1998, pp. 292–3.

10 Theodor W. Adorno, *Hegel: Three Studies*, trans. Shierry Weber Nicholsen, Cambridge, Mass. and London: MIT 1993, p. 88.

## 8 Analogy of Religious and Commodity Fetishism

1 For an exploration of a similar amalgamation of Catholic iconography with pagan elements in Haiti, see Michel Leiris, 'Note on the Use of Catholic Chromolithographs by Haitian Voodooists', in *Brisées: Broken Branches*, trans. Lydia Davis, San Francisco: North Point Press 1989, pp. 143–53.

2 'This revolution is eternal'; 'We believe in dreams'.

3 *Buena Vista Social Club*, dir. Wim Wenders, Cuba/USA, 1999.

4 Norman Geras, *Literature of Revolution: Essays on Marxism*, London: Verso 1986, p. 59.

5 Karl Marx, *Early Writings*, trans. Rodney Livingstone and Gregor Benton, Harmondsworth: Penguin 1992, p. 244 (see 'Zur Kritik der Hegelschen Rechtsphilosophie. Einleitung' in Karl Marx/Friedrich

Engels, *Historisch-Kritische Gesamtausgabe*, Band 1: Erster Halbband, ed. David Rjazanov, Frankfurt am Main: Verlagsgesellschaft MBH. 1927, pp. 607–8).

6 See for example Robert Browning, 'Confessions', *The Poetical Works of Robert Browning: Volume 1*, London: Smith, Elder & Co. 1901, p. 598: 'What is he buzzing in my ears?/ "Now that I come to die,/ "Do I view the world as a vale of tears?"/ Ah, reverend sir, not I!' The phrase originates, according to *Brewer's Dictionary of Phrase and Fable*, in Psalm 84: 6.

7 Jonathan Dollimore, *Death, Desire and Loss in Western Culture*, Harmondsworth: Penguin 1999.

8 Marx, *Early Writings*, p. 244.

9 Lukács, 'Reification and the Consciousness of the Proletariat', p. 199.

10 Ibid., p. 193.

11 Ibid., pp. 119, 157, 192.

12 J. G. Fichte, *The Popular Works of Johann Gottlieb Fichte* (Fourth edn., in two volumes): Volume 1, trans. William Smith, London: Trübner & Co., 1889, p. 402.

13 Ibid., p. 404 (translation modified).

14 Herman Melville, *Moby-Dick or, The Whale*, Harmondsworth: Penguin 1992, p. 183; 'deaf Burkes and blinded Bendigoes' refers to two English prize-fighters in the 1830s and 1840s.

15 Ibid., p. 178.

16 Fichte, *Popular Works*, Vol. 1, p. 454.

17 Ibid., pp. 461–2.

18 Ibid., p. 463.

19 Ibid., p. 456.

20 Ibid., p. 478.

21 Ibid., p. 448.

22 Georg Simmel, 'The Problem of Religion Today', in *Essays On Religion*, trans. Horst Jürgen Helle in collaboration with Ludwig Nieder, New Haven and London: Yale University Press 1997, p. 12.

23 Herman Melville, *The Confidence-Man: His Masquerade*, Oxford: Oxford University Press 1989, p. 178.

24 Lukács, 'Reification and the Consciousness of the Proletariat', p. 193.

25 Søren Kierkegaard, *Papers and Journals: A Selection*, trans. Alastair Hannay, Harmondsworth: Penguin 1996, p. 375.

26 Lukács, 'Reification and the Consciousness of the Proletariat', p. 193.

## 9 The Desire for Transcendence

1 Michel Leiris and Jacqueline Délange, *African Art*, trans. Michael Ross, London: Thames and Hudson 1968, p. 35; Michel Leiris, *Afrique Noire: La Création Plastique,* in *Miroir de l'Afrique*, Paris: Gallimard 1996, p. 1161.

2 G. W. F. Hegel, *Phenomenology of Spirit*, trans. A. V. Miller, Oxford University Press 1977, §702, p. 426.

3 G. W. F. Hegel, *Aesthetics: Lectures on Fine Art*, Vol. 1, trans. T. M. Knox, Oxford: Clarendon 1975, p. 10.

4 Hegel, *Phenomenology of Spirit*, §710, p. 430.

5 Hegel, *Aesthetics*, Vol. 1, p. 13.

6 See Adorno, *Hegel: Three Studies*, pp. 73, 74.

7 Hegel, *Aesthetics*, Vol. 1, pp. 10-11.

8 Theodor W. Adorno, 'Theses Upon Art and Religion Today', *Notes to Literature: Volume Two*, New York: Columbia University Press 1992, p. 295 (orig. in *The Kenyon Review* Vol. VII, No. 4 (Autumn 1945).

9 Ibid., pp. 293, 292.

10 Andrew Bowie, 'Confessions of a "New Aesthete"', *New Left Review* I/225 (September/October 1997), p. 116.

11 Robert Hullot-Kentor, 'Foreword: Critique of the Organic', in Theodor W. Adorno, *Kierkegaard: Construction of the Aesthetic*, trans. Robert Hullot-Kentor, Minneapolis: University of Minnesota Press 1989, p. xiv.

12 Robert Hullot-Kentor, 'Translator's Introduction', Theodor W. Adorno, *Aesthetic Theory*, p. xi.

## 10 Comment on Proust

1 Adorno, *Notes to Literature: Volume Two*, New York: Columbia University Press 1992, p. 297–8.

2 Marcel Proust, *In Search of Lost Time* Volume 1: *Swann's Way*, trans. C. K. Scott Moncrieff and Terence Kilmartin, London: Vintage 1992, p. 422.

3 Ibid., p. 359.

4 Ibid., p. 470.

5 Ibid., p. 482.

6 Ibid., pp. 284–5.

7 Malcolm Bowie, *Proust Among the Stars*, London: HarperCollins 1998, p. 124.

8 Ibid., p. 70.

9 Marcel Proust, *Swann's Way*, p. 283.

10 Ibid., p. 235.

11 Ibid., p. 285.

12 Ibid., p. 510.

13 Theodor W. Adorno, *Notes to Literature: Volume Two*, p. 294. See Bret Easton Ellis, *American Psycho*, New York: Random House 1991; Douglas Coupland, *Girlfriend in a Coma*, London: HarperCollins 1998.

## 11 Hierarchy of Mediation and Immediacy

1 See G.W.F. Hegel, *Aesthetics: Lectures on Fine Art*, Vol. 1, trans. T.M. Knox, Oxford: Clarendon 1975, esp. pp. 56-7.

2 Theodor W. Adorno, *Aesthetic Theory*, trans. Robert Hullot-Kentor, Minneapolis: University of Minnesota Press 1997, p. 143.

3 Ibid., p. 145.

4 Ibid., p. 144.

5 Theodor W. Adorno, *Hegel: Three Studies*, trans. Shierry Weber Nicholsen, Cambridge, Mass. and London: MIT 1993, p. 57.

6 Ibid., p. 59.

7 Hannah Arendt, *The Origins of Totalitarianism*, New York and London: Harcourt Brace Jovanovich, 1973, p. 476.

8 Ibid., p. 477. Luther is commenting upon the Biblical text 'it is not good that man should be alone', from Genesis 2: 18.

9 Ibid., p. 478.

10 Joseph Gabel, *False Consciousness: An Essay on Reification*, trans. Margaret A. Thompson, Oxford; Basil Blackwell 1975, p. xx.

11 Ibid., p. 3.

12 Fredric Jameson, *Late Marxism: Adorno, or, The Persistence of the Dialectic*, London: Verso 1990, p. 16.

13 Jean Baudrillard, 'The Ecstasy of Communication', in Hal Foster, ed., *Postmodern Culture*, London: Pluto 1985, p. 133.

14 Ibid., p. 132.

15 Joseph Gabel, *False Consciousness*, p. 87.

16 Arendt, *The Origins of Totalitarianism*, p. 468.

17 See Arendt, *Eichmann in Jerusalem*, p. 105. 'It could be you!' is the advertising slogan of Camelot, the operators of the British National Lottery.

18 David Runciman, 'The Plot to Make Us Stupid', *London Review of Books* Vol. 18, No. 4 (22 February 1996)

19 Frantz Fanon, *The Wretched of the Earth*, trans. Constance Farrington, Harmondsworth: Penguin 1967, pp. 239ff.

20 Gabel, False *Consciousness*, pp. 12–13.

21 Sigmund Freud, 'The Unconscious', in *Penguin Freud Library* Vol. 11: *On Metapsychology: The Theory of Psychoanalysis*, Harmondsworth; Penguin 1991, p. 204.

22 Gabel, *False Consciousness*, pp. 85, 80.

23 Ibid., p. 81.

24 Gilles Deleuze and Félix Guattari, *Anti-Oedipus: Capitalism and Schizophrenia*, trans. Robert Hurley, Mark Seem and Helen R. Lane, London: Athlone 1984, p. 69.

25 Ibid., p. 318.

26 Ibid., p. 43.

27 Gilles Deleuze and Félix Guattari, *Kafka: Toward a Minor Literature*, trans. Dana Polan, Minneapolis: University of Minnesota Press 1986, pp. 41, 95–6n.

28 Deleuze and Guattari, *Anti-Oedipus*, p. 42.

29 Hegel, *Phenomenology of Spirit*, §25, p. 14.

30 Ibid., §20, p. 11 (my emphases).

31 Theodor W. Adorno, 'The Experiential Content of Hegel's Philosophy' in *Hegel: Three Studies*, p. 72.

32 Georg Lukács, 'Reification and the Consciousness of the Proletariat', p. 170.

33 Ibid., p. 181.

34 Robert Hullot-Kentor, 'Forward: Critique of the Organic', in Adorno, *Kierkegaard*, p. xviii; see also Theodor W. Adorno, 'Aspects of Hegel's Philosophy' in *Hegel: Three Studies*, pp. 8–9.

35 See Theodor W. Adorno, 'Resignation', in *Critical Models: Interventions and Catchwords*, trans. Henry W. Pickford, New York: Columbia University Press 1998.

36 Deleuze and Guattari, *Anti-Oedipus*, p. 293.

37 Marcel Proust, *In Search of Lost Time* Volume 2: *Within a Budding*

*Grove*, trans. C.K. Scott Moncrieff and Terence Kilmartin, London: Chatto & Windus 1992, p. 48.

38 Ibid., p. 46.

12 The Virtue of Obsolescence

1 Theodor W. Adorno, *Hegel: Three Studies*, trans. Shierry Weber Nicholsen, Cambridge, MA and London: MIT 1993, p. 55–6.

2 Jean Baudrillard, *The Perfect Crime*, trans. Chris Turner, London: Verso 1996, p. 100.

3 Ibid., p. 101.

4 Ibid., p. 102.

5 Arendt, *The Origins of Totalitarianism*, p. 467.

6 Ibid., p. 468.

7 John Armitage, 'Dissecting the Data Body: An Interview with Arthur and Marilouise Kroker', *Angelaki* Vol. 4 No. 2 (September 1999), p. 72.

8 'Design guru' Stephen Bayley, quoted in Oliver Burkeman and Emma Brockes, 'Trouble Brewing' (news report on the Seattle WTO riots, November 30 1999), *Guardian*, 3 December 1999.

9 Ibid.

10 Baudrillard, *The Perfect Crime*, p. 1. The impossibility of the perfect crime is for Baudrillard, of course, precisely what makes it perfect. Yet it is also what makes it irrelevant as an epistemological model, and useless as a political analysis.

11 See John Hooper, 'Case of the "perfect pointless murder" grips Italy', *Guardian*, 13 February 1999.

12 Baudrillard, *The Perfect Crime*, p. xi.

13 Giorgio Agamben, *The Man Without Content*, trans. Georgia Albert, Stanford, California: Stanford University Press 1999, p. 8; see Walter Benjamin's analogous distinction between the exhibition value and the cult value of the artwork, in 'The Work of Art in the Age of Mechanical Reproduction', in *Illuminations*, trans. Harry Zohn, New York: Schocken 1968, pp. 224–5.

14 Agamben, *The Man Without Content*, p. 18.

15 Flaubert quoted by Agamben, *The Man Without Content*, p. 9.

16 Julian Stallabrass, *High Art Lite*, London: Verso 1999, p. 123.

17 See Georg Lukács, 'Reification and the Consciousness of the Proletariat', p. 188.

18 Edward Said, 'Traveling Theory', in *The World, the Text, and the Critic*, London: Vintage 1991, p. 239.

19 Gillian Rose, *The Melancholy Science: An Introduction to the Thought of Theodor W. Adorno*, London and Basingstoke: Macmillan 1978, pp. 30–31 and ff.

20 Tony Blair, Speech to Labour Party Conference, 28 September 1999.

21 See my 'Truth and Appearance in Politics: The Mythology of Spin', in Timothy Bewes and Jeremy Gilbert (eds), *Cultural Capitalism: Politics after New Labour*, London: Lawrence and Wishart 2000, pp. 158-76.

22 Marcel Proust, *In Search of Lost Time* Volume 2: *Within a Budding Grove*, trans. C. K. Scott Moncrieff and Terence Kilmartin, London: Chatto & Windus 1992, pp. 120-21.

23 Georg Lukács, 'Reification and the Consciousness of the Proletariat', p. 198.

24 Francis Fukuyama, *The End of History and the Last Man*, New York: The Free Press 1992.

25 Theodor W. Adorno, 'Cultural Criticism and Society', in *Prisms*, trans. Samuel and Shierry Weber, Cambridge, MA: MIT Press 1981, p. 34.

## PART THREE: REDEMPTION

1 Wim Wenders, 'Notebook on Clothes and Cities', in *The Act of Seeing*, London: Faber and Faber 1997, p. 84.

### 1 The Pleasure Tendency

2 *Life and its Replacement with a Dull Reflection of Itself: Preliminary Theses of The Pleasure Tendency*, Leeds: The Pleasure Tendency 1984, p. 2 (§4.1). Due to the obscurity of the text I shall quote at length from it in the following discussion. References are given as page numbers, followed by, in parentheses, the number of the relevant thesis (renumbered from the beginning of each section) as given in the text itself.

3 Ibid., p. 15 (§4.3).

4 Ibid., p. 12 (§1.14).

5 Ibid., p. 1 (§3.11).

6 See Georg Simmel, *The Philosophy of Money* (Second Edition), trans. Tom Bottomore and David Frisby, London: Routledge 1990, p. 53; Theodor W. Adorno, 'Resignation', in *Critical Models: Interventions and Catchwords*, trans. Henry W. Pickford, New York: Columbia University Press 1998.

7 *Life and its Replacement with a Dull Reflection of Itself*, p. 1 (§3.0)

8 Ibid., p. 1 (§2.1)

9 Ibid., p. 22 (§2.1).

10 Valerie Solanas, *SCUM Manifesto*, Edinburgh and San Francisco: AK Press 1996.

11 'The anarchists would have you believe that 'Everything is Permitted' means that you must permit anything to be done to you, and wait until they get tired of doing it – for the sake of the other chap's freedom.' *Life and its Replacement with a Dull Reflection of Itself*, p. 32 (§1.0). 'The Socialist dream – everyone will live in their own council flat . . . Communism is Capitalism without the good bits.' Ibid., p. 18 (§§1.0–2.0).

12 Ibid., p. 25 (§5.1). Elsewhere in the book the 'essence' of femininity is imbued with the following characteristics: 'crudity, vulnerability, wetness, violence, abandon, ecstasy, bloodiness, messiness, non-utility, flexibility, insatiability'. As such, female sexuality is held by the text to be exemplary of 'the perfect world and life' – p. 28 (§2.0).

13 Ibid., pp. 33 (§2.2), 34 (§6.0)

14 Ibid., pp. 10 (§3.0), 30 ( §5.0)

15 Ibid., p. 27 (§§ 2.0–2.1)

16 Ibid., p. 3 (§1.3)

17 'Trying to sustain those moments of joy and empathy that can be found in the arms of a lover is like trying to remember a beautiful half-remembered tune, and is subversive in itself, going against the grain of this consumption-besotted society.' Ibid., p. 7 (§1.3).

18 Ibid., p. 33 (§§ 2.11–2.2)

19 Ibid., p. 2 (§§5.1).

20 Ibid., p. 2 (§§5.2).

21 Ibid., p. 11 (§4.0).

22 Ibid., p. 31 (§3.1).

23 The section on 'Civilization' includes the following revealing sentiments: 'There is no doubt that . . . Britain has "gone" somewhere over the years. Almost wiped off the map of the civilized world, certainly pushed to the edge, nothing has risen to take its place except the

worst American garbage . . . How long is it since we produced an Isaac Newton, a Shakespeare, a Drake, a Wren, a Handel? Since Europe produced a Leonardo, a Galileo, a Beethoven, an Einstein?' Ibid., p. 31 (§§2.0–2.1).

24 Søren Kierkegaard, *The Concept of Anxiety: A Simple Psychologically Orienting Deliberation on the Dogmatic Issue of Hereditary Sin*, trans. Reidar Thomte, Princeton, NJ: Princeton University Press 1980, p. 42.

25 Jean-Paul Sartre, *Being and Nothingness: An Essay on Phenomenological Ontology*, trans. Hazel E. Barnes, London: Methuen 1957, p. 29. (The English translation gives 'anguish' instead of 'anxiety' for Sartre's *l'angoisse,* and I have modified this here.)

26 Georg Simmel, 'Christianity and Art', in *Essays on Religion*, trans. Horst Jürgen Helle in collaboration with Ludwig Nieder, New Haven and London: Yale University Press 1997, p. 72.

27 Frantz Fanon, *Black Skin White Masks*, trans. Charles Lam Markmann, London: Pluto 1986, p. 10.

28 Ibid. (my emphasis).

## 2 Reification as Cultural Anxiety

1 René Girard, *Deceit, Desire and the Novel: Self and Other in Literary Structure*, trans. Yvonne Freccero, Baltimore and London: Johns Hopkins University Press 1965, p. 62.

2 Ibid., pp. 59, 65.

3 Marcel Proust, *In Search of Lost Time* Volume 1: *Swann's Way*, trans. C.K. Scott Moncrieff and Terence Kilmartin, London: Vintage 1992, pp. 509–10.

4 Ibid., pp. 510–11; see above, p. 152.

5 Peter Berger and Thomas Luckmann, *The Social Construction of Reality: A Treatise in the Sociology of Knowledge*, Harmondsworth: Penguin 1971, p. 106.

6 Ibid., p. 13.

7 Ibid., p. 107.

8 Ibid., p. 107.

9 Peter Berger and Stanley Pullberg, 'Reification and the Sociological Critique of Consciousness', *New Left Review* I/35 (January–February 1966), p. 70. More recently, Homi Bhabha has made similarly grand claims for the multicultural, which he says questions the

'very notion of the ipso facto', subverting 'the leaden prose of an inherited world' – 'The Dislocation of Culture', paper given at *All Tomorrow's Parties: 30 Years of Radical Politics and Philosophy* conference, Birkbeck College, University of London, 13 May 2000.

10 Berger and Luckmann, *The Social Construction of Reality*, p. 108.

11 Theodor W. Adorno, *Aesthetic Theory*, trans. Robert Hullot-Kentor, Minneapolis: University of Minnesota Press 1997, pp. 83–4.

12 Berger and Luckmann, *The Social Construction of Reality*, p. 108. Here and throughout their discussion of reification Berger and Luckmann appear to substantiate Adorno's earlier negative judgement upon sociology as counterposed to critical theory: 'critical theory is orientated towards the idea of society as subject, whilst sociology accepts reification, repeats it in its methods and thereby loses the perspective in which society and its law would first reveal themselves.' See Theodor W. Adorno et al., *The Positivist Dispute in German Sociology*, trans. Glyn Adey and David Frisby, London: Heinemann 1976, p. 34.

13 *American Beauty*, dir. Sam Mendes, USA 1999.

14 Philip Kemp, 'The Nice Man Cometh', *Sight and Sound*, Vol. 10 No. 1 (January 2000), p. 25.

15 In *The Truman Show* (dir. Peter Weir, USA 1998) Truman Burbank is played by Jim Carey; in *The Matrix* (dir. The Wachowski Brothers, USA/Australia 1999) Thomas 'Neo' Anderson is played by Keanu Reeves.

16 There is thus something 'homoeopathic', to use Gayatri Spivak's phrase, about the redemption offered by *The Matrix*. The addressee of Neo's final speech ('I know you're out there. I can feel you now. I know that you're afraid. You're afraid of us. You're afraid of change . . . I'm going to show these people what you don't want them to see. I'm going to show them a world without you . . .') is highly ambiguous. It seems as likely that he is talking to the freedom fighters, led by Morpheus (a John the Baptist figure), as to the dehumanizing machines – an interpretation which would endorse the sentiment articulated earlier in the film by Cypher, an unsympathetic character who rejects the reality pietism of his fellow rebels and negotiates a return to the Matrix: 'I think the Matrix can be more real than this world'. *The Truman Show*, meanwhile, represents this 'homoeopathic' perspective in Christof's defence of his programme on a radio phone-in: 'The world, the place *you* live in, is the sick place,' he tells a caller; 'Seahaven is the way the world should be' – a verdict tentatively confirmed by the

film's representation of the *Truman Show*'s viewers as more duped than Truman himself, and by the redemptive effect of Truman himself on what is indisputably a fallen world.

17 Philip Kemp, 'The Nice Man Cometh', p. 25.

18 Leslie Felperin, 'How's it going to end?', *Sight and Sound*, Vol. 8, No. 10 (October 1998), p. 37.

19 Philip Strick, review of *The Matrix*, in *Sight and Sound*, Vol. 9, No. 7 (July 1999), p. 47.

20 See note 16, above.

3 On Reversibility

1 For an example of Agamben's literary readings, not discussed explicitly here, see his 'Bartleby, or On Contingency', in *Potentialities: Collected Essays in Philosophy*, trans. Daniel Heller-Roazen, Stanford, CA: Stanford University Press 1999, pp. 243–71.

2 On a visit to the 'Oracle', a source of wisdom who lives in the Matrix in the form of a cookie-baking matriarch, Neo meets a cross-legged boy dressed in 'Eastern' clothes who is able to bend a spoon at will. The boy gives the spoon to Neo and tells him: 'Do not try and bend the spoon – that's impossible. Instead, only try and realize the truth . . . – there is no spoon! Then you will see that is it not the spoon that bends, it is only yourself.' *The Matrix*, dir. The Wachowski Brothers, USA/Australia 1999.

3 See Karl Marx, 'Postface to the Second Edition', in *Capital: A Critique of Political Economy* Vol. 1, trans. Ben Fowkes, Harmondsworth: Penguin 1976, p. 103.

4 Karl Marx, *Capital: A Critique of Political Economy* Vol. 1, pp. 163–4.

5 Karl Marx, *Das Kapital: Kritik der politischen Ökonomie*, Erster Band, Berlin: Dietz Verlag 1974, p. 27; *Capital: A Critique of Political Economy* Vol. 1, trans. Ben Fowkes, Harmondsworth: Penguin 1976, p. 103; *Capital: A Critical Analysis of Capitalist Production*, Vol. 1, trans. Samuel Moore and Edward Aveling, London: Lawrence & Wishart 1974, p. 29.

6 Karl Marx and Frederick Engels, *The German Ideology*, ed. C.J. Arthur, London: Lawrence & Wishart 1974, p. 52.

7 Georg Lukács, 'Reification and the Consciousness of the Proletariat', in *History and Class Consciousness: Studies in Marxist*

*Dialectics*, trans. Rodney Livingstone, London: Merlin 1971, pp. 180, 181.

8 See Nicholas of Cusa, *The Vision of God*, trans. Emma Gurney Salter, London: J. M. Dent 1928, pp. 43–4: 'I have learnt that the place wherein Thou art found unveiled is girt around with the coincidence of contradictories, and this is the wall of Paradise wherein Thou dost abide.' See also Blaise Pascal, *Pensées and Other Writings*, trans. Honor Levi, Oxford: Oxford University Press 1999, p. 69; Alfred Jarry, 'Concerning the Surface of God', in *Exploits and Opinions of Doctor Faustroll, Pataphysician: A Neo-Scientific Novel*, trans. Simon Watson Taylor, in *Selected Works*, ed. Roger Shattuck and Simon Watson Taylor, London: Jonathan Cape 1969, p. 256; Revelation 22: 12 (RSV).

9 Revelation 1: 8 (RSV).

10 Søren Kierkegaard, *Attack Upon 'Christendom'*, trans. Walter Lowrie, Princeton: Princeton University Press 1968, p. 107.

11 Ibid., p. 139.

12 See Howard A. Johnson, 'Kierkegaard and the Church: A Supplement to the Translator's Introduction', in ibid., p. xxii.

13 Walter Lowrie, 'Introduction by the Translator', in ibid., p. xiv.

14 Johnson, 'Kierkegaard and the Church', p. xxiii.

15 Kierkegaard, *Attack Upon 'Christendom'*, pp. 60, 110; the use of three dots in quotations from this text appears in the translation, and denotes not ellipses but punctuation in Kierkegaard's original, usually a dash, which has been replaced in the English text. See translator's preface in ibid., p. vi.

16 Ibid., p. 84 (my emphasis).

17 Ibid., p. 110.

18 See Søren Kierkegaard, *Papers and Journals: A Selection*, trans. Alastair Hannay, Harmondsworth: Penguin 1996 p. 557 (53 X 5 A 134).

19 Ibid., p. 556 (53 X 5 A 119).

20 As has already been pointed out, Hegel never uses the term reification; Adorno's statement is perhaps more appropriately referred to Herbert Marcuse, who in *Reason and Revolution* reads the opening sections of the *Phenomenology of Spirit* (the first part entitled 'Consciousness') as a critique of reification – by which he means 'positivism', or 'identity thinking'. It is this interpretation of the term that Adorno is attempting to rethink in his letter to Benjamin. Later, in the

*Three Studies* on Hegel, Adorno will mobilize Hegel himself in the service of that rethinking.

21 Letter from Adorno to Benjamin, 29 February 1940, in Theodor W. Adorno and Walter Benjamin, *The Complete Correspondence 1928–1940*, trans. Nicholas Walker, Cambridge: Polity 1999, p. 321.

22 Martin Jay, *Adorno*, Cambridge, MA: Harvard University Press 1984, p. 69.

23 Marcel Proust, *In Search of Lost Time* Volume 1: *Swann's Way*, trans. C. K. Scott Moncrieff and Terence Kilmartin, London: Vintage 1992, p. 50.

24 Ibid., p. 235.

25 Samuel Beckett, *Proust* and *Three Dialogues with Georges Duthuit*, London: John Calder 1965, p. 32.

26 Proust, *Swann's Way*, p. 53.

27 Marcel Proust, *In Search of Lost Time* Volume 2: *Within a Budding Grove*, trans. C. K. Scott Moncrieff and Terence Kilmartin, London: Chatto & Windus 1992, p. 74.

28 Ibid., p. 58; *À l'ombre des jeunes filles en fleurs*, Paris: Nouvelle Revue Française 1918, p. 74.

29 Letter from Adorno to Benjamin, 29 February 1940, pp. 320–21.

30 Bhabha, 'The Dislocation of Culture'.

31 In an earlier letter to Benjamin – another response to an essay by the latter, this time on Kafka – Adorno offers the metaphor of a 'non-fetishistic' conception of photography. Citing his own earlier interpretation of Kafka (now lost), Adorno writes: 'I claimed he represents a photograph of our earthly life from the perspective of a redeemed life, one which merely reveals the latter as an edge of black cloth, whereas the terrifyingly distanced optics of the photographic image is none other than that of the obliquely angled camera itself . . .' In other words, the objectifying gaze of the camera lens is replaced, in Kafka, by a twisted apparatus which records only its own failure to represent objectively. Letter from Adorno to Benjamin, 17 December 1934, in Theodor W. Adorno and Walter Benjamin, *The Complete Correspondence 1928–1940*, p. 66.

32 Beckett, *Proust*, p. 35.

33 Søren Kierkegaard, *Either/Or: A Fragment of Life*, trans. Alastair Hannay, Harmondsworth: Penguin 1992 ('Crop Rotation'), esp. pp. 235–6.

34 Dante, *The Divine Comedy* Vol. II*: Purgatory*, trans. Mark Musa, Harmondsworth: Penguin 1985, p. 304 (Canto XXVIII, ll. 127–32).

35 Ibid., p. 340n (my emphasis).

36 Kierkegaard, *Either/Or*, p. 235.

37 Marx to Ruge, September 1843, in Robert C. Tucker, ed., *The Marx-Engels Reader* (Second edition), New York: W. W. Norton 1978, p. 13.

38 Jacques Derrida, 'Le facteur de la vérité', in *The Post Card: From Socrates to Freud and Beyond*, trans. Alan Bass, London: University of Chicago Press, 1987, p. 444; Jacques Lacan, 'Seminar on "The Purloined Letter"', trans. Jeffrey Mehlman, in John P. Muller and William J. Richardson (eds), *The Purloined Poe: Lacan, Derrida and Psychoanalytic Reading*, Baltimore, Maryland and London: Johns Hopkins 1988, p. 53

39 Kierkegaard, *The Concept of Anxiety*, p. 93 (emphasis mine).

4 The Threatened Intimacy of Creation: Flannery O'Connor

1 Søren Kierkegaard, *The Concept of Anxiety: A Simple Psychologically Orienting Deliberation on the Dogmatic Issue of Hereditary Sin*, trans. Reidar Thomte, Princeton, NJ: Princeton University Press 1980, pp. 36–7; see *Samlede Værker* Bind IV, Copenhagen: Gyldendalske Boghandels Forlag 1902, p. 308.

2 Flannery O'Connor, *Mystery and Manners: Occasional Prose*, ed. Sally and Robert Fitzgerald, New York: Farrar, Straus and Giroux 1969, pp. 147, 148.

3 Ibid., p. 148.

4 Ibid.

5 Ibid., p. 149.

6 Ibid., p. 147.

7 Flannery O'Connor, *The Violent Bear It Away*, London: Faber and Faber 1980, p. 41.

8 Flannery O'Connor, Letter to John Hawkes, 20 November 1959, in *The Habit of Being: Letters*, ed. Sally Fitzgerald, New York: Farrar, Straus and Giroux 1979, pp. 359–60.

9 O'Connor, *The Violent Bear It Away*, pp. 16, 18.

10 Étienne Balibar, 'Violence, Ideality, and Cruelty', *New Formations* 35 (Autumn 1998), p. 15.

11 Ibid., p. 12.

12 Matthew 11: 12.

13 Matthew 11: 11; all Bible quotations, unless otherwise stated, are from the Revised Standard Version (RSV). According to Dante, John the Baptist spent the two years between his death and the resurrection of Christ in Limbo, the first circle of Hell reserved for those of the era before Christ who had no chance of knowing him. Afterwards, the Son raised him to glory in Paradise. See Dante, *The Divine Comedy* Vol. III: *Paradise*, trans. Mark Musa, Harmondsworth: Penguin 1986, p. 377 (Canto XXXII, ll. 31–3). The case of John the Baptist gives further credibility to the argument that Neo's final speech in *The Matrix* is addressed to Morpheus and his followers – heralds of the new order but themselves indisputably figures of the old. See Part Three, section 2, above, note 16' (pp. 307–8).

14 'For John came neither eating nor drinking, and they say, "He has a demon"; the Son of man came eating and drinking, and they say, "Behold, a glutton and a drunkard . . ."': Matthew 11: 18–19.

15 Matthew 5: 3–11, 44. Fanon, in his chapter on violence in *The Wretched of the Earth*, also quotes from Matthew's gospel, appropriating Jesus's words in chapter 19 as a description of decolonization: 'the last shall be first and the first last'. See Matthew 19: 30; Frantz Fanon, *The Wretched of the Earth*, trans. Constance Farrington, Harmondsworth: Penguin 1967, p. 28.

16 O'Connor, 'On Her Own Work', *Mystery and Manners*, p. 113.

17 Ibid., p. 114.

18 O'Connor, *The Violent Bear It Away*, p. 29.

19 Kierkegaard, *The Concept of Anxiety*, pp. 188-9.

20 O'Connor, *The Violent Bear It Away*, p. 73.

21 Ibid., p. 59.

22 Ibid., p. 174.

23 Søren Kierkegaard, *Either/Or: A Fragment of Life*, trans. Alastair Hannay, Harmondsworth: Penguin 1992, p. 486.

24 O'Connor, *The Violent Bear It Away*, p. 157.

25 Kierkegaard, *The Concept of Anxiety*, ch. III, pp. 93 ff.

26 Kierkegaard, *Either/Or*, p. 431.

27 O'Connor, 'Introduction to *A Memoir of Mary Ann*', in *Mystery and Manners*, p. 226.

28 Flannery O'Connor, *A Good Man is Hard to Find and other stories*, London: The Women's Press 1980, pp. 28-9.

29 O'Connor, 'On Her Own Work', in *Mystery and Manners*, p. 113.

30 Proust, *Swann's Way*, pp. 164–5, 216–18

31 O'Connor, *The Violent Bear It Away*, pp. 21-2.

32 Ibid., p. 113.

33 Ibid., pp. 113–14.

34 See Lukács, 'Reification and the Consciousness of the Proletariat', p. 135.

35 This is confirmed in O'Connor's correspondence with John Hawkes about the novel: 'The modern reader will identify with the schoolteacher,' she wrote, 'but it is the old man who speaks for me.' Flannery O'Connor, Letter to John Hawkes, 13 September 1959, in *The Habit of Being: Letters*, p. 350.

36 O'Connor, *The Violent Bear It Away*, p. 242.

37 Stanley Spencer to Richard Carline, quoted in Richard Carline, *Stanley Spencer at War*, London: Faber and Faber 1978, p. 172. See the brief discussion and reproduction of the painting in Part One, above, p. 45.

38 David Eggenschwiler, *The Christian Humanism of Flannery O'Connor*, Detroit: Wayne State University Press 1972, p. 19.

## 5 The Coincidence of Contraries

1 Karl Marx, *Capital: A Critique of Political Economy* Vol. 1, trans. Ben Fowkes, Harmondsworth: Penguin 1976, p. 173; *Das Kapital: Kritik der politischen Ökonomie*, Erster Band, Berlin: Dietz Verlag 1974, p. 94.

2 Søren Kierkegaard, *The Concept of Anxiety*, trans. Reidar Thomte, Princeton, NJ: Princeton University Press 1980, p. 160.

3 Søren Kierkegaard, *Either/Or: A Fragment of Life*, trans. Alastair Hannay, Harmondsworth: Penguin 1992, p. 266.

4 Ibid., p. 339.

5 Ibid., pp. 237–8.

6 Ibid., p. 463.

7 Ibid., p. 392.

8 Ibid., p. 461.

9 Ibid., p. 465.

10 Ibid., p. 432.

11 Ibid., p. 507. See 'Crop Rotation' for an example of such an 'inner emigration' at first hand: A tells the story of finding a certain acquaintance unutterably dull, until one day he noticed that the man

sweated so profusely during his monologues that drops of perspiration would slide down his nose and hang off its extreme end – at which point his listener began to find a new and perverse pleasure in observing his discourses: ibid., pp. 239–40.

12 Flannery O'Connor, Letter to Cecil Dawkins, 23 December 1959, in *The Habit of Being: Letters*, ed. Sally Fitzgerald, New York: Farrar, Straus and Giroux 1979, p. 364.

13 Flannery O'Connor, Letter to 'A', 2 August 1955, in *The Habit of Being*, p. 92.

14 Hieronymus Wierix, *Christ in the Wine Press*, c. 1600.

15 Flannery O'Connor, Letter to Cecil Dawkins, 23 December 1959, in *The Habit of Being: Letters*, ed. Sally Fitzgerald, New York: Farrar, Straus and Giroux 1979, p. 365. The films of Jean-Luc Godard have a similar 'intractable' quality; indeed, Susan Sontag has pointed this up both in an article on Godard and in the famous essay where she makes a case 'against interpretation'. Godard himself comments as follows: 'People didn't like *Une Femme est une femme* because they didn't know what it meant. But it didn't mean anything. If you see a bouquet of flowers on a table, does it mean something? . . . I meant it to be contradictory, juxtaposing things which didn't necessarily go together, a film which was gay and sad at the same time.' Quoted by Tom Milne, 'Jean-Luc Godard and *Vivre sa vie*', in David Sterritt (ed.), *Jean-Luc Godard: Interviews*, Jackson, Mississippi: University Press of Mississippi 1998, p. 6. See Susan Sontag, 'Godard', in *Styles of Radical Will*, London: Secker & Warburg 1969, esp. pp. 179–85; *Against Interpretation*, London: Vintage 1994, p. 11.

16 Søren Kierkegaard, *The Book on Adler*, trans. Howard V. Hong and Edna H. Hong, Princeton, NJ: Princeton University Press 1998, p. 235.

17 Michele Nicoletti, 'Politics and Religion in Kierkegaard's Thought: Secularization and the Martyr', in George B. Connell and C. Stephen Evans (eds), *Foundations of Kierkegaard's Vision of Community: Religion, Ethics, and Politics in Kierkegaard*, New Jersey and London: Humanities Press 1992, p. 191.

18 Kierkegaard, *The Book on Adler*, p. 232.

19 Ibid., p. 235.

20 Søren Kierkegaard, *Letters and Documents*, trans. Henrik Rosenmeier, Princeton, NJ: Princeton University Press 1978, no. 186, p. 262.

21 Kierkegaard, *The Book on Adler*, p. 236.

22 Ibid., pp. 230-31.

23 Ibid., pp. 231-2.

24 Nicoletti, 'Politics and Religion in Kierkegaard's Thought: Secularization and the Martyr', p. 192.

25 Gillian Rose, *Hegel Contra Sociology*, London: Athlone 1981, p. 218.

26 Søren Kierkegaard, *Papers and Journals*, p. 102 (39 II A 420).

## 6 Kierkegaard as a Theorist of Reification

1 Søren Kierkegaard, *Either/Or: A Fragment of Life*, trans. Alastair Hannay, Harmondsworth: Penguin 1992, p. 428.

2 Ibid., pp. 375–6.

3 Ibid., p. 428.

4 Ibid., p. 463.

5 Ibid., p. 411.

6 Ibid., p. 572.

7 Jean-Luc Godard, *Two or Three Things I Know About Her*, trans. Marianne Alexander, in *Three Film Scripts: A Woman is a Woman, A Married Woman, Two or Three Things I Know About Her*, London: Lorrimer 1975, pp. 135–6.

## 7 Total Reification (III): Reading Hardt and Negri

1 Michael Hardt and Antonio Negri, *Empire*, Cambridge, MA and London: Harvard University Press 2000, pp. 18, 38, 201.

2 See, for example, Gilles Deleuze and Félix Guattari, *A Thousand Plateaus: Capitalism and Schizophrenia*, trans. Brian Massumi, London: Athlone 1988, pp. 3–25; Michel Foucault, 'On Power', in *Politics, Philosophy, Culture: Interviews and Other Writings 1977–1984*, ed. Lawrence D. Kritzman, London: Routledge, 1988, pp. 102-6; Jacques Derrida, *Of Grammatology*, trans. Gayatri Chakravorty Spivak, Baltimore and London: Johns Hopkins University Press 1976, pp. 44–65.

3 Hardt and Negri, *Empire*, p. 356.

4 Ibid., p. 361; Georg Lukács, *A Defence of* History and Class Consciousness: *Tailism and the Dialectic*, trans. Esther Leslie, London: Verso 2000, p. 92.

5 Hardt and Negri, *Empire*, p. 21.
6 Ibid., p. xiv
7 Ibid., pp. 379–80.
8 Søren Kierkegaard, *The Concept of Anxiety*, trans. Reidar Thomte, Princeton, NJ: Princeton University Press 1980, p. 155.
9 William F. Fischer, *Theories of Anxiety* (Second Edition), Washington DC: University Press of America 1988, p. 89.
10 Kierkegaard, *The Concept of Anxiety*, p. 49.
11 Ibid., p. 157.
12 Ibid., p. 158.
13 Ibid., p. 159.
14 *Vivre sa vie*, dir. Jean-Luc Godard, France 1962.
15 See Kierkegaard, *The Concept of Anxiety*, p. 150.
16 For information on the life and work of Brice Parain, see the special issue of *La Nouvelle Revue Française* No. 223 (July 1971). See also Maurice Blanchot's interesting discussion of Parain, 'Studies on Language', *Faux Pas*, trans. Charlotte Mandell, Stanford, CA: Stanford University Press 2001.
17 Hardt and Negri, *Empire*, pp. 296-7.
18 Ibid., p. 361.

## 8 Conclusion: Towards Intimacy

1 Naomi Klein, *No Logo*, London: HarperCollins 2001, p. xiii.
2 Ibid., p. 143.
3 *Guardian* (G2), 9 June 2001.
4 Klein, *No Logo*, p. 21.
5 Ibid., p. 143.
6 Ibid., p. 325.
7 Ibid., p. 224.
8 Ibid., p. 23.
9 Karl Marx, *Capital: A Critique of Political Economy*, Volume 1, trans. Ben Fowkes, Harmondsworth: Penguin 1990, p. 163.
10 Klein, *No Logo*, p. 196.
11 Ibid., pp. 291–2.
12 Ibid., p. 203–4.
13 Ibid., pp. 143–4.
14 Ibid., p. 283.
15 Ibid., p. 350.

16 Ibid., p. 442.

17 'Power has decentralized; it hides in fragments behind the wood that we can't see for the trees.' *Life and its Replacement with a Dull Reflection of Itself: Preliminary Theses of The Pleasure Tendency*, Leeds: The Pleasure Tendency 1984, p. 30 (§1.1).

18 T. W. Adorno, 'On Kierkegaard's Doctrine of Love', *Zeitschrift für Sozialforschung*, Vol. VIII (1939), No. 3, München: Kösel-Verlag 1970, p. 413.

19 Ibid., p. 415.

20 Gordon D. Marino, 'Anxiety in *The Concept of Anxiety*', in Alastair Hannay and Gordon D. Marino (eds), *The Cambridge Companion to Kierkegaard*, Cambridge: Cambridge University Press 1998, pp. 310, 313.

21 Adorno, 'On Kierkegaard's Doctrine of Love', p. 414.

22 Theodor W. Adorno, *Kierkegaard: Construction of the Aesthetic*, trans. Robert Hullot-Kentor, Minneapolis: University of Minnesota Press 1989, p. 40.

23 Ibid., p. 39.

24 Søren Kierkegaard, *Fear and Trembling and Repetition*, trans. Howard V. Hong and Edna H. Hong, Princeton: Princeton University Press 1983, p. 27.

25 Søren Kierkegaard, *The Concept of Anxiety*, trans. Reidar Thomte, Princeton, NJ: Princeton University Press 1980, pp. 81 ff.

26 Ibid., p. 95.

27 Ibid., p. 94.

28 Ibid., p. 95.

29 I cannot be sure of this assertion, the precise content of religious belief being, even on a mass scale, as unverifiable as the solitary cogitations of Abraham on Mount Moriah.

30 Theodor W. Adorno, *Kierkegaard: Construction of the Aesthetic*, p. 40.

31 Karl Marx and Frederick Engels, *Manifesto of the Communist Party*, trans. Samuel Moore, Peking: Foreign Languages Press 1975, p. 47.

32 Ibid., p. 62.

33 G. W.F. Hegel, *Science of Logic*, trans. A. V. Miller, London: George Allen & Unwin 1969, p. 139.

34 See Nicholas of Cusa, *The Vision of God*, trans. Emma Gurney Salter, London: J. M. Dent 1928, esp. pp. 61–63.

35 Herbert Marcuse, *One Dimensional Man*, London: Sphere 1968, p. 200.

36 Karl Marx, 'Theses on Feuerbach', in *Early Writings*, Harmondsworth: Penguin 1975, p. 422.

37 Slavoj Žižek, *The Fragile Absolute, or, Why is the Christian legacy worth fighting for?*, London: Verso 2000, p. 16.

38 Theodor W. Adorno, 'Resignation', in *Critical Models: Interventions and Catchwords*, trans. Henry W. Pickford, New York: Columbia University Press 1998, p. 291.

39 Adorno, 'Resignation', p. 291.

40 Ibid.

# Index